COLL

BRITISH

POSTMARKS

Third Edition

A HANDBOOK

TO

BRITISH POSTAL MARKINGS

AND THEIR VALUES

Compiled by

DR J. T. WHITNEY

LONGMAN
London and New York

Longman Group Limited
Longman House, Burnt Mill, Harlow, Essex CM20 2JE, England

Associated companies throughout the world

Published in the United States of America by Longman Inc., New York

© Dr J. T. Whitney, 1979, 1980, 1983
© Picton Publishing (Chippenham) Limited, 1983

1st Edition (Printed by Accent Office Services) February 1979
Reprinted August 1979
2nd Edition (Picton Publishing) May 1980
3rd Edition (Longman Group Limited) May 1983

British Library Cataloguing in Publication Data
Whitney, J. T.
   Collect British postmarks, to 1983.—
   3rd ed
   1. Postmarks — Great Britain — Catalogs
   I. Title
   769'.S6941   HE6184.C3
ISBN 0-582-40622-6

Library of Congress Cataloging in Publication Data
Whitney, J. T.
   Collect British postmarks
   1. Postmarks — Great Britain — Catalogs.   I. Title.
HE6185.G62W46   1983   769.56'7'0750941   82-20808
ISBN 0-582-40622-6 (pbk.)

Typeset by Chippenham Typesetting, Chippenham.
Printed in Great Britain by Picton Print, (PP38934)
Citadel Works, Bath Road, Chippenham, Wilts SN15 2AB

Acknowledgements

Acknowledgement for illustrations is given to the British Post Office, the
Railway Philatetic Group, Robson Lowe and especially to the House of Alcock
for the following illustrations from *British Postmarks* and its Supplements:
   20, 21, 23, 28, 42, 58, 102, 120, 133, 136, 155, 157, 165, 166, 173, 218, 220, 221,
222, 237, 247, 322, 327, 328, 352, 353, 355, 675, 676, 688, 726, 728, 830, 833,
853, 1017, 1024, 1029, 1053, 1062, 1064, 1067, 1075, 1076, 1099, 1109, 1111,
1160, 1180, 1181, 1184, 1190, 1192, 1196, 1201, 1205, 1208, 1209, 1212, 1213,
1293, 1309, 1311, 1362, 1363, 1364, 1533, 1562, 1580, 1590, 1591, 1595, 1683,
1707, 1895, 1896, 1897, 1900, 1901, 1903, 1904, 1905, 1907, 1908, 1910, 1933,
1958, 1974, 1987, 2003, 2004, 2009, 2011, 2012, 2024, 2031, 2032, 2047, 2058,
2059, 2062, 2066, 2067, 2069, 2072, 2092, 2093, 2095, 2097, 2099, 2100, 2101,
2171, 2587, 2651.

Thanks are also expressed to Edmond Chambers for drawings and to Messrs
C. R. H. Parsons, C. G. Peachey and G. R. Pearson for permission to use their
numbers in the sections on Slogan Machines and Special Events.

CONTENTS

USING THIS BOOK

The strong interest in Postal History and postmark collecting continues. Despite the effects of the recession on some other aspects of philately, prices have generally held steady and actually increased in several sections of the hobby. Collectors are becoming noticeably more insistent on fine quality and condition.

This Handbook aims to provide a 'Postmark Simplified'. *Collect British Postmarks* surveys and prices the main types of postal markings which are collected. It should be possible to use the Handbook with little or no previous knowledge but C.B.P. should be equally useful to the specialist for ready reference and for fields outside his own specialisation.

In this Third Edition a thorough price revision has been carried out in line with current values. The scope of the book has been expanded especially – a start has been made in providing a more thorough pre-1840 coverage, Provincial Penny Posts, Uniform Penny Posts, Maltese Crosses, Spoons, sideways duplex and railway stations are now priced individually. A basic price is now given for every major First War type. The Royalty section has been expanded and there is a wholly new chapter on British Post Offices abroad.

It is important to realise that, in most instances, this is a Catalogue of postmark types rather than of actual postmarks. Behind a single entry there may be several hundred or even thousand versions, varying in value depending on the date and place of use. Even where lists have been given (e.g. T.P.O., Paquebot or Camp) variations such as punctuation and size of mark have been ignored – only a change of wording would produce a separate entry. So all that can be done in a work of this type is to give a *minimum* price for each type of postmark. *All prices should be treated as though the word 'From' were printed before them.* Secondly because no attempt has been made to include every known variety *the omission of a mark does not imply it is rare or even scarce.*

All marks were struck in black unless otherwise stated. A solidus (/) is used to indicate new lines of type in describing postmarks, ⊠ indicates a postmark on cover, △ on piece, ◯ on loose stamp. Illustrations are not necessarily full size. The term 'postmark' is used for convenience to describe all kinds of mark applied in the processing of the mails though the function may vary considerably, e.g. obliterating or cancelling the stamps, giving information, advertising an event, raising a surcharge, etc.

A general work of this kind cannot be written unless much specialised work has already been done. The Bibliography (and references in the text) will make clear my major sources and collectors are urged to acquire their own copies of relevant publications from our advertisers. In addition to the Acknowledgements I would like to thank the many collectors who have written letters of encouragement and sent suggestions for additional material, etc. Constructive criticism will always be welcome. Finally I wish especially to thank Keith Brooker for his help with the First War section, Tony Goodbody for advice on the Railway section and Philip Parker for work on the abbreviations list.

HOW TO PRICE A COVER

1. Prices given are for clear strikes on a clean card or cover. Some dealers describe the quality of a mark with a star rating others attempt more precision by the use of percentages. Prices stated are for at least Three Star or 85% quality.

   : Halve prices for Two Star or 55%

   : Quarter prices for One Star or when less than half the mark is clear.

   Collectors are strongly advised to insist on these standards when purchasing items. Covers in pristine condition or with other attractive features will command a premium above catalogue value.

2. Postmarks, in the Compiler's opinion, should always be collected on full entire, cover or card (or on a piece as large as an envelope in the case of parcel or packet marks).

   : Fronts are worth up to three-quarters of Catalogue value.

   : Pieces (or 'squares') are worth between a third and a half of Catalogue value.

   : Loose stamps on which a substantial (at least half) part of the postmark can be positively identified are worth about a quarter of Catalogue value.

3. To assess the basic value of a cover—

   : First check the value of all postmarks on the cover in this Catalogue.

   : Take the highest value and add to it half the value of other marks priced over 50p ignoring others.

   : Then check the value of the stamps in a stamp catalogue. Ignore all stamps valued at 20p or less. Add full Catalogue value thereafter.

Dr J. T. Whitney

1. THE GENERAL POST 1661–1840

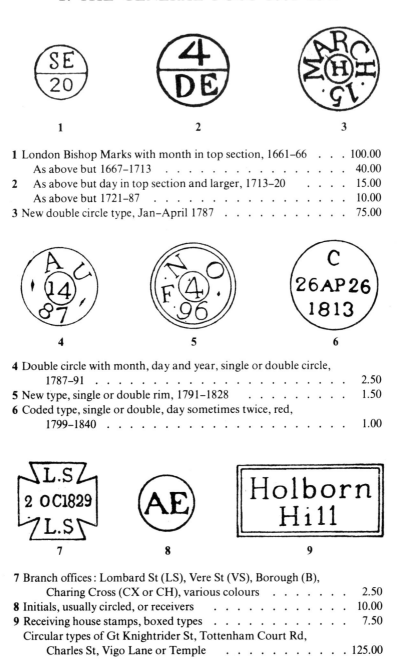

1 London Bishop Marks with month in top section, 1661–66 . . . 100.00
   As above but 1667–1713 . . . . 40.00
2 As above but day in top section and larger, 1713–20 . . . . 15.00
   As above but 1721–87 . . . . 10.00
3 New double circle type, Jan–April 1787 . . . . 75.00

4 Double circle with month, day and year, single or double circle,
   1787–91 . . . . 2.50
5 New type, single or double rim, 1791–1828 . . . . 1.50
6 Coded type, single or double, day sometimes twice, red,
   1799–1840 . . . . 1.00

7 Branch offices: Lombard St (LS), Vere St (VS), Borough (B),
   Charing Cross (CX or CH), various colours 2.50
8 Initials, usually circled, or receivers 10.00
9 Receiving house stamps, boxed types 7.50
   Circular types of Gt Knightrider St, Tottenham Court Rd,
   Charles St, Vigo Lane or Temple 125.00

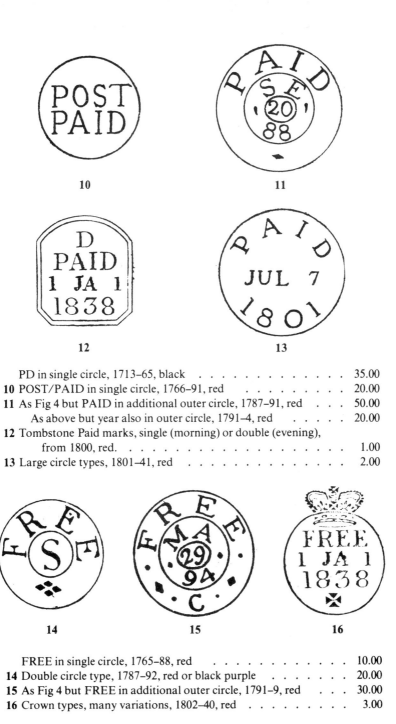

PD in single circle, 1713–65, black	. . . .	35.00
10 POST/PAID in single circle, 1766–91, red	. . . .	20.00
11 As Fig 4 but PAID in additional outer circle, 1787–91, red	. . .	50.00
As above but year also in outer circle, 1791–4, red	. . . . .	20.00
12 Tombstone Paid marks, single (morning) or double (evening), from 1800, red.	. . . .	1.00
13 Large circle types, 1801–41, red	. . . .	2.00

FREE in single circle, 1765–88, red	. . . .	10.00
14 Double circle type, 1787–92, red or black purple	. . . .	20.00
15 As Fig 4 but FREE in additional outer circle, 1791–9, red	. . .	30.00
16 Crown types, many variations, 1802–40, red	. . . .	3.00

7

2. LONDON LOCAL POST

Dockwra's Post, 1680–82

17

A private post organised by William Dockwra and collaborators. Triangular stamps show abbreviations for offices: L, Lime Street, B, Bishopsgate, W, Westminster, P, St Paul's and T, Temple. Willcocks states that only twenty-three examples are known, only six of which are in private hands (the remainder being in archives) and that, if one were sold, it might be expected to fetch above £10,000.

Government Penny Post, from 1682

18   19

18 Dockwra-type marks, several types, with office abbreviation and day

B/CH	Bishopsgate	. . . . ?		P	St Paul's	75.00
B	Bishopsgate	. . 150.00		S	Southwark . . .	75.00
G	General	. . . . 75.00		T	Temple	120.00
H	Hermitage	. . . 125.00		W	Westminster . .	75.00

19 Circular time markings 20.00
As above but in other shapes (e.g. heart-shaped) 50.00

Reorganised Penny Post, from 1794 (Two Penny Post from 1801)

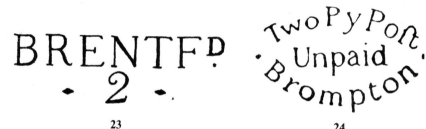

20   21   22

20 Indented sides types, 1794–1822, red	. . . .	3.00
As above but in black, 1794–1822	. . . .	10.00
Oval, 1795–1822, red	. . . .	1.00
Small oval with double frame, 1824–33, red	. . . .	0.75
21 As above but single frame, 1834–35, red	. . . .	1.00
22 Small stamp with indented sides, 1836–43, red	. . . .	0.75
As above but with oval frame, 1836–43, red or black	. . . .	2.50

23   24

25

23 Receiving House unpaid stamps with Office and 1, 2 or 3 below	.	125.00
As Fig 24 but Penny Post, 1795–1801	. . . .	20.00
24 Two Py Post Unpaid, from 1801	. . . .	6.00
25 Step types, framed or unframed, 1816–50	. . . .	4.00

26

Aldgate 2py P·Paid

27

26 Receiving House Paid 1d stamps, 1796–1801 . . . . 30.00
    As above but Paid 2d, 1796–1801 . . . . 50.00
27 Two line type, 1802–45 . . . . 6.00
    As above but 3 py P. Paid, 1805–39 . . . . 15.00
    As above but 1 py P. Paid, before 1840 . . . . 10.00
    1 py P. Paid after 1840 . . . . 4.00
    As above but 1D PAID, before 1840 . . . . 10.00
    1D PAID after 1840 . . . . 3.00
    As above but 2D PAID 5.00
    As above but 3D PAID 40.00

28

29

28 London Instructional marks, 'Postage Not Paid to London', 'Too
    late for Morning Post' etc 40.00
    Star marks, in red 3.50
    Crown marks 10.00
29 Sunday stamps 7.50

REMEMBER!
Prices in C.B.P. are minimum values
for a **clear strike on a clean card or cover**.
Have you read the notes
at the beginning?

---

3. THE PROVINCIAL POST

'Bishop' Types

30

30 Initial containing date, used at Bristol 1697–1720 . . . . 500.00
As above but E for Exeter 1697–1709 . . . . 700.00

Regular Types

STOCKTON

31

32

33

34

35

36

31 Straight lines

Before 1730 . . . 90.00	1730–70 . . . . 20.00
1770–1805 . . . 15.00	After 1805 . . . 10.00

As above but in two straight lines

Before 1770 . . . 35.00	After 1770 . . . 20.00

As above but in three straight lines 50.00
Abbreviated types, e.g. AB.N.DON, 1705–20 . . . . 150.00
Framed by lines, 1720–65 . . . . 100.00
32 Town name in convex or concave arc, 1789–1810 . . . . 25.00
33 Horseshoe types, 1789–1801 . . . . 20.00
As above but reversed horseshoe 35.00
34 Town name in circle with stop, 1798–1845 . . . . 15.00
35 Town name with undated double arc, from 1829 . . . . 12.50
36 As above but dated, from 1829 . . . . 2.50
As above but dated and sans serif letters, from 1844 . . . . . 1.00

Mileage Types

98 LYMING TON

37

LYMINGTON [98]

38

39

Straight line with mileage from London below town name,
1784–95 . . . . 50.00
37 As above but mileage first, town in one or two lines, 1784–95 . 40.00
As above but mileage after, 1784–95 . . . . 75.00
38 Town name with boxed mileage beneath, 1801–30 . . . . . . 7.50
As above but pair of bars, not box, 1804–40 . . . . 5.00
39 Circular dated mileage types, 1804–40 . . . . 5.00
As above but undated, 1809–28 . . . . 7.50

Distinctive Town Stamps, (many types, various colours) 'A'

40   41   42   43

Penny Posts

AYLSHAM
Penny Post

44 'B'

Atherstone
P.y Post

45 'C'

Cheltenham
Penny Post

46 'D'

Isfield
Penny Post

47 'E'

Fifth Clause Posts

NEWCASTLES
5"Clause Post

48 'F'

Newcastle
5"Cls Post

49 'G'

SHEPT^N MALLET
5th Clause Post

50 'H'

Haverford West
5" Clause Post

51 'J'

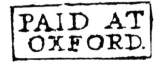

52

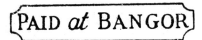

53

54

Abbotts Ann, E . . . . ?	Askrigg, E . . . . ?
Abingdon, D £75	Atherstone, B £60
Adderbury, G £275	C £60
Addlestone, E £80	D £75
Aigburth, E . . . . ?	Attercliffe, D £75
Allendale, E . . . . ?	Attleborough, B £60
Alnmouth, E . . . . ?	D £60
Alnwick, D £55	Auckland, D £75
E £75	Austerlands, distinctive £70
Aldborough, E £80	Axminister, B £50
Allonby, E . . . . ?	distinctive £40
Althorne, E . . . . ?	K £80
Altrincham, distinctive £60	Aycliffe, E . . . . ?
Alston, distinctive £60	Aylesbury, C £50
K £30	Aylsham, B £50
Alton, B £30	Ayton, E £75
E £60	Bagshot, B £30
Ambleside, E £75	C £40
Amesbury, E £55	D £60
Ancoats, distinctive £75	E £40
Andover, E £50	Barnborough, E . . . . ?
Appleby, D £60	Bampton, E £75
Appleshaw, E . . . . ?	Banbury, B £70
Ardwick, distinctive £30	Bangor, K £80
Arundel, B £50	Barford, E £75
C £45	Barnby, B £75
Ashbourne, distinctive £60	Barnet, B £50
Ashburton, B £50	C £70
distinctive £40	D £60
Ashby DLZ, A £50	E £60
D £50	Barnstable, C £50
Ashford, B £5	Bartley, E . . . . ?
E . . . . ?	Baschurch, E . . . . ?
K £65	Bath, A £10
Asht . . . . ?	B £35
Ashton-under-Line, distinctive . . £40	distinctive £8

Battle, C	£50	Bolton-Le-Sands, E	£75
E	£75	Bootle, E	£75
Bawtry, B	£40	Boston, B	£60
Beaconsfield, B	£60	Botesdale, D	£75
E	?	Botley, E	?
Beaford, E	£75	Bournemouth, E	?
Beaulieu, E	?	Bowness, E	£75
Beaumaris, K	?	Box, E	?
Beckford, E	?	Brackley, E	?
Bedale, B	£30	Bradford, K	£25
C	£20	Bradwell, E	?
E	?	Brancaster, E	£75
Bedlington, E	?	Brandford, C	£40
Beeston, D	£60	D	£75
Benenden, E	?	Braintree, B	£40
Benson, C	£75	D	£40
E	£60	Brecknock, A	£100
Benwick, A	£150	Brenchley, E	?
distinctive	£40	Brentford, E	£75
Bevois Hill, E	?	Bridgewater, B	£50
Bewdley, B	£40	C	£60
C	£30	E	£30
E	£75	Bridport, B	£40
Bideford, E	£80	Brigg, D	£75
Billericay, K	£65	Brighouse, D	£30
Billingshurst, E	?	E	?
Bingham, A	£150	Brighton, B	£30
Birch, E	£75	D	£40
Birchington, E	?	E	£75
Birmingham, A	£600	Bristol, A	£35
C	£35	B	£50
distinctive	£30	distinctive	£10
K	£10	F	£90
Birstal, D	£50	G	£200
Bishops Stortford, B	£40	J	£90
C	£40	K	£16
E	£55	Brittel Lane, E	?
Bishopstoke, E	?	Broadwater, E	?
Bittern, E	?	Brockley, E	?
Blackburn, C	£70	Brompton, E	£75
D	£70	Brooke, E	?
E	£60	Brookend, E	?
K	£100	Broomsgrove, E	?
Blackpool, E	?	Broughton, E	£75
Blackwater, E	?	Buckingham, E	?
Blandford, B	£50	Burford, K	£110
distinctive	£20	Burley, E	?
Bletchingey, K	£75	Burnham, Berks, E	£75
Blofield, E	£75	Burnham, Essex, E	?
Blunham, E	?	Burnham, Norfolk, D	£60
Blythe, E	£75	Bursledon, E	?
Bollington,	?	Burton, B	£75
Bolton, B	£75	Burwarton, E	?
distinctive	£75	Burwash, E	£75
Bolton-Le-Moors, A	£100	Burwaston, E	?

Bury Lancashire, A	£40
B	£60
C	£75
Bury St Edmunds, B	£40
E	£60
Bushley, E	£75
Buxted, E	?
Caistor, A	£90
Calderbridge, E	?
Callington, E	£75
Camborne, C	£75
E	£75
Canbridge, D	£75
distinctive	£60
Campden, E	?
Canterbury, C	£50
E	£60
Carnarvon, K	£110
Carnforth, E	?
Castle Cary, C	£75
Castle Rising, E	?
Castletown, IOM, A	£180
Catton, E	?
Chalford, C	£50
Chard, C	£40
E	£60
Chartham, E	?
Cheadle, distinctive	£75
Chelmsford, A	£80
B	£75
E	£75
K	£110
Cheltenham, C	£40
D	£40
Chertsey, E	£75
Chessington, E	£75
Chester, A	£30
D	£60
E	£75
Chichester, B	£75
C	£75
D	£50
E	£75
Chilbolton, E	?
Chilham, E	?
Chippenham, B	£75
C	£75
E	£60
Chipping Norton, E	£75
Chobham, E	?
Christchurch, E	£60
Chudleigh, B	£50
C	£75
E	£75
Church Street, distinctive	?
Cirencester, D	£60

Cleckheaton, D	£75
Clenchwarton, E	£75
Coatham Mandeville, E	?
Colchester, B	£30
C	£30
E	£50
Coleford, D	£40
E	?
K	?
Colnbrook, B	£60
C	£75
D	£50
Compton, E	?
Congleton, K	£85
Conte, E	?
Copplestone, E	?
Cotherstone, E	?
Coltishall	?
Cottingham	£75
Coventry, A	£25
B	£40
C	£30
E	£75
Cowfold, E	?
Crabtree, E	?
Cranford Bridge, E	?
Crawley, B	£50
E	?
Crawley, Hants, E	?
Crediton, C	£60
E	?
Crewkerne, C	£50
E	?
G	£175
Croft, E	?
Cromer, C	£60
E	£75
Crosby, E	£60
Cross, D	£40
E	£60
Cross In Hand, E	?
Croydon, E	£40
Cuckfield, B	£50
D	£75
Cullercoats, E	?
Cullumpton, B	£60
Cullompton, E	£60
Curdworth, distinctive	£75
Darlington, E	?
Dartford, D	£60
Dartmouth, D	£50
Daventry, B	£50
C	£50
E	£40
Dawley Green, E	£75
Deal, B	£50

Debenham £75	Everton, distinctive £75
Delph, distinctive £40	Exeter, distinctive £20
Dent, E £75	Exmouth, B £60
Denton, D £75	Falmouth, A £175
Derby, A £50	B £60
B £40	Fareham, B £50
C £40	C £75
K £160	D £50
Devizes, B £60	Faringdon, D £50
D £60	Farnham, D £50
E £60	Farnborough, E £75
distinctive £60	Faversham, D £50
K £75	Fawley, E £75
Devonport, C £60	Feckenham, E . . . . ?
distinctive £50	Feltham, E . . . . ?
Didsbury . . . . ?	Filby, E £75
Distington, E . . . . ?	Finchley, E £75
Dobcross, distinctive £30	Five Lanes, D £75
Dorchester, C £20	Fleet, E . . . . ?
K £55	Fleetwood, E . . . . ?
Douglas IOM, E £400	Fletching, E . . . . ?
distinctive £1100	Flixton, distinctive £75
Daver, C £50	Folkestone, distinctive £50
Downham, E £60	Four Posts, E . . . . ?
Dudley, D £75	Framfield, E . . . . ?
Dunkirk, E . . . . ?	Framlingham, B £50
Dunstable, K . . . . ?	D £50
Dunster, D £75	Frimley, E . . . . ?
Durham £75	Frame, K £65
Dursley, B £75	Gainford, E . . . . ?
C £60	Garnick, distinctive . . . . . . ?
D £60	Gateshead, D £60
Eagleshurst, E . . . . ?	Gateshead Highfell, E . . . . . ?
Earsdon, E . . . . ?	Gedney, E . . . . ?
Eastbourn, B £50	Gee Cross, D £75
Eastbourne, E . . . . ?	Gerards Cross, D £60
East Grinstead, A £250	Gisburne, E . . . . ?
B £50	Glastonbury, D £75
E £60	Glossop, distinctive £60
distinctive £75	Gloucester, B £50
East Hoathley, E . . . . ?	C £50
East Moulsey, E . . . . ?	K £20
East Strotten, E . . . . ?	Godnostham, E £75
Eaton, E . . . . ?	Godstone, B £60
Eccles, distinctive . . . . . . ?	D £60
Eccleshill, E . . . . ?	Goldhanger, E . . . . ?
Edgbaston, D £75	Gomersall, D £20
Edgehill, distinctive . . . . . . ?	Gooderich, E . . . . ?
Edgeware, B £75	Goodhurst, E . . . . ?
Elland, E . . . . ?	Goodworth, Clatford, E . . . . . ?
Elmdon, distinctive £75	Goring, E . . . . ?
Enstone, B £40	Gorleston, D £75
D £60	Gorton, D £75
Epsom, E £75	Gosberton, B £75
Erdington, distinctive £75	Gosforth, E . . . . ?
Ermebridge, D £75	Gosport, D £75

Grantham, B	£60
D	£60
Gravesend, C	£50
Great Barford, E	?
Great Barr, distinctive	£75
Great Malvern, D	£50
Greenacres, distinctive	£50
Green Street, E	?
Guernsey, A	£250
Guildford, B	£50
D	£60
K	£45
Guisboro, D	£50
E	?
Guiseley, D	£60
Hadleigh, B	£60
C	£60
E	£75
Halifax, C	£30
E	£30
K	£35
Halstead, B	£50
C	£40
D	£75
E	?
Haltwhistle, C	£75
Hamble, E	?
Hambledon, E	?
Hammersmith, E	?
Handley, distinctive	£75
Handsworth, distinctive	£75
Hanworth	?
Harewood, E	£75
Harewood End, E	?
Harleston, K	£75
Harlington, E	?
Harrogate, B	£75
C	£60
distinctive	£75
K	£65
Harrowgate, E	£75
Harlow, K	£75
Hartlebury, E	?
Hartle Pans, E	?
Harwich, B	£60
Haslingden, D	£40
Hastings, D	£60
Hatfield, B	£75
Hatherley, A	£250
Hathersage, E	£75
Haudley, E	£75
Havant, E	£100
K	£135
Hawes, D	£60
Haweshead, E	?
Hawkeshead, E	£75
Hay, E	?

Hayling Island, E	?
Heacham, E	£75
Heathfield, E	£75
Hebdon Bridge, E	£75
Heckmondwike, D	£50
Heighington, E	£75
Henley, E	£75
Hereford, D	£60
Hertford, B	£60
E	£75
K	£100
Heshett, E	?
Hethersett, A	£120
Hevingham	£75
Highfield	£75
High Gate	£75
Highworth	£75
High Wycombe, B	£60
K	?
Hilborough, E	£75
Hinckley, B	£60
D	£60
Hindon	£60
Hitchin, distinctive	£75
Hochcliffe, E	?
Hockley, E	?
Holbeach, D	£75
E	£75
Holdsworthy, distinctive	£60
G	£275
Holkham, A	£75
Hollinsgreen, E	?
Hollinwood, distinctive	£75
Holmfirth, B	£40
Holsworthy, E	£75
Honiton, B	£60
E	£60
distinctive	£50
Hoogreen, E	?
Hook	?
Horndean, E	£60
Horsemonden, E	?
Horsforth, D	£60
Horsham, B	£60
D	£60
E	£60
Houghton-le-Spring, E	£75
Hounslow, C	£50
E	£60
Hove, E	£75
Howden, K	£75
Howden Pans, E	?
Huddersfield, B	£60
C	£75
D	£75
E	£30
K	£30

Hull, A	£50
D	£40
Hunsdon, E	?
Hunstanton, E	?
Huntingdon, C	£60
E	£60
Hursley, E	?
Hurst, E	?
Hurstbourne, E	?
Hurstbourne Tarrant, E	£75
Horworth, E	?
Hyde, E	?
Hythe, B	£60
E	?
Ideford, E	?
Idle, E	£75
Ightham, E	£75
Ilfracombe, distinctive	£60
Ilkley, E	?
Ilminster, D	£60
distinctive	£50
G	£150
Ipswich, D	£60
E	£60
Ironbridge, D	£60
E	£75
Isfield, E	£75
Isle of Man, E	£300
Itchen, E	?
Ivybridge, D	£60
Ixworth, D	£40
Jarrow, E	?
Jersey, A	£250
D	£350
Kelveden, B	£40
Kelvedon, D	£60
Kemp Town, distinctive	£60
Kendal, B	£40
C	£60
Kenilworth, E	£50
Kentchurch, E	?
Kenyon, E	?
Kessingland, A	£70
Kettering, E	£75
Kcy Street, E	?
Kilsby, E	£75
Kilvedon, C	£60
Kimmerton, E	?
Kineton, B	£75
Kingsbridge, A	£200
B	£75
E	£75
Kings Norton, distinctive	£75
Kingston, B	£50
E	£75
Kinvar, E	?

Kirby Lonsdale, D	£75
Kirkdale, distinctive	£75
Kirkham, E	?
Kirkoswald, E	£80
Kirkstall, D	£60
Knaresborough, E	£75
Knott Hill, distinctive	£75
Knowle, E	£75
Laleham	?
Lamberhurst, B	£60
E	£60
Lancaster, A	£150
D	£50
K	£70
Landrake, E	?
Lapford, E	?
Latchingdon, E	?
Lawncester, C	£75
D	£60
K	£50
Lea, D	£75
Leamington, D	£50
E	£60
Leatherhead, D	£75
Lechmere Heath, E	?
Leeds, D	£50
E	£35
K	£8
Leek, A	£60
Lees, D	£75
Leicester, E	£75
K	£40
Leigh, E	£75
distinctive	£60
Leominster, D	£60
E	£75
Letton, E	?
Lewos, B	£75
C	£50
K	£75
Leyburn, E	£75
Lindale, E	?
Liskeard, B	£75
Litchfield, E	£60
Liverpool, A	£3
K	£5
Lodsworth, E	£75
Loftus, E	£75
London Colney, E	£75
London Road, distinctive	?
London (St James St.), K	£80
Long Benton	£75
Long Ditton	?
Long Parish	?
Long Sutton	?
Lostwithiel, B	£75

Lower Wallop, E	?
Ludgershall, E	?
Ludlow, E	?
Luton, E	?
Lutterworth	£75
Lydney	£75
Lymington, C	£60
Lynn, B	£50
D	£50
E	£60
Lytchett	?
Maidenhead, D	£60
Maidstone, B	£60
D	£30
Maldon, B	£60
D	£40
Malton, E	£75
Malvern, B	£40
Malvern Wells, B	£40
Manchester, A	£30
D	£75
distinctive	£40
K	£10
Maresfield, E	?
Margate, A	£200
Market Harborough, E	£75
Marlborough, K	£60
Marsfield, E	?
Marske, E	?
Masham, E	?
Mayfield, E	?
M. Dean, C	£75
Melksham, C	£75
D	£60
Melton Mowbray, E	£75
Middle Claydon, E	?
Middleham, E	?
Middlesbro, E	?
Middleton, A	£50
distinctive	£40
Middleton-one-Row, E	?
Middle Wallop, E	?
Middlewich, F	£275
Midhurst, K	£65
Mildenhall, C	£60
Millbridge, D	£30
Millbrook, E	?
Milnthorpe, D	£75
Miton, E	?
Minchinhampton, D	£50
Minehead, E	£60
Minster, E	?
Mitcheldever, E	?
Monk Wearmouth, E	£80
Moreton-in-Mush, D	£75
Moreton-in-the-Marsh, E	£75

Morley, D	£40
Morpeth, C	£75
E	£75
Morton	£75
Mortram, distinctive	£60
Mountsorrel, A	£50
Mundford, E	?
Mundon, E	?
Neasham, E	?
Newark, B	£50
E	£75
Newbiggin, E	?
Newbury, B	£50
C	£75
D	£50
Newby Bridge, E	£75
Newcastle, N'thumb, D	£60
E	£75
Newcastle, Staffs, A	£140
F	£70
G	£90
J	£70
Newcross, distinctive	?
Newent, distinctive	£40
New Ferry, E	?
Newick, E	?
Newington Kent, E	?
Newmarket, D	£50
Newnham, D	£75
Newnham Kent, E	?
Newport IOW, E	?
New Romney, E	£60
Newton Abbot, B	£50
C	£50
D	£60
Newton Heath, E	?
distinctive	£75
Newton Lancashire, E	£75
Northaw, E	?
Northfield, distinctive	?
Northshields, B	£60
D	£75
E	£75
North Sunderland, E	?
North Tawton, E	£75
Northwich, D	£75
Norton, E	?
Norwich, B	£40
D	£40
K	£50
Nottingham, A	£135
Nuthurst, E	?
Okehampton, C	£70
G	£75
Old Down, A	£40
distinctive	£20

Old Hall Green, E	?
Old Hall Street, distinctive	?
Oldham, A	£90
distinctive	£30
Olney, K	£75
Orford, A	£60
Ormokirk, B	£60
D	£75
Ossett, D	£40
Oswaldkirk, E	?
Oswestry, B	£50
C	£60
Otley, E	?
K	£75
Otterbourne, E	?
Otterton, C	£50
D	£60
Ottery, distinctive	£60
Ottery St Mary, E	£75
Oxford, D	£60
K	£30
Oxford St, distinctive	£75
Parkstone, E	?
Peel Town IOM, A	£150
Pembury, E	?
Pencraig, E	?
Penny Bridge, E	£75
Penrith, B	£50
distinctive	£60
Penshurst, E	?
Penzance, D	£75
Peterborough, B	£50
D	£50
Peterchurch, E	?
Petersfield, B	£75
D	£75
Pewsey, E	£60
Pickering, E	£75
Pierre Bridge, E	?
Plymouth, B	£40
C	£50
E	£50
distinctive	£30
K	?
Plymouth Dock, B	£60
Poole, E	£50
Portsmouth, A	£60
B	£60
C	£50
Potters Bar, E	?
Potton, D	£40
Poulton, B	£60
Prescot, B	£75
D	£75
E	?
Preston, A	£200
B	£30
K	£55
Preston Brook, distinctive	?
Prittlewell, E	?
Puckeridge, E	£75
Pudsey, D	£60
Radcliffe, distinctive	£75
Rainham, E	?
Ramsey, Hants, K	?
Ramsey IOM, A	£130
Ramsgate, D	£50
E	£60
Rawdon, D	£60
Rawtenstall	£60
Reading, A	£200
B	£50
D	£40
Redbridge, E	?
Redcar, E	£75
Redland, E	?
Regent Road, distinctive	?
Reigate, C	?
Richmund, D	£75
Rickmansworth, D	£75
Ridge, E	?
Ringwood, E	£75
Ripley, B	£10
Ripon, D	£60
Rochdale, B	£50
E	?
Rochford, B	£50
C	£60
distinctive	£60
Romford, B	£50
C	£50
D	£50
E	£60
distinctive	£50
Ross, B	£50
Rotherfield, E	?
Rottingdean, E	?
Rougham, B	£40
E	£60
Roydon, E	?
Royston, E	£75
Rudgewick, E	£75
Rugeley, distinctive	£75
Rushyford, D	£60
Ruyton, E	?
Ryde, D	£60
Rye, B	£50
Ryton, E	?
St Albans, E	£60
St Austell, E	£75
St Columb, E	£75
St Cross, E	?

St Faith's, E . . . . ?	Skipton, distinctive £50
St Germans, E . . . . ?	Slinfold, E . . . . ?
St James, distinctive . . . . . . ?	Smarden, E . . . . ?
St John's Common, E £75	Smethwick, distinctive £75
St Mary Bourne, E . . . . ?	Snettisham, E . . . . ?
St Neots, A £65	Somerton, D £60
Salford, distinctive £60	South Shields, D £75
Salisbury, B £50	Southall, D £60
distinctive £50	E . . . . ?
Sandhurst, E . . . . ?	Southampton, B £60
Sarre, E . . . . ?	D £50
Scarborough, E . . . . ?	distinctive £30
Scotland Road, distinctive . . . . ?	Southbourne, E . . . . ?
Seacomb, E £75	Southend, E . . . . ?
Sea Houses, E . . . . ?	South Mims, E . . . . ?
Seaton, E £75	Southminster, E . . . . ?
distinctive £75	Southwold, D £60
Sedberg, E £75	E £30
Seddlecomb, E . . . . ?	Spalding, D £60
Settle, D £60	E £60
Sevenoaks, B £60	Spilsby, D £60
C £60	Stafford, B £75
Shaftesbury, B £60	Staines, B £50
D £30	Staleybridge, distinctive £60
distinctive £30	Stalham, E £75
F £100	Stanstead, E . . . . ?
G £65	Stewkley, E £75
H £85	Steyning, B £75
Sheffield, A £100	C £60
B £75	Stillington, E . . . . ?
distinctive £60	Stockbridge, E £50
Shefford, B £75	Stockport, A £35
D £60	distinctive . . . . ?
E . . . . ?	Stockton, D £60
Shernley, E £75	E . . . . ?
Shepton Mallet, G £150	Stoke Climsland, E . . . . . . ?
H £150	Stoke Ferry, E £75
J £125	Stokesley, D £60
Sherbourne, A £150	Stoney Cross, A £85
B £50	Stonham, E . . . . ?
Shiere, E £75	Stourbridge, E . . . . ?
Shiffnall, B £60	Stratford, B £60
C £50	K £40
Shildon, E . . . . ?	Stratford-on- Avon, C £60
Shipstone-on-Stour, D £60	D £60
Shirley, E . . . . ?	E £75
Shirley Street, distinctive £75	Stratton, distinctive £75
Shooters Hill, E £50	Stretford, distinctive £60
Shoreham, B £60	Stretton, E . . . . ?
D £60	Stroud, E £75
E £75	Sudbury, B £50
Shrewsbury, D £60	D £60
Sidmouth, C £75	E £75
Sittingbourne, E . . . . ?	Sunderland, D £60
distinctive £50	Sunninghill, A £75
Skelton, E . . . . ?	E £75

Sutterton, B	. . . .	£75
Sutton, E	. . . .	?
Sutton-in-Ashfield, E	. . . . . .	£75
Sutton Scotney, E	. . . .	?
Swaffham, E	. . . .	£75
Swanwick, E	. . . .	£75
Swamling, E	. . . .	?
Swineshead, distinctive	. . . .	£60
Swinshead, distinctive	. . . .	£60
Taplow, E	. . . .	?
Taunton, A	. . . .	£100
B	. . . .	£20
distinctive	. . . .	£10
F	. . . .	£220
Tavistock, C	. . . .	£60
K	. . . .	£70
Teignmouth, D	. . . .	£50
E	. . . .	£50
Temple Sowerby, E	. . . . . .	?
Tempsford, E	. . . .	?
Terrington, E	. . . .	?
Tetbury, K	. . . .	£100
Tetsworth, B	. . . .	£50
D	. . . .	£60
Tewkesbury, D	. . . .	£50
E	. . . .	£50
distinctive	. . . .	£60
Thame, E	. . . .	£75
Thames Ditton, E	. . . .	?
Thaxsted, D	. . . .	£75
Thornham, E	. . . .	£75
Thorpe, E	. . . .	£75
Thrapstone, D	. . . .	£60
distinctive	. . . .	£60
Ticehurst	. . . .	?
Tid	. . . .	?
Tillingham	. . . .	?
Tiverton, B	. . . .	£60
E	. . . .	?
Todmorden, E	. . . .	?
Tolleshurst D'Arcy, E	. . . . . .	?
Tolworth, E	. . . .	?
Torquay, E	. . . .	£60
Torrington, E	. . . .	?
Totnes, D	. . . .	£50
E	. . . .	£50
K	. . . .	£100
Totton, E	. . . .	£75
Truro, C	. . . .	£50
K	. . . .	£40
Trysall, E	. . . .	?
Tunbridge, D	. . . .	£75
E	. . . .	?
Tunbridge Wells, A	. . . . .	£15
Turnham Green, E	. . . . . .	£75
Turville, E	. . . .	?

Twickenham, E	. . . .	£75
Twyford, E	. . . .	£75
Tynemouth, E	. . . .	?
Uckfield, B	. . . .	£60
C	. . . .	£50
Ulverstone, D	. . . .	£50
Upper Mill, D	. . . .	£60
Uppingham, A	. . . .	£75
Usworth, E	. . . .	£75
Uttoxeter, B	. . . .	£75
Uxbridge, E	. . . .	£75
Vauxhall Road, distinctive	. . . .	?
Wadesmill, E	. . . .	?
Wadhurst, E	. . . .	?
Wakefield, D	. . . .	£75
K	. . . .	£100
Wakering, E	. . . .	?
Waldron, E	. . . .	?
Walling Ford, B	. . . .	£50
D	. . . .	£75
Wallsall, B	. . . .	£50
Wallsend, E	. . . .	?
Waltham Cross, B	. . . . . .	£50
C	. . . .	£60
D	. . . .	£75
E	. . . .	£60
K	. . . .	£60
Wangford, B	. . . .	£50
Wapping, distinctive	. . . . . .	?
Ware, B	. . . .	£75
C	. . . .	£50
D	. . . .	£60
E	. . . .	?
Wargrave, E	. . . .	?
Warnham, E	. . . .	?
Warrington, B	. . . .	£60
D	. . . .	£60
E	. . . .	£75
Warwick, B	. . . .	£40
C	. . . .	£50
D	. . . .	£50
Watchet	. . . .	?
Watford, B	. . . .	£75
E	. . . .	?
Wath, A	. . . .	£90
Watton, E	. . . .	£80
Wavertree, E	. . . .	£75
Wednesbury, K	. . . .	£60
Weldon Bridge, E	. . . . . .	£80
Wellington Com, E	. . . . .	£80
Wells, B	. . . .	£60
C	. . . .	£50
F	. . . .	£60
K	. . . .	£140
Weobley, E	. . . .	£75
West Burton, E	. . . .	?

23

Westbury, E	. . . .	?
West Drayton, E	. . . .	?
West-End, E	. . . .	?
Westfield, E	. . . .	?
West Grinstead, E	. . . .	?
West Moulsey, E	. . . .	?
Weston Green, E	. . . .	?
West Tarring, E	. . . .	?
Wetherby, D	. . . .	£30
Weyhill, E	. . . .	£75
Weymouth, K	. . . .	?
Whalton, E	. . . .	?
Whetstone, E	. . . .	?
Whickham, E	. . . .	?
Whitchurch, Hants, D	. . . . .	£60
Whitchurch, Salop, D	. . . . .	£50
Whitchurch, Somerset, E	. . . . .	?
Whitehaven, D	. . . .	£60
E	. . . .	?
Whiteparish, E	. . . .	?
Whitfield, E	. . . .	?
Whitford, E	. . . .	?
Whittingham, E	. . . .	?
Widford, E	. . . .	?
Wigan, A	. . . .	£160
distinctive	. . . .	£75
K	. . . .	£70
Wigton, E	. . . .	?
Wiley, E	. . . .	£75
Willenhall, D	. . . .	£60
Willingdon, E	. . . .	?
Wilmslow, distinctive	. . . . .	£60
Wimbourne, E	. . . .	?
Wincanton, F	. . . .	£115
J	. . . .	£115
K	. . . .	£100
Winchester, E	. . . .	£75
Windlesham, E	. . . .	?
Windsor, D	. . . .	£60
distinctive	. . . .	?

Wingham, E	. . . .	£75
Winkfield, E	. . . .	?
Winkleigh, E	. . . .	?
Winlaton, E	. . . .	?
Winstow, E	. . . .	?
Winwick, E	. . . .	?
Wirksworth, B	. . . .	£40
Wisbeach, E	. . . .	£75
Wisborough Green, E	. . . . . .	?
Witney, B	. . . .	£50
C	. . . .	£50
E	. . . .	£75
Wittersham, E	. . . .	?
Woking, E	. . . .	?
Wolston, E	. . . .	?
Wolverhampton, B	. . . .	£60
C	. . . .	£60
E	. . . .	£75
Woodbridge, E	. . . .	£40
Woodside, E	. . . .	£50
Woodstock, C	. . . .	£60
E	. . . .	£60
Woodgates, E	. . . .	£75
Woolton, E	. . . .	£75
Wootton Bridge, E	. . . . . .	£75
Worcester, B	. . . .	£55
D	. . . .	£45
Wordesley, D	. . . .	£75
E	. . . .	?
Worksop, B	. . . .	£75
Worthing, E	. . . .	?
Wootton-O-Edge, E	. . . . . .	£75
Wrentham, E	. . . .	£60
Wykeham, E	. . . .	£75
Yarmouth, E	. . . .	£75
K	. . . .	£70
Yeadon, D	. . . .	£60
Yealand Conyers, E	. . . . . .	£80
Yeovil, D	. . . .	£50
York, E	. . . .	£75

Missent marks (e.g. Missent to Leicester)	. . . . from	£35
Returned marks (e.g. Retd from Worthing)	. . . . . from	£100
Late marks (e.g. Too Late)	. . . . from	£18

REMEMBER!
Prices in C.B.P. are minimum values
for a **clear strike on a clean card or cover.**
Have you read the notes
at the beginning?

---

4. EARLY SCOTTISH MARKS

55	56	57	58

55 Small Edinburgh Bishop marks, 1693–1725 . . . . 10.00
56 Larger Edinburgh Bishop marks, 1725–1806 . . . . 5.00
57 Circular Edinburgh types with year in full, 1801–1857 . . . . . 1.00
58 Williamson's post, circular marks, 1773–1793 . . . . 75.00

EDDLESTONE
59

62 JEDBURGH 374 — B

60    **61**

59 Straight line town stamps, from 1730 . . . . 6.00
60 Illustrated types, e.g. Fort William 'Thistle', Perth 'Lamb' . . . 150.00
61 Circular types, with or without lines 5.00
62 Mileage types, boxed or unboxed from 1808 . . . . 2.50
    As above but mileage removed, from 1829 . . . . 2.00
    Dated town stamps, from 1800 . . . . 2.00

63    **64**    **65**

Missent marks, boxed, unframed, etc 4.00
63 'Too Late', 'Mae West' types 2.50
64 Other types of 'Too Late' marks 5.00
65 Additional Halfpenny, boxed or unboxed with or without 'Addl'

. . . . 4.00

5. EARLY IRISH MARKS

66 　　**67** 　　**68**

　　　　　　　　　　　　69

70 　　　　　**71**

66 Small Dublin Bishop marks, 1670–1746 . . . . 65.00
67 Larger Dublin Bishop marks, 1746–95 . . . . 20.00
68 Circular year marks, 1796–1807 . . . . 7.50
69 'Mermaids', 1808–14 . . . . (average quality) 30.00
70 Octagonals, 1818 . . . . 2.50
71 Diamonds, in red, 1820–46 . . . . 1.00
　　 'Mermaid' paid marks, in red, 1808–15 . . . (average quality) 150.00
　　 Octagonal or rectangular paid marks, in red, 1814–46 . . . . . 2.50

WATERFORD
72

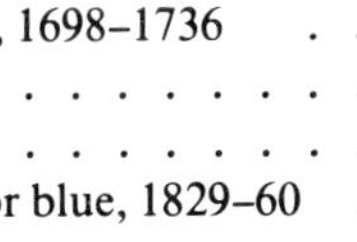

DERRY

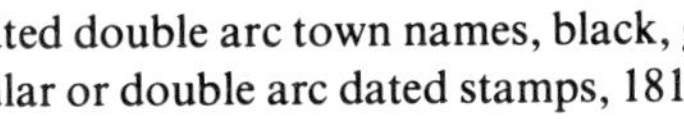

BELFAST
　　　73

118
74

72 Town stamps, straight line with large first letter, 1698–1736 . . 150.00
73 　As above but uniform height, 1713–1855 . . . . 13.00
　　 　As above but contracted names 80.00
　　 Undated double arc town names, black, green or blue, 1829–60 . 12.00
　　 Circular or double arc dated stamps, 1818–65 . . . . 1.50
74 Mileage stamps, boxed or unboxed, various colours, 1808–32 . . 8.50
　　 Provincial paid stamps 10.00

6. THE GREAT POST OFFICE REFORM, 1839–40

Uniform 4d Post, 5 Dec 1839–9 Jan 1840

75 Arundel

76 Oxford

77 Wakefield

78 Scottish Standard type    **79 Galashiels**    **80 Dublin**

Manuscript '4', 'P4', 'Pd 4' or 'Paid 4', black for unpaid letters . 35.00
As above but in red for paid letters 60.00
Handstruck '4' from English or Welsh towns

75 Arundel	Cullompton	Ipswich	Scarborough
Ashburton	Dorchester	Kington	Sherborne
Ashby	East Winch	Leamington	Stockton
Baldock	Grimsby	Leominster	77 Wakefield
Blackburn	Halifax	Norwich	Welshpool
Carlisle	Hawes	Nottingham	Whitchurch
Catterick	Hertford	76 Oxford	Woodbridge
Chester	Horsham	Rushyford	Worcester

from 500.00

78 Handstruck '4' from Scottish towns (standard type):

Aberdeen	Edinburgh	Perth
Ayr	Haddington	Stonehaven
Dundee	Inverness	
Glasgow	Leith (blue)	from 85.00

As above but individual Scottish types:

Coldstream	. . .£250	Hawick	£400
79 Galashiels	. . £300	Kirkwall . . .	£300
Glasgow . . .	£200	Stromness . .	£250
Golspie	£250	Wigtown . . .	£250

Handstruck '4' from Irish towns:

Armagh (blue) .	£750	Drogheda . . .	£750	Galway	£750
Ballymena . .	£750	**80** Dublin	£350	Newry	£750
Belfast	£750	Dundalk . . .	£750	Roscrea . . .	£750
Derry	£750	Enniskillen . .	£750	Stanorlan . . .	£750

Uniform 1d Post, from 10 Jan 1840

81
London

82
Newcastle on Tyne

83
Marlborough

84
Maidstone

85
Northampton

ABBEYLEIX

PAID

PDI

1^D

86 Braemar

87 Abbeyleix

88 Verner's Bridge

Manuscript '1' in red, paid letters 1.50

Handstruck '1', 'Pd 1', 'Paid 1d', 'P1', etc, from English or Welsh towns (usually in red):

Abergavenny . . £40	Clifton £30	Leeds £20
Aberystwyth . . £50	Colchester . . . £35	Leicester £40
Addingham . . . £40	Coleford £40	Liverpool £8
Amlwch £40	Colne £50	81 London £1
Andover . . . £100	Cranbrook . . . £40	Long Stratton . . £80
Arundel £35	Crawley £20	Loose £40
Ashbourn £20	Croydon £40	Lowestoft £20
Attleborough . . £45	Darlington . . . £15	84 Maidstone . . . £15
Aylsham £30	Dorking £40	Manchester . . . £35
Banbury . . . £100	Dowlais £45	83 Marlborough . . £40
Bangor £30	Edgware £45	Merthyr Tydfil . . £50
Barmouth . . . £35	Englefield Green . £50	Middleham . . . £35
Barnet £35	Epsom £40	Nantwich £30
Basingstoke . . . £8	Esher £40	82 Newcastle on Tyne £15
Bath £15	Falmouth £30	Newcastle-u-Lyme £30
Battle £40	Folkestone . . . £50	Newmarket . . . £20
Bawtry £50	Gateshead . . . £25	Newport Pagnell . £35
Beaconsfield . . £25	Goole £25	New Romney . . £35
Beaumaris . . . £50	Grantham . . . £35	Newton Abbott . £30
Beverley £15	Guernsey . . . £200	85 Northampton . . £10
Biddenden . . . £40	Guildford £25	Nottingham . . . £25
Bingham £60	Hadleigh £20	Oldham £40
Birkenhead . . . £20	Halifax £30	Olney £70
Bishop's Stortford £45	Harleston £20	Otney £55
Blackburn . . . £12	Hastings £35	Petworth £18
Bognor £15	Havant £60	Port Madoc . . . £40
Bolton £65	Haverford West . £40	Portsmouth . . . £40
Bradford £20	Hereford £20	Presteigne £30
Braintree £50	Hertford £75	Ramsgate £10
Brenchley £50	High Wycombe . £40	Redruth £40
Brentford £35	Hoddesdon . . . £60	Rickmansworth . £25
Bridgend £50	Horsham £30	Ripley £30
Bridgenorth . . . £18	Horwich . . . £100	Robertsbridge . . £30
Brighton £15	Huddersfield . . £15	Rochdale £20
Bungay £40	Hull £10	Rochford £25
Buntingford . . . £30	Hurst Green . . . £30	Romford £30
Burnley £30	Hythe £50	Romsey £30
Bury St. Edmunds £15	Ipswich £15	St. Leonards . . . £40
Carlisle £25	Isle of Man . . £200	Salisbury £20
Carnarvon . . . £50	Ixworth £75	Sawbridgeworth . £30
Chard £50	Jersey . . . £200	Scarborough . . £25
Chelmsford . . . £40	Kingston £20	Selby £30
Chertsey £30	Lamberhurst . . £45	Settle £20
Chester £20	Lancaster £35	Sevenoaks . . . £40
Chichester . . . £20	Lawkland £40	Sheerness £15
Chippenham . . £15	Leamington . . . £30	Sheffield £40
Clare £100	Ledbury £30	Skipton £75

Slough £30	Ulverston £60	Whitchurch . . . £12
Southampton . . £10	Uxbridge £25	Whitehaven . . . £12
Stafford £40	Wadhurst £45	Wigan £40
Staplehurst . . . £50	Waltham Cross . £75	Windsor £35
Stevenage £80	Walworth £30	Woburn £30
Swindon £40	Warwick £40	Wokingham . . . £18
Thetford £50	Watton £35	Wolverhampton . £20
Ticehurst £30	Wednesbury . . . £30	Worthing £35
Thrapston . . . £35	Wells £30	Wrexham £25
Tunbridge . . . £30	Welwyn £35	York £12
Topcroft . . . £100	West Bromwich . £50	
Tunbridge Wells . £45	West Drayton . . £30	

Handstruck '1', etc, from Scottish towns (usually in red):

Aberdeen £5	Dumfries £10	Kinghorn £10
Aberdour £10	Dunbar £10	Kirkcaldry . . . £10
Alloa £20	Dundee £10	Kirkcudbright . . £10
Annan £30	Dunfermline . . £15	Kirkwall £10
Anstruther . . . £10	Dunoon £15	Lanark £10
Arbroath £15	Dunse £15	Langholme . . . £15
Appin £10	Ecclefechan . . . £15	Largs £10
Auchterarder . . £20	Edinburgh . . . £4	Lauder £10
Auchtermuchty . £10	Elgin £10	Laurencekirk . . £15
Ayr £10	Falkirk £6	Leith £10
Ayton £10	Fisherrow £10	Lerwick £40
Ballantrae . . . £10	Forfar £10	Lesmahago . . . £20
Banff £12	Forres £10	Leven £20
Bathgate £10	Fort William . . £10	Linlithgow . . . £15
Beith £10	Fraserburgh . . . £12	Lochgilphead . . £15
Biggar £10	Galashiels . . . £10	Lockerby £10
Boness £15	Garliestone . . . £25	Maybole £10
Braco £20	Gatehouse . . . £15	Mauchline . . . £10
86 Braemar £30	Girvan £15	Melrose £15
Bridge of Earne . £10	Glasgow £50	Midcalder £15
Callender £10	Glenluce £20	Moffatt £15
Campbelton . . . £10	Golspie £18	Montrose £10
Canonbie £10	Greenoch £10	Musselburgh . . £10
Cockburnspath . £15	Haddington . . . £10	Newburgh £10
Coldstream . . . £10	Hamilton £10	Newport £15
Collinsburgh . . £15	Hawick £10	Newton Stewart . £20
Crail £10	Holytown £15	North Queensferry £10
Crieff £25	Huntly £25	Paisley £10
Culross £15	Inverkeithing . . £15	Peebles £10
Cumnock £10	Inverness £15	Perth £10
Cupar £10	Jedburgh £10	Peterhead £10
Dalkeith £10	Kelso £10	Pittenweem . . . £15
Denny £15	Kettle £15	Port Patrick . . . £15
Douglas £12	Kilmarnock . . . £10	Port William . . £15
Dumbarton . . . £15	Kincardine . . . £10	Prestonkirk . . . £15

Rhymie £30	Stirling £10	Tobermory . . . £40
St. Andrews . . . £10	Stonehaven . . . £25	Whitehorn . . . £15
St. Boswells . . . £15	Stow £15	Wick £15
Sanquhar £15	Stranraer £10	Wigtown £15
Selkirk £10	Tarbert £10	
Stewarton £10	Thornhill £15	

Handstruck '1d', etc, from Irish towns (usually in red):

87 Abbeyleix £25	Cookstown . . . £50		Maryborough . . £30
Armagh £20	Derry £20		Navan £20
Athlone £25	Donaghadee . . £25		Parsonstown . . £15
Athy £25	Down £15		Portarlington . . £60
Ballymena . . . £20	Drogheda £30		Portglenone . . . £30
Ballymoney . . . £30	Dublin £10		Roscrea £20
Borrisakane . . . £30	Dundalk £20		Tallow £40
Carrickfergus . . £30	Dungarvan . . . £30	88	Verner's Bridge . £40
Castleburn . . . £30	Maghera £20		

89
Blackburn

90
Colchester

91
Stirling

92
Ballyjamesduff

Manuscript '2' or '2d', black, for unpaid letters 4.00
Handstruck '2' or '2d', from English towns (usually black,
        sometimes blue or green):

Abingdon	Braintree	Chelmsford	Folkestone
Ashburton	Bridgenorth	Cheltenham	Gloucester
Ashton-u-Lyne	Broadway	Chester	Glossop
Bangor	Buckingham	Chippenham	Gravesend
Barmouth	Bungay	90 Colchester	Great Malvern
Barnard Castle	Burnley	Darlington	Guernsey
Basingstoke	Bury	Derby	Guildford
Bedale	Bury St. Edmunds	Diss	Hadleigh
Beverley	Canterbury	Dudley	Halifax
Birmingham	Carlisle	Dunmow	Halstead
89 Blackburn	Carnarvon	Durham	Harwich
Bolton	Catterick	Ely	Haverfordwest

Hawes	Liverpool	Reading	Trowbridge
Hayle	London	Rochford	Torquay
Hereford	Loughborough	Romford	Wakefield
Hertford	Lynn	Romsey	Waltham Cross
High Wycombe	Manchester	Ross	Warwick
Hounslow	Monkwearmouth	Ryde	Wells
Huddersfield	Narbeth	Selby	Weymouth
Hythe	Newbury	Scorton	Wigan
Ipswich	Newcastle on Tyne	Southampton	Wigton
Ironbridge	Newcastle-u-Lyme	Spilsby	Windsor
Isle of Man	Northampton	Stafford	Worcester
Jersey	Nottingham	Stockport	Wolverhampton
Kendal	Oldham	Stoneham	Woodbridge
Leamington	Plymouth	Stourbridge	York
Leeds	Portsmouth	Sudbury	
Leominster	Preston	Sunderland	from 15.00

Handstruck '2' from Scottish towns (usually black, sometimes blue or green):

Aberdeen	Dunbar	Jedburgh	Newburgh
Alloa	Dunblane	Kelso	Newport
Annan	Dundee	Kettle	Paisley
Auchtermuchty	Dunfermline	Kirkwall	Peebles
Ayr	Dunse	Kirmarnock	Perth
Ayton	Edinburgh	Kinross	Pittenweem
Ballantrae	Falkirk	Kirkcaldy	Portobello
Beith	Galashiels	Lamgholm	St. Boswells
Bridge of Earne	Glasgow	Largs	Sanday
Cairnryan	Glen App	Leith	Selkirk
Canonbie	Glenluce	Lerwick	**91** Stirling
Carsphairn	Greenock	Leven	Stonehaven
Cockburnspath	Haddington	Linlithgow	Stow
Creetown	Hamilton	Lochgilphead	Stranraer
Crieff	Hawick	Maybole	Tranent
Dalry	Inverkeithing	Melrose	Whitehorn
Dumbarton	Irvine	Moffatt	from 20.00

Handstruck '2' from Irish towns (usually black, sometimes blue or green):

Abbeyleix	Derry	Lisnaskea	Roscrea
Armagh	Donaghadee	Longford	Stradone
Athlone	Donegal	Lurgan	Tipperary
Bailyboro	Drogheda	Magherafelt	Tralee
92 Ballyjamesduff	Dublin	Maryborough	Tuam
Ballymena	Dungannon	Monaghan	Warren Point
Ballymonte	Dundalk	Moneymore	
Banbridge	Enniskillen	Mullinger	
Belfast	Kells	Newry	
Castlebar	Kilbeggan	Newtownlimavady	
Cookstown	Killucan	Portadown	from 10.00

Maltese Cross Cancellations, from 1840

93
General
(England)

94
General
(Scotland)

95
Alderney

96
Kilmarnock

97
Leeds

98
Manchester

99
Mulligar

100
Norwich or
Plymouth

101
Wotton-
under-Edge

102
York

103
London

| Colours: | One Penny Imperf | | | | Two Penny Blue Imperf | | | |
| | 1840 Black | | 1841 Red | | 1840 No Lines | | 1841 White Lines | |
	◯	✉	◯	✉	◯	✉	◯	✉
Red	£25	£100	£300	£3000	£100	£250	£1500	—
Black	£75	£150	£2	£15	£100	£200	£20	£40
Blue	£450	£2000	£25	£85	£1000	£3000	£150	£750
Brown	£150	£350	—	—	—	—	—	—
Green	—	—	£200	£900	—	—	—	—
Magenta	£300	£750	—	—	£1000	£3000	—	—
Orange	£100	£250	—	—	—	—	—	—
Ruby	£150	£300	—	—	£1000	£2500	—	—
Vermilion	£100	£200	—	—	—	—	—	—
Violet	£250	£900	£250	£1100	—	—	—	—
Yellow	£2000	—	—	—	—	—	—	—

	Types:	One Penny Imperf 1840 Black ○	1840 Black ✉	1841 Red ○	1841 Red ✉	Two Penny Blue Imperf 1840 No Lines ○	1840 No Lines ✉	1841 White Lines ○	1841 White Lines ✉
93	General	£25	£100	£2	£15	£100	£200	£20	£40
94	Scottish	—	—	£10	£20	—	—	—	—
95	Alderney	—	—	£750	£4000	—	—	—	—
	Belfast	—	—	£15	£40	—	—	£90	£180
	Brighton	—	—	£30	£100	—	—	—	—
	Cork	—	—	£60	£150	—	—	£90	£180
	Coventry	—	—	£90	£300	—	—	—	—
	Dublin	£190	£350	£15	£40	£350	£750	£75	£150
	Dursley	—	—	£50	£125	—	—	—	—
	Eyrecourt	—	—	£100	£500	—	—	—	—
	Greenock	—	—	£20	£40	£500	£1000	—	—
	Hollymount	—	—	£200	£1000	—	—	—	—
	Kelso	—	—	£50	£180	£400	£1000	£200	£400
96	Kilmarnock	£1000	—	£100	£500	£1000	£2000	£200	£400
	Leamington	—	—	£25	£65	—	—	—	—
97	Leeds	£200	£600	£40	£125	£400	£1000	£150	£500
	Limerick	—	—	£50	£100	—	—	—	—
98	Manchester	£75	£225	£30	£50	£400	£800	—	—
	Montrose	—	—	£35	£100	—	—	—	—
99	Mullingor	£1000	£1800	£200	£1000	£1000	£2000	—	—
100	Norwich	—	—	£35	£100	£400	£1000	£200	£400
	Perth	—	—	£20	£50	—	—	—	—
100	Plymouth	£250	£600	—	—	£500	£1100	—	—
	Settle	—	—	£150	£800	—	—	—	—
	Stirling	—	—	£20	£60	—	—	—	—
	Stonehaven	£200	£1900	£100	£300	£450	£1000	—	—
	Welshpool	—	—	£60	£300	—	—	—	—
	Whitehaven	—	—	£100	£700	—	—	—	—
101	Wootton	£500	£1000	£400	£1500	£1200	£2250	—	—
102	York	—	—	£60	£200	£800	£1800	£200	£400
	London 1	£1000	—	£15	£60	£1500	—	£60	£200
	London 2	£750	£2000	£15	£60	£1500	—	£60	£200
	London 3	£750	£2000	£25	£65	—	—	£60	£200
	London 4	£750	£2000	£40	£70	£1500	—	£60	£200
	London 5	£750	£2000	£15	£60	£1800	—	£65	£400
103	London 6	£750	£2000	£12	£40	£1500	—	£60	£200
	London 7	£750	£2000	£12	£40	£1500	—	£100	£400
	London 8	£750	£2000	£10	£40	£2000	£5000	£90	£350
	London 9	£750	£2000	£15	£40	£1800	—	£100	£500
	London 10	£750	£2000	£23	£65	£1800	—	£120	£550
	London 11	—	—	£27	£65	—	—	£100	£450
	London 12	£750	£2000	£38	£70	£1500	—	£45	£100

Maltese Crosses on piece are worth about 50% above the price for loose stamp.

TO ALL POSTMASTERS.

GENERAL POST OFFICE,
Edinburgh, April, 1840.

I BEG to inclose you two Specimens of the Penny and Two-penny stamped Covers and Envelopes, and two of the Penny adhesive Labels. (the Two-penny one is not yet ready) which I must beg you will carefully preserve, in order to compare them in case of doubt with the stamped Letters that may pass through your Office. In the event of your suspecting that the Stamps used on any Letters are forged, you will not detain the Letter, but simply take the Address, and report the circumstance to me without loss of time, in order that the Party to whom the Letter is directed may be at once applied to. You will observe, however, that the adhesive Stamps vary almost in all cases, one from the other, having different Letters at the bottom corners, and I point this out that you may not be misled by the circumstance, and be induced to suspect Forgery, where the variation of the Stamps has been intentional. The Numbers on the Covers and Envelopes also vary. You will carefully Stamp with the Cancelling Stamp that has been forwarded to you, the stamped Covers and Envelopes, as well as the adhesive Stamps, the two former must be struck on the figure of Britannia, and in case of more than one adhesive Stamp being attached to a Letter, each Stamp must be separately obliterated. The use of the Cancelling Stamp, however, will not dispense with that of the ordinary dated Stamp, which will be struck on the Letter as usual. Where the value of the Stamps is under the rate of Postage, to which the Letter if pre-paid in Money would be subject, you will Surcharge the Letter with a Pen in the usual manner.

You will acknowledge the receipt of this Letter and the Specimen Stamps by return of Post.

By Command,

EDWARD S. LEES,

SECRETARY.

Official notice informing Postmasters of regulations for cancelling the first adhesive postage stamps. The cancellations are known to collectors as 'Maltese Crosses'.

7. NUMERAL AND DUPLEX POSTMARKS

London: Inland Section

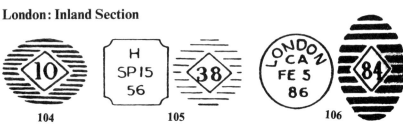

104   105   106

104 Horizontal oval with number in diamond, single, 1–44 and 50–75,
from 1844 . . . .   2.00
     As above but twin 45, 46 or 47 . . . .   7.50
     As above but triple 48 or 49 . . . . 70.00
105 Duplex type with datestamp as square with indented corners,
from 1853 . . . .   7.50
106 Duplex, circular datestamp, number in diamond, upright oval,
1–107 . . . .   1.75
     As above but datestamp with double circle 4.50
     Single obliterators with number with or without diamond,
upright oval or circular 2.50

London: District Post and Suburban Offices

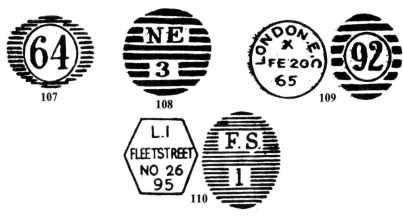

107   108   109

110

107 Horizontal oval with number in circle, 1–98, from 1844 . . . .   3.50
     Duplex, circular datestamp with horizontal oval, 1853–7 . . .   2.50
108 Single obliterators with District initials, upright oval or circular .   3.00
109 Duplex with upright oval, several series, from 1858 . . . . . .   1.50
     Sideways duplexes of London W or SE, 1857–62 . . . . . .   4.00
110 Duplex with hexagonal datestamps, for late fees 6.50

Numbers used:

1. Highgate
2. Finchley
   E. Finchley
3. Whetstone
4. Hampstead
5. Hendon
6. Edgware
   E.C.
   Churton St
7. Stoke Newington
8. Tottenham
   W. Brompton
9. Kentish Town
10. Edmonton
    S. Kensington
11. Enfield
    Chelsea
12. Bow
13. Stratford
14. Leyton
    St. Martin's Place
15. Woodford
    Highbury
16. Chigwell
    Victoria St
    E.C.
17. Ilford
    Leytonstone
18. Deptford
19. Halfway St
    Finsbury Pk.
20. Greenwich
21. Woolwich
    Wanstead
22. Eltham
    Plaistow
23. Bexley
    Brockley
24. Dulwich
25. Sydenham
26. Beckenham
    Kensal Town
    North Kensington
27. Clapham
28. Tooting
29. Mitcham
    Forest Gate
30. Carshalton
    Lee
31. Wandsworth
32. Putney
33. Mortlake
34. Richmond
    Earl's Court
35. Twickenham
    Bethnal Grn.
36. Hampton
    Walthamstow
    Balham
37. Brompton
38. Kensington
39. Hammersmith
40. Acton
    Hse of Commons

41. Brentford
    Barnes
42. Paddington
    Walworth
43. Charing Cross
    Sutton
    Aldgate
44. Nth Row
    Wimbledon
    Manor Pk
45. Portland St
    Tottenham
    Nth Woolwich
46. Stepney
    Palmer's Grn
47. Southwark
    Finchley Church End
48. Shoreditch
    N. Finchley
49. Sidmouth St
    Royal Hill, Greenwich
50. Chief Letter Carrier
    Victoria Docks
51. Registration Clerk
    New Southgate
52. Chief Office
    Herne Hill
53. Chief Office
    Woodford Green
    Homerton
54. Chief Office
    Norwood
55. Chief Office
    Leyton St
    W. Kensington
56. Chief Office
    Smallbury Gn.
    Isleworth
    Sth Woodford
57. Chief Office
    Sutton
    Chiswick
58. Chief Office
    Wimbledon
    Mill Hill
59. Unpaid Letter Div.
    Plaistow
60. Chief Office
    Kilburn
61. Chief Office
    Willesden
62. Chief Office
    Harrow
    Sth Tottenham
63. Chief Office
    E.C.
    Elstree
    Wimbledon
64. Chief Office
    E.C.
    Cheshunt
    Ealing Dean
    W. Ealing

65. Chief Office
    Camberwell
66. Chief Office
    E.C.
    Lewisham
67. Chief Office
    E.C.
    Peckham
68. Chief Office
    E.C.
    Kennington
69. Chief Office
    E.C.
    Blackheath
70. Chief Office
    E.C.
    Anerley
71. Chief Office
    Catford
72. Chief Office
    Lower Norwood
    W. Norwood
73. Chief Office
    Shooter's Hill
    W.C. District Office
74. Chief Office
    Tottenham
    Bedford St
75. Chief Office
    Edmonton
    Paddington
76. Chief Office
    New Cross
77. Chief Office
    E. Dulwich
78. Chief Office
    S.E. Dist. Office
79. Chief Office
    S.W. Dist. Office
80. E.C.
    Tottenham
81. E.C.
    Lower Edmonton
82. E.C.
    Leyton
83. E.C.
    Up. Edmonton
84. E.C.
    Chingford
85. E.C.
    Walthamstow
86. E.C.
    N.W. Dist. Office
87. E.C.
    N. Dist. Office
88. E.C.
    E. Dist. Office
89. E.C.
    W. Dist. Office
90. E.C.
    Muswell Hill
91. E.C.
    Cricklewood
92–98 E.C.

37

B and C Series, issued from 1861

1B. Ponders End	21B. Rotherhithe	37C. Notting Hill
2B. Colney Hatch	22B. Welling	38B. Paddington
3B. Hornsey	23B. Brixton Hill	38C. Paddington
4B. Southgate	Brixton	39B. Shepherds Bush
5B. Holloway	24B. Camberwell	40B. Southall
6B. Clapton	25B. Merton	41B. St. John's Wood
7B. Loughton	26B. Sth Lambeth	42B. Stanmore
8B. Hackney	27B. Stockwell	43B. Sudbury
9B. Canning Town	28B. Streatham	44B. The Hyde
10B. Chadwell	29B. Thornton Heath	45B. Barking
11B. Poplar	30B. Walworth	46B. Waltham Grn
12B. Charlton	Maida Hill	Fulham
13B. Chislehurst	31A. New Wandsworth	47B. Sunbury
14B. Erith	31B. Battersea	48B. Forest Hill
15B. Foots Cray	32B. Petersham	49B. Sth Norwood
16B. Lessness Heath	33B. Teddington	51B. Winchmore Hill
17B. Lewisham	34B. Acton	52B. Wood Green
18B. Peckham	35B. Ealing	53B. Upper Holloway
19B. Penge	36B. Hanwell	Junction Rd.
20B. Plumstead	37B. Notting Hill	U. Holloway

England and Wales

Numerals

111

112

111 Numbered cancellations in horizontal oval, from 1844 . . . . 2.50
112 Numbered cancellations in upright oval, 1864 . . . . 7.00

Numbered cancellations used with Edward VII stamps 2.50
   As above but George V period 3.50
   As above but George VI period 4.50
   As above but Elizabeth II period 8.00

Spoons and Sideways Duplexes

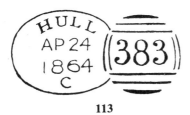

113

114

115

116

Office No	Office	Spoon 113	Sideways Duplex 114	Office No	Office	Spoon	Sideways Duplex
3	Abingdon		£15	258	Dover		£9
046	Aldershot Camp		£85	263	Dudley	£90	£18
32	Ashton-under-Lyne		£10	267	Durham		£12
47	Bangor		£15	285	Exeter		£10
50	Barnstaple		£9	288	Fakenham		£30
53	Bath		£8	290	Falmouth		£12
54	Battle		£40	023	Farnborough Station		£40
61	Bedford		£15	303	Folkestone	£5	
74	Birkenhead	£100	£9	309	Gateshead		£12
75	Birmingham	£5	£7	312	Gloucester	£20	£10
92	Bolton		£15	320	Gosport		£20
94	Boston		£10	321	Grantham		£10
107	Bradford		£5	322	Gravesend		£20
118	Brentwood		£9	497	Great Malvern		£18
122	Bridgenorth	£45		325	Guildford		£10
132	Brighton		£8	330	Halifax		£7
134	Bristol	£10	£4	336	Harleston		£45
147	Bungay		£30	338	Harrogate		£20
150	Burnley		£18	342	Hastings		£8
152	Burton-u-Trent	£25		344	Havant		£30
154	Bury, Lancs		£10	345	Haverfordwest		£10
97	Bury St. Edmunds		£12	351	Helston		£40
158	Cambridge		£6	357	Hereford		£10
84	Canterbury		£10	359	Hertford		£17
162	Cardiff		£8	376	Honiton		£6
165	Carlisle		£9	387	Huddersfield		£10
167	Carmarthen		£9	383	Hull	£10	£5
108	Carnarvon		£9	396	Huntingdon		£18
173	Chatham		£15	428	Hurst Green		£12
176	Chelmsford		£17	405	Ipswich		£10
177	Cheltenham	£120	£5	407	Isle of Man		£80
179	Chertsey		£17	411	Kendal		£6
180	Chester	£20	£7	415	Kidderminster	£100	£10
186	Chesterfield		£8	422	Kingston		£40
190	Chichester		£9	436	Lancaster		£10
204	Cirencester		£17	439	Launceston		£40
959	Clifton		£10	444	Leamington	£60	£20
210	Colchester		£15	447	Leeds	£30	£5
223	Coventry		£10	449	Leicester		£9
938	Croydon		£35	451	Lewes		£12
233	Darlington		£7	458	Lincoln		£10
236	Dartford		£35	466	Liverpool	£5	
242	Derby		£7	478	Lowestoft		£12
249	Devizes		£20	488	Lynn		£18
250	Devonport		£30	492	Maidenhead		£15
620	Devonport		£10	493	Maidstone		£10
255	Doncaster		£10	498	Manchester	£8	£5
256	Dorchester		£10	506	Margate		£10
257	Dorking		£10	523	Merthyr Tydfil		£12

Office No	Office	Spoon	Sideways Duplex	Office No	Office	Spoon	Sideways Duplex
541	Newark		£10	730	Stafford	£100	£7
544	Newbury		£15	742	Stamford		£10
545	Newcastle on Tyne		£8	939	Staplehurst		£18
557	Newmarket		£15	733	Stockport		£15
561	Newport, Mon		£10	547	Stoke on Trent	£100	
567	Newton Abbot		£10	750	Stourbridge		£12
048	Normanton		£15	757	Stroud		£17
570	Northampton	£35	£7	761	Sunderland		£10
573	North Shields		£10	763	Swansea		£10
575	Norwich		£7	766	Swindon		£15
583	Nottingham		£6	776	Taunton		£10
595	Oswestry	£50		780	Tavistock		£15
603	Oxford		£9	784	Tenby		£10
368	Pembroke Dock		£12	790	Thetford		£30
606	Penrith		£10	800	Tiverton		£35
612	Peterborough		£9	805	Torquay		£10
620	Plymouth	£25	£6	814	Truro		£35
624	Poole		£10	820	Tunbridge Wells		£10
625	Portsmouth		£6	830	Uxbridge		£12
628	Preston		£8	831	Wakefield		£6
634	Ramsgate		£10	834	Wallsall	£100	
635	Reading 115	£50 'Biscuit'		847	Warrington	£35	£10
637	Reigate		£20	859	Wellington, Salop		£10
973	Rhyl		£10	860	Wellington, Somerset		£7
648	Rochdale		£10	864	Wells, Somerset		£10
650	Rochester		£15	871	Weston Super Mare		£10
655	Rotherham		£10	873	Weymouth		£9
658	Royston		£18	878	Wigan		£15
659	Rugby 116	£90 'shoe'		888	Winchester		£10
683	Salisbury		£10	890	Windsor		£10
693	Scarborough		£8	897	Wisbeach		£10
699	Sheerness		?	905	Wolverhampton	£25	£7
700	Sheffield		£5	907	Woodbridge		£20
708	Shrewsbury	£20	£8	918	Worcester	£15	£6
717	Slough		£15	924	Wrexham	£75	£18
723	Southampton		£6	927	Yarmouth		£10
727	Spalding		£12	930	York	£35	£6

Note: There are several types of 'Spoons' and 'Sideways Duplex' marks. Some towns used more than one type. Prices are for the cheapest type.

Duplex

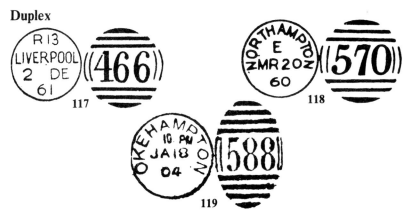

117 Duplex cancellations, oval numeral, town across datestamp,
from 1857 . . . . 4.00

118 Duplex cancellations, oval numeral, town round datestamp . . 2.50

119 Duplex cancellations, upright oval with three or four bars, on
cover with 1d, red 2.00

As above but with 1d Lilac 0.85

As above but card or cover with Edward VII ½d or 1d 0.50

As above but card or cover with George V ½d or 1d 1.50

Numbers used:

1. Abergavenny	41. Bakewell	79. Knowle
2. Aberystwyth	42. Baslow	80. Bishop Auckland
3. Abingdon	Chiswick	81. Stanhope
4. Wantage	Login	82. Bishops Castle
5. Accrington	43. Stoney Middleton	83. Bishops Stortford
6. Alfreton	Turnham Grn.	84. Canterbury
7. Crick	Docking	85. Bishops Waltham
Longhope	44. Tideswell	86. Blackburn
8. Alnwick	Resolven	87. Blandford
9. Hoarwithy	45. Baldock	88. Bodmin
10. Alresford	46. Banbury	89. Wadebridge
11. Alton	47. Bangor	90. Padstow
12. Altrincham	48. Barnards Castle	91. Bognor
13. Ambleside	Barnard Castle	92. Bolton
14. Amersham	49. Barnsley	93. Borough Bridge
15. Chesham	50. Barnstaple	94. Boston
16. Missenden	51. Barton-on-Humber	95. Alford
Gt. Missenden	52. Basingstoke	96. Stickney
17. Amesbury	53. Bath	Aldershot Camp
18. Ampthill	54. Battle	97. Bury St. Edmunds
19. Gilfach Goch	55. Bawtry	98. Dinas Mawddwy
20. Silsoe	56. Gringley	99. Caldicot
21. Andover	Forest Row	100. Botesdale
22. Andover Rd.	57. Beaconsfield	Ruardean
Micheldever Station	58. Beaumaris	101. Ixworth Alnmouth
23. Whitchurch	59. Beccles	102. Woolpit Leyton
Senny Bridge	60. Bedale	103. Bourn
24. Overton	61. Bedford	Bourne
25. Appleby	62. Belford	104. Brackley
26. Arrington	63. Wooler	105. Bracknell
Cray	64. Belper	106. Bradford, Wilts
27. Arundel	65. Berkhamstead	107. Bradford, Yorks
28. Ashbourne	66. Berwick	108. Carnarvon
29. Ashburton	Berwick Station	109. Walthamstow
30. Ashby DLZ	67. Beverley	110. Keighley
31. Ashford, Kent	68. Bewdley	111. Bingley
Ashford, S.O.	69. Bicester	112. Braintree
32. Ashton U.L.	70. Bideford	113. Brampton
33. Atherstone	71. Biggleswade	114. Brandon
34. Attleborough	72. Billericay	115. Stoke Ferry Hilborough
35. Axminster	73. Bilston	116. Brecon
36. Colyton	74. Birkenhead	117. Trecastle
Modley	75. Birmingham	Tottenham
37. Seaton	Five Ways, Birmingham	Trindon Colliery
Buckfastleigh	Gt. Hampton St., Birmingham 118. Brentwood	
38. Aylesbury	Smethwick, Birmingham	119. Edmonton
39. Aylsham	76. Campden	120. Bridgend, Glam
40. Bagshot	77. Halesowen	121. Pyle West Cross
Newtown Tredegar	78. Henley-in-Arden	122. Bridgenorth
Chapel Town, Mon	Aldershot	123. Bridgewater

124. Bridlington
125. Bridlington Quay
126. Hunmanby
    Spennymoor
127. Bridport
128. Beaminster
    St. Ann's Head
129. Brigg
130. Caistor
131. Limber
132. Brighton
    Alma Terr Hove Brighton
    Bedford St Brighton
    Hove B.O. Brighton
    Kemptown B.O. Brighton
    Lewes Rd Brighton
    Preston Rd Brighton
    St. George's Rd Brighton
    St. James's St Brighton
    Victoria Rd Brighton
    Western Rd B.O. Brighton
    West-Pier B.O. Brighton
133. Catterick
134. Bristol
    Clifton Bristol
    North St Bristol
    Redcliffe Bristol
135. Caxton
    Ton-yr-efail
    Corbridge
136. Brixham
137. Broadway
138. Bromyard
139. Bromsgrove
140. Redditch
141. Studley
142. Brough
143. Temple Sowerby
    Pontardawe
144. Bromley
    Shortlands, Kent
145. Buckingham
146. Builth
147. Bungay
148. Buntingford
149. Burford
150. Burnley
151. Colne
152. Burton-on-Trent
153. Burton, Westm'land
154. Bury, Lancs
155. Buxton
156. Chapel le Frith
    Maesycwmmer
157. Calne
158. Cambridge
159. Chard
160. Camelford
161. Five Lanes
    Bardney
162 Cardiff
    Barry Dock B.O. Cardiff

    Bute Docks Cardiff
    East Dock Cardiff
163. Pontypridd
164. Cardigan
165. Carlisle
166. Haltwistle
167. Carmarthen
168. Kidwelly
169. Prestbury
170. Newcastle Emlyn
171. Chalford
    Campsea Ash
172. Minchinhampton
173. Chatham
174. Chatteris
    West Felton
175. Cheadle
176. Chelmsford
177. Cheltenham
178. Chepstow
179. Chertsey
180. Chester
181. Abergele
182. Hawarden
    Betchworth
183. Mochdrai
184. Neston
    Shipley, Yorks
185. Northop
186. Chesterfield
187. Staveley Consett
188. Chester le Street
189. Leadgate
190. Chichester
    Chichester Station Office
191. Chippenham
192. Malmesbury
193. Sodbury
194. Charmouth
195. Chipping Norton
196. Chirk
197. Ruabon
198. Chorley
200. Christchurch
201. Chiselhurst
202. Chudleigh
203. Chumleigh Bwlch
204. Cirencester
205. Dunkirk
    Worcester Park
206. Clare
    Bream
207. Clitheroe
208. Cobham
209. Cockermouth
210. Colchester
211. Boxford
    Derri
212. Coleford
213. Coleshill
    Woodville
214. Cullompton

215. Colsterworth
    Repton
216. Congleton
217. Monksheath
    Barton-u-Needwood
    Preston-u-Needwood
218. Conway
219. Corwen
220. Bala
221. Barmouth
222. Dolgelly
223. Coventry
224. Cowbridge
225. Cowes
226. Cranbrook
    Tutbury
227. Biddenden
    Swadlincote
228. Crawley
229. Crediton
230. Crewkerne
231. Crickhowell
232. Cuckfield
233. Darlington
234. Smeaton
    Llansamlet
235. Staindrop
236. Dartford
237. Dartmouth
238. Daventry
239. Dawlish
240. Deal
241. Denbigh
242. Derby
243. Melbourne, Derby
244. Ticknall
    Tally
245. Dereham
246. Briningham
    Mountain Ash
247. Elmham
248. Guist
    Felstead
249. Devizes
250. Devonport
251. St. Germans
252. Torpoint
    Seascale
253. Dewsbury
254. Diss
255. Doncaster
256. Dorchester
257. Dorking
258. Dover
    Dover Station Office
259. Walmer
    New Walsingham
    Walsingham, Nflk
260. Downham
261. Driffield
262. Droitwich
263. Dudley

264. Dunchurch
    Woolwich
265. Dunmow
266. Dunstable
267. Durham
268. Seaham
    Broseley
269. Dursley
270. Berkeley
271. Eastbourne
272. East Grinstead
273. Eccleshall
274. Ellesmere
275. Ely
276. Much Wenlock
277. Emsworth
278. Enstone
279. Epping
280. Epsom
281. Ermebridge
    Madeley
282. Modbury
282. Modbury
    Dawley
283. Esher
284. Evesham
285. Exeter
286. Exmouth
287. Eye
288. Fakenham
289. Walsingham
    Coalbrookdale
290. Falmouth
291. Fareham
292. Farnham
293. Faringdon
294. Fairford
295. Highworth
296. Letchlade
297. Fazeley
298. Felton
299. Fenny Stratford
    Horsehay
300. Ferry Bridge
301. Feversham
    Faversham
302. Folkingham
303. Folkestone
304. Fordingbridge
305. Fowey
306. Frome
307. Gainsborough
308. Garstang
309. Gateshead
310. Gerrard's Cross
    Malpas
311. Glastonbury
312. Gloucester
313. Lea
    Cromford
314. Painswick
315. Thornbury
316. Godalming

317. Godstone
    Chelford
318. Bletchingley
    Lalnfymach
319. Goole
320. Gosport
321. Grantham
322. Gravesend
323. Grimsby
324. Guernsey
325. Guildford
326. Guisborough
327. Gretabridge
    Shrewton
328. Hadleigh
    Edgware
329. Halesworth
330. Halifax
331. Sowerby Bridge
    Nantymoel
332. Todmorden
333. Northowram
    Blackmill
334. Halstead
335. Haverhill
    Leckhampton
336. Harleston
337. Harlow
338. Harrowgate
    Harrogate
339. Hartfordbridge
340. Harwich
341. Haslemere
    Westbury on Severn
342. Hastings
    Hastings Station Office
    High St Hastings
    White Rock Hastings
    St. Leonard's-on-Sea Station Office
    Kings Rd. St. Leonard's-on-Sea
    St. Leonard's-on-Sea Kings Rd. B.O.
    St. Leonard's-on-Sea Marina
343. Hatfield
344. Havant
345. Haverfordwest
346. Hawes
347. Hay
348. Bruntless
    Coity
349. Glasbury
350. Haydonbridge
351. Helston
352. Hayle
353. Hemel Hempstead
354. Kings Langley
355. Henley-on-Thames
356. Nettlebed
    Charing
357. Hereford
358. Eardisley
    Radstock
359. Hertford
360. Hexham

361. Heytesbury
    Loughor
362. Deptford Inn
    Brizenorton
363. Higham Ferrers
364. High Wycombe
365. Hinckley
366. Hindon
367. Hitchin
368. Hobbs Point
    Pembroke Dock
369. Hoddesdon
370. Holbeach
371. Holt
372. Blakeney
373. Cley
374. Holyhead
375. Holywell
376. Honiton
377. Ottery St. Mary
378. Horncastle
379. Old Bolingbroke
    Charlton
    Church Lane Charlton, Kent
    Lower Rd. Charlton, Kent
    Old Charlton
380. Homdean
381. Horsham
382. Howden
383. Hull
    Hull Sorting Tender
    Hull – S.T.
384. Filey
385. Hedon
    Shooters Hill
386. Barrow-on-Humber
    Welling
387. Huddersfield
388. Marsden
    Bexley Heath
389. Slaithwaite
    Bexley
390. Hungerford
391. Aldbourne
392. Lambourne
    Lambourn
393. Ramsbury
394. Hounslow
395. Southall
396. Huntingdon
397. Buckden
    Crayford
398. Hythe, Kent
399. Ilchester
400. Ilfracombe
401. Ilminster
402. Ingatestone
403. Rayleigh
    Erith
404. Wickford
    Belvedere
405. Ipswich
406. Ironbridge

407. Douglas, IOM
408. Ivy Bridge
409. Jersey
410. Kelvedon
411. Kendal
412. Bowness
    Picardy Belvedere
413. Keswick
414. Kettering
415. Kidderminster
416. Kimbolton
417. Kineton
    Hucknall Torkard
418. Kingsbridge
419. Kington
420. Pennybont
421. Radnor
    Long Eaton
422. Kingston
    Kingston on Thames
423. Kirkby Lonsdale
    New Charlton
424. Knaresborough
425. Knutsford
426. Lamberhurst
    Crowhill Ross
427. Hawkhurst
428. Hurst Green
429. Newenden
    Broxbourne
430. Northiam
    Headcorn
431. Peasmarsh
432. Rolvenden
    Croesgoch
433. Sandhurst
    Maesteg
434. Lampeter
435. Aberayron
436. Lancaster
437. Kirkby Stephen
438. Sedbergh
439. Lauceston
440. Holsworthy
441. Stratton
442. Bude
443. Lowton
    Aberkenfig
444. Leamington
445. Leatherhead
446. Ledbury
447. Leeds
    Chapletown Rd. B.O. Leeds
    Hunslet B.O. Leeds
    Hyde Park B.O. Leeds
    Hyde Park Corner B.O. Leeds
448. Leek
449. Leicester
450. Leighton Buzzard
451. Lewes
    Lewes Station Office
452. Newhaven
    Porthcawl

453. Seaford
    Llanfairfechan
454. Leominster
455. Pembridge
456. Shobden
    Shobdon
457. Lichfield
458. Lincoln
    Lincoln Sorting Tender
459. Kirton-in-Lindsey
    Kirton-Lindsay
460. Wragby
461. Linton
    Upper Bangor
462. Liphook
463. Liskeard
464. Looe
    Hessle
465. Polperro
    Llangennech
466. Liverpool
    Exchange Liverpool
    Bootle Liverpool
    Bootle-cum-Linacre Liverpool
    Liverpool E.
    Liverpool N.
    Liverpool S.
    Liverpool E.D.
    Liverpool N.D.
    Liverpool S.D.
    Liverpool W.D.
467. Llandilo
468. Llandovery
469. Llanelly
470. Ponterdulais
    Pontardulais
471. Llangadock
472. Llangollen
473. Long Stratton
474. Lostwithiel
475. Loughborough
476. Mountsorrel
477. Louth
478. Lowestoft
479. Ludlow
480. Knighton
481. Leintwardine
    Haslemere
482. Luton
483. Lutterworth
484. Lyme
    Lyme Regis
485. Lymington
486. Yarmouth, IOW
487. Lyndhurst
488. Lynn
    Kings Lynn
489. Burnham
    Hildenborough
490. Holkham
    Ham Street
491. Macclesfield
492. Maidenhead

493. Maidstone
    Maidstone Station Office
494. Maldon
495. Malton
496. Sledmere
    Kew
497. Malvern
498. Manchester
    Manchester E.
    Manchester N.
    Manchester N.W.
    Manchester S.
    Manchester S.DO.
    Manchester S.E.
    Manchester S.W.
    Manchester W.
499. Glossop
500. Haslingden
    Keymer
501. Rawstenstall
502. Stalybridge
503. Manningtree
504. Mansfield
505. March
506. Margate
507. Marazion
508. Market Deeping
509. Market Drayton
510. Woore
511. Market Harborough
512. Market Raisin
    Market Rasen
513. Market Street
    Merstham
514. Market Weighton
515. South Cave
    Warlingham
    Whyteleafe
516. Marlborough
517. Great Bedwin
518. Marlow
519. Maryport
520. Matlock Bath
521. Melksham
522. Melton Mowbray
523. Merthyr Tydfil
524. Middlewich
525. Holmes Chapel
526. Winsford
    Boston Spa
527. Midhurst
528. Mildenhall
529. Milford
    Milford Haven
530. Milnthorpe
531. Mold
532. Monmouth
533. Ragland
    Raglan
534. Moreton-in-Marsh
535. Stow on the Wold
536. Winchcombe
537. Morpeth

538. Namptwich
    Nantwich
539. Narberth
540. Neath
541. Newark
542. Southwell
543. Carlton-on-Trent
    Liss
544. Newbury
545. Newcastle on Tyne
    Quayside Newcastle on Tyne
546. Newcastle-under-Lyme
    Newcastle, Staffs
547. Stoke
    Stoke on Trent
548. Tunstall
549. Hanley
550. Cobridge
    Kenley
551. Burslem
552. Lane Delph
    Sandgate
553. Lane End
    Longton
554. Etruria
555. Long-Port
    Longport
556. Shelton
557. Newmarket
558. Newnham
559. Lydney
560. Newport, IOW
561. Newport, Mon
    Newport Docks Newport, Mon
562. Caerleon
563. Tredegar
564. Newport Pagnell
565. Newport, Salop
566. New Romney
567. Newton Abbott
568. Newtown
569. Northallerton
570. Northampton
571. Northleach
572. Andoversford
572. Andoversford
    Wighton
573. North Shields
574. Northwich
575. Norwich
576. Acle
    Rolvenden
577. Cromer
578. Loddon
    Appledore, Kent
579. North Walsham
580. Reepham
    Lamberhurst
581 Scatton
    Burnham, Som
582. Worstead
583. Nottingham
584. Bingham
    Woodchurch

585. Ilkeston
586. Stapleford
    Bowness, Westm'land
587. Oakham
588. Oakhampton
    Okehampton
589. Hatherleigh
    Grasmere
590. Odiam
    Billingshurst
591. Oldham
592. Ollerton
593. Ormskirk
594. Southport
595. Oswestry
596. Cerrig-y-druidon
    Fittleworth
597. Llanrwst
598. Pentre Voylas
599. Otley
600. Addingham
601. Oundle
602. Ongar
603. Oxford
604. Pembroke
605. Penkridge
606. Penrith
607. Alston
608. Penryn
609. Penzance
610. Scilly
611. Pershore
612. Peterborough
613. Petersfield
614. Petworth
615. Fittleworth
616. Pulborough
617. Storrington
618. Pewsey
619. Pickering
620. Plymouth
621. Plympton
622. Pocklington
623. Pontefract
624. Poole
625. Portsmouth
    Portsmouth H.P.O.
    High St B.O. Portsmouth
    Landport Portsmouth
    Portsea Portsmouth
626. Prescot
627. Presteign
628. Preston
629. Fleetwood
630. Preston Brook
631. Frodsham
632. Pwllheli
633. Queenborough
634. Ramsgate
635. Reading
636. Redruth
637. Reigate
638. Retford
639. Rhayader

640. Devils Bridge
641. Richmond, Yorks
642. Ravenglass
643. Rickmansworth
644. Ringwood
645. Ripley
646. Ripon
647. Robertsbridge
648. Rochdale
649. Littleborough
    Snodland
650. Rochester
651. Rochford
652. Rockingham
    Crymmych
653. Romsey
654. Ross
655. Rotherham
656. Wath
    Bingham
657. Rougham
658. Royston
659. Rugby
    Rugby Station
660. Rugeley
661. Great Heywood
    Rotherfield
662. Shirlewich
    Sowerby Bridge
663. Wolseley Bridge
    Feltham
664. Rushyford
    Ilkley
665. Ruthin
666. Ryde, IOW
667. Rye
668. Romford
669. Saffron Walden
670. St. Austell
671. Grampound
672. St. Mawes
    West Woodburn
673. Mevagissey
674. Tregoney
    Great Chesterford
675. St. Albans
676. St. Asaph
677. St. Clear's
678. St. Columb
679. St. Helen's
680. St. Ives, Hunts
681. Somersham
    Dukinfield
682. St. Leonard's
    St. Leonard's on Sea
    Borough Green, Kent
683. Salisbury
684. Downton
685. Wilton
686. St. Neots
687. Sandbach
688. Sandwich
689. Sawbridgeworth
690. Saxmundham

691. Aldborough
    Eglwyswrw
692. Yoxford
    Velindre
693. Scarborough
694. Scole
695. Selby
696. Settle
697. Sevenoaks
698. Shaftsbury
    Shaftesbury
699. Sheerness
700. Sheffield
701. Shepton Mallet
702. Sherborne
703. Queen Camel
    Hatherleigh
704. South Shields
705. Shiffnall
    Shifnal
706. Shipston
    Shipston on Stour
707. Shoreham
708. Shrewsbury
709. Church Stretton
710. Llanidloes
711. Wem
712. Sidmouth
713. Sittingbourne
714. Skipton
715. Cross Hills
716. Sleaford
717. Slough
718. Colnbrook
    Manorbier
719. Solihull
    Fourstones
720. Somerton
721. Langport
722. Southam
723. Southampton
724. South Molton
725. South Petherton
726. Martock
727. Spalding
728. Spilsby
729. Spittal
730. Stafford
    Stafford Station
731. Stilton
    Spelter Works
    Caerau Bridgend
731. Stilton
    Spelterworks
732. Stockbridge
    South Stockton
    Thornaby on Tees
733. Stockport
734. Disley
    Whalley
735. Hazelgrove
    Trecastle
736. Stockton

    Stockton on Tees
737. Castle Eden
    Broadstairs
    Broadstairs Station Office B.O.
738. Stokenchurch
    Byfield
739. Stokesley
740. Ingleby
    Crawley Down
741. Staines
742. Stamford
743. Stevenage
744. Steyning
745. Stone, Staffs
746. Stoneham
747. Thwaite
    Nantyfyllon
748. Stoney Cross
    Newton Heath
749. Stoney Stratford
    Stony Stratford
750. Stourbridge
751. Stourport
752. Stowmarket
753. Needham Market
754. Stratford on Avon
755. Alcester
756. Henley in Arden
    Budleigh Salterton
757. Stroud
758. Kingscote
759. Uley
760. Sudbury
761. Sunderland
762. Swaffham
763. Swansea
    The Docks Swansea
    The Docks B.O. Swansea
    Swansea Mumbles
    St. Helens Swansea
    Swansea Walters Rd.
764. Brinmawr
    Brynmawr, Brec
765. Reynoldstone
    Partridge Green
766. Swindon
    New Swindon
767. Cricklade
768. Wootton Bassett
769. Wroughton
770. Stanmore
771. Shooters Hill
    Caerphilly
772. Tadcaster
773. Taibach Aberavon
    Port Talbot
774. Tamworth
775. Tarporley
776. Taunton
777. Williton
778. Dunster
779. Minehead
780. Tavistock

781. Callington
782. Teignmouth
783. Tenbury
784. Tenby
785. Tenterden
786. Tetbury
787. Tetsworth
788. Tewkesbury
789. Thame
790. Thetford
791. Harling
    E. Harling
792. Larlingford
    New Tredegar
793. Shipdam
    Sandringham
794. Watton
    Watton, Norfolk
795. Thirsk
796. Osmotherley
    West Wickham
797. Thorne
    Kibworth Harcourt
798. Thrapstone
    Thrapston
799. Tipton
800. Tiverton
801. Wimbledon
    Ton-y-refail
802. Bampton
803. Dulverton
804. Topsham
805. Torquay
806. Torrington
807. Totness
    Totnes
808. Towcester
809. Merton
    Eastgate
810. Tring
811. Montford Bridge
812. Risborough
    Princes Risborough
813. Trowbridge
814. Truro
815. Camborne
816. Sunbury Common
817. St. Ives
818. Tonbridge
    Tonbridge Station Office
819. Aspatria
820. Tunbridge Wells
    High St B.O. Tunbridge Wells
    Calverley Tunbridge Wells
    High St Tunbridge Wells
821. Tuxford
    Ashford, Middx
822. Uckfield
823. Hailsham
824. Ulverstone
825. Uppingham
826. Usk
827. Uttoxeter

828. Abbot's Bromley
    Lanchester
829. Sudbury
    Crowborough
830. Uxbridge
831. Wakefield
832. Wallingford
833. Benson
    Chingford
    Cowshill
834. Walsall
835. Waltham Cross
836. Wangford
837. Wrentham
    Reeth
838. Southwold
839. Wansford
840. Deane
841. Weldon
    Hednesford
842. Ware
843. Wareham
844. Corfe Castle
845. Swanage
846. Warminster
847. Warrington
848. Warwick
849. Watford
850. Wednesbury
851. Weedon
852. Welshpool
853. Machynlleth
854. Montgomery
855. Chirbury
    South Ferndale
    Tylorstown
856. Churchstoke
    Pumpsaint
857. Welford
    Silloth
858. Wellingboro'
859. Wellington, Salop
860. Wellington, Som
861. Onllwyn
862. Milverton
863. Wells, Norfolk
864. Wells, Som
865. Welwyn
866. Crynant
867. Wendover
868. West Bromwich
869. Port Dinorwic
870. Westbury
871. Weston-super-Mare
872. Wetherby
873. Weymouth
874. Wheatley
    Godstone Station
    South Godstone
875. Whitby
876. Whitchurch, Salop
877. Whitehaven
878. Wigan

879. Wigton
880. Allonby
    Didsbury
881. Swindon Station
882. Wimborne
883. Wincanton
884. Henstridge Ash
    Aberbeig
885. Milborne Port
    Abertillery
886. Crumlin
887. Stalbridge
    Cwmtillery
888. Winchester
889. Elland
890. Windsor
891. Godstone
892. Eton
    Chatteris
893. Wingham
894. Winslow
895. Wirksworth
896. Abbots Langley
897. Wisbeach
    Wisbech
898. Brightlingsea
899. Hunstanton St. Edmonds
    Hunstanton
900. Witham
901. Pangbourne
902. Witney
903. Wiveliscombe
904. Wokingham
905. Wolverhampton
906. Woburn
907. Woodbridge
908. Wembley
909. Harrow Station
910. Woodstock
911. Elmham
912. Deddington
    Hebron
913. Woodyates
    Crook Loc
    Bexley Heath
914. Cranbourne
    Cranbourn
915. Wotton-under-Edge
916. Furness Abbey
917. Wickwar
    Askam
918. Worcester
919. Llanfalteg
920. Upton-on-Severn
921. Workington
922. Worksop
923. Worthing
    Worthing Station Office
    Worthing Station B.O. Worthing
    Montague St Worthing
924. Wrexham
925. Wymondham
926. Yarm

927. Yarmouth
    Great Yarmouth
928. Yealmpton
    Crowboro' Cross
929. Yeovil
930. York
    Micklegate, York
    Strensall Camp, York
931. Easingwold
932. Escrick
    Barnetby
933. Hamerton
    Hilborough
934. Helmsley
    Mundford
935. Kirby Moorside
    Castle Acre
936. Whitwell
937. Barnet
938. Croydon
    Croydon E.
    Croydon S.
    Croydon W.
    New Thornton Heath Croydon
    Thornton Heath
    Thornton Heath High St
939. Staplehurst
940. Alne
    Litcham
941. Burton Agnes
    Three Cocks
942. Bradbury
943. Beaminster
944. Lynton
945. Runcorn
946. Middlesboro'
947. Hartlepool
948. Bruton
949. Castle Cary
950. Kenilworth
951. Pontypool
952. Hollytroyds
    Greenhithe
953. Blackpool
    South Shore Blackpool
954. Longtown
955. Otterton
    Southboro'
956. Hurstpierpoint
957. Nuneaton
958. Leigh
    Fence Houses
959. Clifton
    Long Sutton
960. Crewe
961. Sutton Bridge
962. Middleham
963. Winchfield
964. Euston Square Station
965. Alderney
966. Hadlow
967. Edenbridge
968. Winchelsea

970. Washford	024. Stonehouse, Glos	Rhydyfelin
971. Ventnor	025. Bletchley Station	076. Knottingley
972. Flint	026. Southend, Essex	077. Aston on Clun
973. Rhyl	027. Southend-on-Sea	078. Brampton Brian
974. Sedbergh	Houghton-le-Spring	079. Bromfield
975. Easingwold	028. Ramsey, Hunts	080. Clun
976. Windermere	St. Keyne	081. Castletown Portland
977. Ferry Hill	029. West Hartlepool	082. Leintwardine
978. Littlehampton	030. Tremadoc	083. Little Brampton
979. Acklington	031. Port Madoc	084. Lydbury North
980. Rhymney	032. Festiniog	085. Craven Arms
982. Dowlais	033. Tanybwlch	086. Fortuneswell
983. Soham	034. Smethwick	087. Goginan
984. Mere	035. Oldbury	088. Sunninghill
985. Aberdare	036. Ramsey, IOM	089. Usk
986. Treherbert	037. Castletown, IOM	090. Winstantow
987. Burbage	038. Chathill	091. Kirkby Lonsdale
Treorchy	039. Willenhall	092. Fence Houses
988. Ystrad Rhondda	040. Whittlesea	093. Harwell
989. Ton-y-pandy	Duloe	Crowthorne
990. Collingbourn	041. Crowland	093. Crowthorne
Dinas	Kirkbythore	094. Steventon
991. Porth, Glam	042. Eggesford	095. Drayton, Berks
992. Tidworth	Sandplace	096. Colwyn Bay
Pen-y-graig	043. Yatton Keynell	097. Shiplake
993. Chalderton	Looe	Mitcheldean
Ferndale	044. Lacock	099. Whitchurch, Hants
Blaenllecha	Polperro	A16. Newcastle-on-Tyne Station
994. Axbridge	045. Sutton Benger	A19. Appledore
Treallaw	Temple Sowerby	A20. Wickham Market
995. Brierley Hill	046. Aldershot Camp	A21. Red Hill
996. Sturminster	Trawsfynydd	A22. Boxmoor
997. Shillingstone	047. Crewe Station	A23. Fremington
Pinxton	048. Normanton	A24. Instow
998. Charfield	Normanton Station Office	A84. Brasted
999. Paulton	Normanton Station	A85. Talog
001. Pensford	049. Paddington Station	A86. Upper Cwmtwrch
002. Ulceby	050. Bampton	A87. Forestfach
003. Weobley	051. Tickhill	A88. Ynyshir
004. Redcar	052. Shotley Bridge	A89. Pontyclown
005. Corsham	053. Hackmondwike	A90. East Liss
006. Templecloud	054. Farnworth	A91. Southsea B.O. Portsmouth
007. Brough, Yorks	055. Beaford	A92. Masham
008. Clutton	056. Bow	A93. Llanfarian
009. Farrington Gurney	057. Brandis Corner	A94. Penarth
010. Copplestone	058. Bridestowe	A95. Newport, Yorks
011. Hallatrow	059. Chulmleigh	A96. North Cave
012. Highampton	060. Newent	A97. South Cave
013. North Tawton	061. Eynsford	A98. South Bank
014. Witheridge	062. Dolton	A99. Chwilog
015. Milford Junction	063. Exbourne	B03. Northfleet
South Milford	064. Lewdown	B04. Par Station, St. Austell
016. Brockenhurst	065. Lifton	B05. Scorrier
017. Upper Clevedon	066. Capel Bangor	B06. Hatt, Plymouth
Rainham, Kent	067. Morchard Bishop	B07. St. Issey
018. Egham	068. Ponterwydd	B08. St. Mellion
019. New Malden	069. Devil's Bridge	B09. Washaway
020. Lower Clevedon	070. Sampford Courtenay	B10. Perranarworthal
Clevedon	071. Wembworthy	B11. Devoran
021. St. Just	072. Winkleigh	B12. Bickley Station
022. Ripley, Yorks	073. Waltham	Bickley
023. Farnboro' Station	074. Probus	B13. Kingsland, Leominster
Farnboro'	075. Newton in Cartmel	B14. Staunton-on-Arrow

B15. Titley, Leominster	B79. Boscastle	C48. Chipping Sodbury
B16. Plymouth & Bristol S.C.	B80. Blackawton, Totnes	C49. Stretford
B17. Brownydd Arms	B81. Harberton, Totnes	C50. Ashton on Mersey
B18. Mardy	B82. Harbertonford, Totnes	Sale
B19. Wolverton	B83. Halwell, Totnes	C52. Godshill
B20. Nailsea	B84. Mounts, Totnes	C53. Rookley
B21. Yatton, Bristol	B85. Malvern Link	C54. Brading
B22. Congresbury, Bristol	B86. Matlock Bridge	C55. Wooton Bridge
B23. Wrington	B87. Weybridge Station	C65. Heywood
B24. Langford	Weybridge	C66. Woking Station
B25. Burrington	B88. Sandown	Woking
B26. Blagden	B89. Shanklin	C67. Droylsden
B28. Moreton Hampstead	B90. Starcross	C68. London and Dover T.P.O.
B29. Chagford	B91. Saltash	C69. Newton-le-Willows
B30. Petersham	B92. Rainhill	C70. Cosham
B33. Grampound Rood	B93. Lelant	C71. Willington
B34. North Western TPO	B94. Saltburn-by-the-Sea	C72. Cheetham Hill
Irish Mail	B95. Horrabridge	C73. Eccles
B35. Shrivenham	B96. Jump	C74. Middleton, Manchester
B36. Stratton St. Margaret	Roborough	C75. Newchurch, Manchester
Llanwrda	B97. Knockersknowle	C76. Prestwich, Manchester
B37. Longcot, Faringdon	Skegness	C77. Radcliffe, Manchester
B38. Pinner	B98. Princetown	C78. Wilmslow
B39. Herne Bay	B99. Abermule	C79. Purley, Surrey
B40. Hundred House, Knighton	C01. Berriew	C80. Helperby
B41. Nantmel	C02. Borth	C84. Aberayron
B42. Walton	C03. Bow St	C85. Enfield
Whitstable	C04. Caersws	C89. Dudley
B43. Washington Station	C05. Carno	C90. Burgess Hill
B44. Flax Bourton	C06. Cemmaes	C91. Harrow
B45. West Town, Bristol	C07. Chirbury	West Malling
B46. Rhyddlan	C08. Churchstoke	C92. Nayland
B47. Llandudno	C09. Commins Coch	C93. Twickenham
B48. Trefriw	C10. Garthmyl	C94. Teddington
B49. Amlwch	C11. Glandovey	C95. Hampton
B50. Llangefni	C12. Llanbrynmair	C96. Sunbury
B51. Menai Bridge	C13. Llandinam	C97. Elstree
B52. Hatch End, Watford	C14. Taliesin	C98. Newhaven
B54. Cramlington	C15. Pateley Bridge	C99. Broughton-in-Furness
B55. Beal	C16. Chorley	D01. Holborn Hill, Ulverston
B56. Troedyrhiw	East Cowes	Millom
B57. Bagshot	C17. Brighouse	D02. Grange-over-Sands
B58. Bucknell	C18. Bilton	D03. Seaford, Lewes
B59. Shap, Westm'land	C19. Holmfirth	D04. Dowlais
B60. Bournemouth	C20. Great Haywood	D05. Chislehurst
B61. Gowerton	C21. St. Columb Minor	Chislehurst Station Office
B63. Blaydon	C22. New Quay, Cornwall	Lower Camden Chislehurst
Blaydon-on-Tyne	C23. Tywyn	D06. Erwood
B66. Briton Ferry	C24. Plymouth and Exeter N.M.T.	D07. Llanuwchllyn
B67. Winsford	C25. Mostyn Quay	Yalding
B68. Lympstone	Mostyn	D08. Llyswen
B69. Paignton	C26. Darwen	D09. Rhydymaen
B70. Dalton-in-Furness	C27. Cleckheaton	D10. Gretna
B71. Barrow-in-Furness	C29. Jarrow	D11. Framlingham
B72. Malvern Wells	C31. Castleford	D12. Burgh
B73. Wylam	C32. Aberdovey	D13. Beckenham
B74. Blyth, Northumberland	C33. Towyn	D15. Aldborough
B75. Bedlington	C34. Pennal	Aldeburgh
B76. Cowpen	C44. Fishguard	D16. Leiston
Emma Colliery	C45. Mossley	D18. Newbridge-on-Wye
B77. Cowpen Lane	C46. Hayland	D19. Burnopfield
Bebside	Everthorpe	Bowers Gifford
B78. Nedderton	C47. Mirfield	D20. Blackhill

D21. Richmond, Surrey	D91. Lavenham	E56. Treforest
D23. Sutton, Surrey	D92. Clare	E57. Haughley
D24. Mitcham, Surrey	D93. Shefford	E59. Llanpumpsaint
D25. Llandyssil	D94. Woodford Bridge	E60. Llangunllo
D31. Pool, Cornwall	D95. Yoxford	E61. Dolau
Carn Brea	Peasenhall	E62. Llandridod
D32. Llanvihhangelar-Arth	D96. West Drayton	E63. Llangammarch
D33. Newport, Essex	D97. Carshalton	E64. Beulah
D34. Waterfoot	D98. Pentre	E65. Llanwrtyd
D35. Talybont	D99. Hakin	E66. Havingham
Talybont on Usk	E01. Brinscomb	E67. Slingsby
D36. Hopkinstown	E02. Mill Street, Aberdare	E68. New Quay, Cardigan
D37. Coggeshall	E03. Letterston	E69. Winforton
D38. Earl's Colne	E04. Dinas Cross	E70. Whitney
D39. Bourton-on-the-Water	E05. Solva	E71. Clifford
D40. Dafen	E07. Newport, Pem	E72. Talgarth
D41. Padiham	E08. St. David's Haverfordwest	E73. Camforth
D42. Blaenellecha	E09. Tangiers Haverfordwest	E74. Penmaenmawr
D43. Llanarth	E10. Treffgarne	E75. Leamside
D44. Potter's Bar	E11. Wolfcastle	E76. Didcot
D45. Brydon	E12. Dwrbach	E77. Ferryside
D46. Cockfield	E13. Camrose	E78. Chigwell Road
D49. Treharris	E14. Roch	E79. Burwash
D50. Wroxall	E15. Penycwm	E80. Mortimer
D51. Peel, IOM	E16. Altywalis	E81. Etchingham
D52. Figure Four	E17. New Inn, Carmarthen	E82. Norham
D53. Llanilar	E18. Llanbyther	E83. Caterham Valley
D54. Crosswood	E19. Llanwren	E84. Garth
D55. Clydach Vale	E20. Talsam	E85. Begelly
D56. Olney	E21. Cilion Aeron	E86. Saundersfoot
D57. Bute Docks B.O. Cardiff	E22. Aberarth	E87. Crook
D58. Harrington	E23. Llanon	E89. Tyne Docks, South Shields
D59. Marske-by-the-Sea	E24. Llanrhystid	E90. Pencader
D60. The Valley	E25. Brimfield	E91. Conwill
D61. Barrasford	E26. Cenarth	E92. Burry Port
D62. Southwick, Sussex	E27. Llechyryd	E93. Horley
D63. Nawton	E28. Cwmamon	E94. Gloucester Station
D64. Kirby Moorside	E29. South Benfleet	E95. Brentford
D65. Helmsby	E31. Little Haywood	E96. Pontrilas
Yoxford	E32. Pontlottyn	E97. Isleworth
D66. Gillingham	E33. New Barnet	E98. Aberavon
D67. Dublin & Cork Rly.	E34. Llandore	E99. Carnarvon
D68. Post Office	E35. Morriston	F01. Haywards Heath
D69. Castle Eden Colliery	E36. Clydach	Crickfield
D70. Castle Eden Station	E37. Pontardine	F02. Bethonia
D71. Wingate	E38. Ystalyfera	F03. Bagilt
D72. Trimdon Grange	E39. Ystradgynlais	F04. Four Crosses
D73. Coxhoe Trimdon Grange	E40. Abergwilly	Blaenau Festiniog
D75. Harrow	E41. Llanarthney	F05. Rhiwbryfdir
D76. Buckhurst Hill	E42. Nantgaredig	F06. Tanygrissian
D77. Loughton	E43. Glanbrydan	F07. Ilford
D78. Brancepeth	Manordilo	F08. Barking
D79. Sandy	E44. Golden Grove	F09. Holm Rook
Twyford	E45. Fulbourne	F10. Chadwell
D80. Potton	E46. Sketty	F11. Ramsbottom
D81. Bures	E47. Parkmill	F12. Batley
D82. Llwyngwril	E48. Penclawdd	F13. Wotton, Dorking
D83. Blaina	E49. Reynoldstown	F14. Askrigg
D84. Beaufort	E50. Ynysmudw	F15. Parkend
D85. Ebbw Vale	E51. Cwmburla, Greenhill	F16. Falfield
D86. Nantyglo	E52. Henfield	F17. Alveston
D88. Linton	E54. Cross Inn, Llanelly	F18. Rudgeway
D89. Haverhill	Ammanford	F19. Almondsbury
D90. Long Melford	E55. Cwmamman	F20. Woodford Green

F21. Ermington	F90. Sharpness Point	G62. Haltwhistle
F22. Whitecroft	F91. Northumberland Dock	G63. Snettisham
F23. Cains Cross	F92. Llantrissant	G64. Burnham, Norfolk
F24. Whitland	F93. Paddock Wood	Burnham Market
F25. Llanfairpwllgwyngll	F94. Ripley, Derby	G65. Bankyfelin
F26. Gaerwen	G01. London and Exeter T.P.O.	G66. Upleatham
F27. Llanerchymedd	G02. Walton-on-Thames	G67. Clarbeston Road
F28. Rhosybol	G03. Buckland	G68. Marden, Kent
F29. Nant Gate	G04. Rothbury	G69. Roche, Cornwall
F30. Charlbury	G05. Widnes	G70. Skelton R.S.O.
F31. Maesycraigian	G07. Bacup	Skelton-in-Cleveland
F32. Bettws	G08. Highbridge	G71. Cleobury Mortimer
Bettws-y-Coed	G09. St. Mary Cray	G72. Angmering
F33. Ystrad Meurig	G10. Dale	G73. Angmering Station
F34. Llandewi Brefi	G11. Llanio Road	G74. Hampton Hill
F35. Tregaron	G12. Harewood End	New Hampton
F36. Surbiton	G17. Used for Autumn Manoeuvres	G75. Ascot
F37. Gensing Station Road	G18. Used for Autumn Manoeuvres	G76. Shillingstone
Wrotham	G19. Used for Autumn Manoeuvres	G77. Heytesbury
F38. Stanford-le-Hope	G20. Much Marcle	G78. Upper Edmonton
F39. Leigh, Chelmsford	G21. Narbeth Road, Glynderwen	G79. Stalbridge
F40. Grays	G22. Eltham	G80. Lower Edmonton
F41. Purfleet	G23. Cleator	G81. Llansantffraid
F42. Rainham	G24. Cark-in-Cartmel	G82. Cemmws
F43. Hyde, Manchester	G25. Egremont, Cumberland	G83. Pandy
F44. Denton, Manchester	G26. St. Bees	G84. Cranbrook
F45. Patricroft, Manchester	G27. Cleator Moor	G85. Churston Ferrers
F46. Shorncliffe Camp	G28. Garn Dolbenmaen	G86. Eglwysbach
F47. St. Mellons	G29. Eastwood, Notts	G87. Cemmaes Rd.
F48. Criccieth	G30. Stantonbury	G88. Lytham
F49. Dyffryn	G31. Castle Donnington	G89. Corris
F50. Croeslon	G32. Duffield	G90. Tow Law
F51. Harlech	G33. Kegworth	G91. Wainfleet
F52. Llanbedr	G34. Quaker's Yard	G92. Portfield Gate
F53. Penygroes	G35. Lesbury	G93. Orpington
F54. Penrhyn Deudraeth	G36. Bloxwich	G94. Ebchester
F55. Talysam	G37. Grosmont, Yorks	G95. Swalwell
F56. Alderley Edge	G38. St. Peter's, Kent	G96. Whickham
F57. Leyburn	G39. Rhoshill	G97. Sarnau
F58. Ponder's End	G40. Rhostryfan	G98. Cross Inn, Cardigan
F59. Talysarnau	G41. Fishponds	G99. Fostrassol
F60. Llangranog	G42. Gorseinon Station	H01. Cenarth
F61. Blaenyffos	Gorseinon	H02. Maesllyn
F62. Kilgerran	G43. Blaenavon	H03. Tunstall
F63. Boncath	G44. Cookham	H04. Orford
F64. Llanymynech	G45. Bourne End	H05. Dymock
F65. Llanfyllyn	G46. Wooburn	H06. School Green
F66. Sutton Benger	G47. Birchington	Freshwater
F67. Little Haven	G48. Westgate-on-Sea	Freshwater Station
F68. Rhyd Lewis	G49. Long Buckby	H07. South Tottenham
F70. Linton Ross	G50. Dolwyddelan	Ynysmudw
F71. St. Weonards	G51. Morecambe	H08. Stanley, Durham
F72. Woodchester	G52. Beckermet	H09. Pevensey
F73. Slade's Bridge	G53. Frizington	H10. Tram Inn
F74. Walton-on-the-Naze	G54. Tilbury, Essex	H11. Birchgrove
F75. Cefn Coed	Tilbury Docks, Essex	H12. Caldicot
F76. Weston-under-Penyard	G55. Gorleston	H13. Rockingham
F77. Lintz Green	G56. Ton Pentre	H14. Llanbadam Fawr
F78. Tebay	G57. Hollinwood	H15. Wivenhoe
F79. Sandy	G58. Bootle, Cumberland	H16. Brotton
F82. Warcop	G59. Ravenglass	H17. Carlin How
F86. Skewen	G60. Hersham Road	H18. Easington, Yorks
F89. Six Mile Bottom	G61. Cottingham	H19. Staithes

H20. Loftus	H82. Whitgift	J44. Thornton-le-Moor
H21. Longfield, Kent	H83. Hook, Yorks	J45. Newton
H22. Seaton	H84. Sancton	Southborough
H23. Hassocks, Sussex	H85. Longwathby	J46. Virginia Water
H24. Aberllechan	H86. Kirkoswald, Cumb	J47. Newbridge, Mon
H25. Wheatley	H87. Lazonby	J48. Wickford
H26. Hinderwell	H88. Dedham	J49. Ripley, Surrey
H27. Pensam	H89. Llanfaelog	J50. Ewell
H28. Abinger Hammer	H90. Abercarne	J51. West Tanfield
H29. Bures	H91. Rhosgoch	J52. Broadstone
H30. Pocklington	H92. Baildon	J53. Llangwyllog
H31. Wawnllwyd	H93. Saltaire	J54. Carnforth and Whitehaven T.P.O.
H32. Llansawell	H94. Llanfinangel	J55. Wrafton
H33. Llanderfel	H95. Hylton	J56. Braunton
H34. Waterlooville	H96. Talsyam	J57. Morthoe Garland
H35. Mersham	H97. Chelsfield	J58. Abersychan
H36. Lydd	H98. Glanamman	J59. Wallsend
H37. Horley Station	H99. Thames Ditton	J60. Bodorgan
H38. Shoeburyness	J01 Englefield Green	J61. Whitley
H39. Great Horkesley	J02. Butterknowle	J62. Bisley
H40. Llanwddyn Reservoir	J03. Trefnant	J63. Wallington
H41. Willesboro'	J04. Rhyddlan	J64. Sudbury, Middx
H42. Llantwit Vardre	J05. Talgarig	J65. Camberley
H43. Coalville	J06. Upper Brynamman	J66. Ramsey, Hunts
H44. Whitefield	J07. Oxted	J67. Chapel-en-le-Frith
H45. Coonah's Quay	J08. Limpsfield	J68. Wool
H46. Carlton Iron Works	J09. Wellington College	J69. Boscombe
H47. Sedgefield	J10. Langley Park Station	J70. Shapperton
H48. West Cornforth	J11. Armley	J71. Hockley
H49. Wingate Station	J12. Birstall	J72. Cambo
H50. Sidcup	J13. Morley	J73. Eastleigh
H51. Heathfield	J14. Pudsey	J74. Totton
H52. Church	J15. Jackfield	J75. Blackwater, Hants
H53. Nelson-in-Marsden	J16. Farnborough, Kent	J76. Horwich
Nelson	J17. Gt. Harwood	J77. Marton, Yorks
H54. Heathfield Station	J18. Brierfield	J78. Medomsley
H55. Ingleton	J19. Stoke-under-Ham	J79. Thatcham
H56. Greenfield	J20. Hinstock	J80. Beenham
H57. St. Dogmael's	J21. Tycroes	J81. Woolhampton
H58. Northiam	J22. Westerham	J82. Wadhurst Station
H59. Wittersham	J23. Long Compton	Wadhurst Station Rd.
H60. Brandon Colliery	J24. Green Street, Kent	J83. Datchet
H61. Stantonbury	J25. Addlestone, Surrey	J84. Ossett
H62. Snaith	J26. Upper Teddington	J85. Church Lane, Old Charlton
H63. Clivetown	J27. Bissoe	J86. Woolwich Road, Old Charlton
H64. Seaham Harbour	J28. Stamford Bridge	J87. Cloughfold
H65. Velindre, Carmarthen	J29. Llandrillo	J88. Haslingden
H66. Greatham	J30. Tywyn	J89. Summerseat
H67. Seaton Carew	Deganwy	J90. Luddenden
H68. Purton	Llandudno	J91. Luddendenfoot
H69. Stratton St. Margaret	J31. Bethersden	J92. Mytholmroyd
H70. Bramley, Yorks	J32. East Molesey	J93. Yeadon
H71. Harrow Weald	J33. Willingdon	J94. Ingleby Greenhow
H72. Llandebie	J34. Cranleigh	J95. Bradford, Lancs
H73. Wealdstone	J35. Burnopfield	J96. Bodenham
H74. Parkstone	J36. Takeley	J97. Willington Quay
H75. Hotham	J37. Bramley, Surrey	J98. Eston
H76. North Newbald	J38. Llanuwchllyn	J99. Normanby, Middlesborough
H77. Adlingfleet	J39. East Cowton	K01. Felling
H78. Garthorpe	J40. Great Ayton	K02. Hebburn
H79. Ousefleet	J41. Great Smeaton	K03. Walker
H80. Nunthorpe	J42. Newby Wiske	K04. Helmshore
H81. Reedness	J43. South Otterington	K05. Stacksteads

K06. Little Hereford	K38. Brayton Station	K73. Newbiggin Kirkby Stephen
K07. Shaw	K39. Dalston	K74. Grimsby
K08. Lymm	K40. Littlestone	Peterborough Night Mail
K09. Woodborough, Wilts	K41. Swinton	K75. Greenfield
K10. Howden-le-Wear	K42. Northwood, Herts	K76. Gwaun-cae-Gurwen
K11. Sinnington, Yorks	Northwood, Mddx	K77. Cholsey
K12. Earlestown	K43. Collingbourne Ducis	K78. Witton Park
K13. Brenchley	K44. Mayfield	K79. Lakeside
K14. Liversedge	K45. Saltford	K80. Calderbridge
K15. Ryton	K46. Mangotsfield	K81. Danby
K16. Brotherton	K47. Warmley	K82. Royton
K17. Purston	K48. London and Holyhead T.P.O.	K83. Aynho
K18. Melplash	K49. Minster Ramsgate	K84. Heyford
K19. Carlton	K50. Boot	K85. King's Sutton
K20. Rawcliffe	K51. Eskdale	K86. Somerton
K21. Rawcliffe Bridge	K52. Gosforth	K87. Souldern
K22. Whitley Bridge	K53. Ravenglass	K88. Hook Norton
K23. Ravenstonedale	K54. Arnside	K89. Loddiswell
K24. Llanwnda	K55. Silverdale	K90. Haworth
K25. Plasmarl	K56. Bigrigg	K91. Silsden
K26. Bexhill	K57. Bootle	K92. Pitsea
Bexhill-on-Sea	K58. Bootle Station	K93. Waskerley
K27. Bexhill Station	K59. Silecroft	K94. Clacton-on-Sea
K28. Fawley Station	K60. The Green	K95. Shipton-under-Wychwood
K29. Whitchurch	K61. Kirkby-in-Furness	K96. Hebden Bridge
K30. Goodrich	K62. Furness Abbey	K97. Grimsby and Peterborough S.T.
K31. Goudhurst	K63. New Oxted	K98. Brighton and Hastings S.C.
K32. Comshall	K64. Lindal	K99. Sheringham
K33. Coniston	K67. Goring	L01. London and Queenborough S.T.
K34. Haswell	K68. Littleport	L02. Lincoln S.T.
K35. Murton Colliery	K69. Wavnarllwyd	Lincoln S.C.
Murton	K70. Shrewsbury and Nonmanton T.P.O.	L03. Rushden
K36. South Hetton	K71. Blockley	L04. Charlton-cum-Hardy
K37. Mumbles	K72. Lynmouth	L05. Norwich S.C.

Numbers not included above were either not allocated or used abroad.
Many office numbers were re-used in later marks (eg Instructional and
Triangles).

Scotland

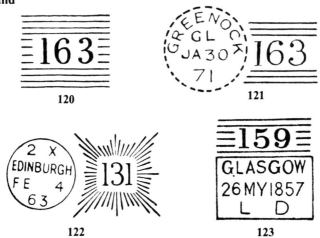

120   121   122   123

53

120 Numbered cancellations between horizontal bars, from 1844 . .		2.50
Duplex cancellations, circular datestamp from 1857		1.00
121 Duplex cancellations, dotted circle types		4.00
122 Duplex cancellations, Edinburgh 'Brunswick Star' types		7.50
123 Glasgow 'Madelaine Smith' type		10.00

1. Aberdeen	Bogroy	76. Carnoustie
2. Aberfeldy	Blackridge	77. Chance Inn
3. Aberdour	43. Bervie	Crossmichael
Achnacroish	44. Blair Athole	78. Colinsburgh
4. Aboyne	Blair Atholl	79. Comrie
5. Aberchirdir	45. Dalnacardoch	Coll
Abernethy, Strathspey	Bankfoot	80. Crail
Nethy Bridge	46. Blairgowrie	81. Cromdale
6. Alford	47. Blair Adam	82. Craigellachie
Advie	48. Bonaw	83. Creetown
7. Alloa	Bunessan	84. Crieff
8. Aberlour	49. Bonar Bridge	85. Cromarty
9. Alexandria	Ardgay	86. Craigellachie
10. Alness	50. Bogroy	Station
11. Annan	Ballachulish	87. Cullen
12. Auchenblae	Ballachulish Ferry	88. Culross
Ardgour	Ballachulish Quarries	Corstorphine
13. Arbroath	51. Blackburn	89. Crosshill
14. Ardersier	Buckhaven	90. Cumnock
Fort George Station	52. Borrowstouness	91. Cupar Angus
Gollanfield	or Boness	Coupar Angus
15. Ardrossan	Bunchrew	92. Cupar
16. Abington	53. Bowmore	93. Cluny
17. Airdrie	Bridgend	Colintraive
18. Arisaig	54. Braco	94. Castleton
Ardersier	Buchlyvie	Colinton
19. Aultbea	55. Blackhillock	95. Crinan
20. Arrochar	Buchlyvie	Crianlarich
Avoch	56. Braemar	96. Cruden
21. Auchnacraig	Bothwell	Cowdenbeath
22. Anstruther	57. Brechin	97. Cockburnspath
23. Aros	58. Edzell	98. Dalkeith
24. Appin	Brodick	99. Delny
25. Auchterarder	59. Broadford	100. Dalmally
26. Auchtermuchty	60. Bridge of Earn	101. Dalry
27. Ayr	61. Buckie	102. Denny
28. Ayton	62. Burntisland	103. Dingwall
29. Assynt	63. Brucklaw	104. Dornoch
Auchnasheen	Burnbank	105. Dunbeath
Achnasheen	64. Callander	106. Douglas
30. Alyth	65. Campbelton	Dalmellington
31. Ballater	Campbeltown	107. Doune
32. Crathie	66. Canonbie	108. Dumfries
Bannockburn	67. Carluke	109. Drimnin
33. Ballantrae	68. Cairnryan	110. Dumbarton
34. Ballindalloch	Catrine	111. Dunbar
35. Banchory	69. Carnwath	112. Dunblane
36. Banff	70. Carsphairn	113. Dunfermline
37. Macduff	Carstairs Junction	114. Dundee
Birnam	71. Castle Douglas	115. Broughty Ferry
38. Bathgate	72. Cairndow	116. Lochee
39. Bauley	Castle Kennedy	Drummore
40. Beith	73. Coldingham	117. Kincaldrum
41. Biggar	74. Coldstream	118. Dunkeld
42. Blackshiels	75. Carrbridge	119. Dunphail

120. Dunning	163. Greenock	211. Kirkintulloch
121. Dunoon	Iona Steamer/Greenock	Kirkintilloch
122. Dunse	Columba Steamer/Greenock	212. Kirriemuir
Duns	Iona Steamer	213. Kirkmichael
123. Dunvegan	164. Glenlivat	Lochwinnoch
124. Durness	Garve	Largs
Dunalastair	165. Glamis	214. Kincardine O'Neil
125. Dunnett	Garlieston	Lamlash
Dunragit	166. Grantown	215. Lanark
126. Drumnadrochit	Grantown on Spey	216. Langholm
127. Dysart	167. Golspie	217. Largs
128. Eaglesham	168. Brora	Upper Largo
Ettrick	169. Gartly	218. Lauder
129. Earlston	170. Glenmorriston	Lochgelly
Elvanfoot	171. Haddington	219. Laurencekirk
130. Ecclefechan	172. Hallkirk	220. Leadhills
131. Edinburgh	173. Hamilton	221. Leith
Edin. – Carlisle	174. Hawick	222. Leithlumsden
Sorting Tender	175. Helmsdale	Lumsden
Carstairs &	176. Helensburgh	Leuchars
Edinr. Sorting	177. Harris	223. Lerwick
Tender	178. Huntly	224. Lynwilg
132. Eddleston	179. Holytown	Ledaig
Easdale	Innellan	225. Laggan
133. Elgin	180. Huna	Lentran
134. Ellon	Innerleithen	226. Lochcarron
135. Elie	181. Inverary	227. Lochearnhead
136. Errol	182. Inverkeithing	228. Lesmahagow
137. Evanton	183. Inverness	Lochgoilhead
138. Eyemouth	184. Inchture	229. Leven
Fairlie	185. Invergordon	230. Linlithgow
139. Falkirk	186. Irvine	231. Lochalsh
140. Falkland	187. Jedburgh	Balmacara
Fasnacloich	188. Johnstone	232. Lochgilphead
141. Fenwick	Innerwick	233. Lockerby
Forgandenny	189. Invergarry	Lockerbie
142. Fettercairn	190. Jura	234. Lochmaddy
143. Fochabers	Inverkip	235. Lochmaben
144. Forfar	191. Kinaldie	Lossiemouth
145. Forres	192. Keith	236. Lochinver
146. Fort Augustus	193. Kelso	Luib
147. Fortrose	194. Keith Hall	237. Lairg
148. Fort William	Invervrie	238. Longhope
149. Fort George	195. Kettle	Longniddry
150. Fraserburgh	Kildonan	239. Luss
151. Fushie Bridge	196. Kenmore	240. Lybster
Fossoway	Kirkliston	241. Markinch
152. Finhaven	197. Kennoway	242. Mauchline
Finstown	Kilmartin	243. Maybole
153. Farr	198. Killin	244. Melrose
Greenlaw	199. Kirknewton	245. Meigle
154. Fyvie	200. Kingussie	246. Melvich
155. Galashiels	201. Kintore	247. Mey
156. Garlieston	202. Kilsyth	Moy
Garmouth	Kirn	248. Mintlaw
157. Gatehouse	203. Kilmarnock	249. Methlic
158. Girvan	204. Kincardine	Macduff
159. Glasgow	Kilwinning	250. Moneymusk
Glasgow Carlisle Sorting Tender	205. Kinghorn	Milnathort
Hope St. Glasgow	206. Kinross	251. Montrose
160. Glenluce	207. Kirkwall	252. St. Cyrus
161. Grangemouth	208. Kippen	Monkton
162. Greenlaw	209. Kirkcudbright	253. Mossat
Gairloch	210. Kirkcaldy	Millport

393. Chirnside
394. Edrom
395. Grantshouse
396. Charlotte Place
    Edinburgh, Lyncdock Place
    Edinburgh
397. Govan
398. Hillhead
399. Greenburn
400. Shotts
401. Pollockshaws
402. Perth and Aberdeen
    Sorting carriage
403. Causewayhead
404. Strathyre
405. Murthly Station
    Murthly
406. Johnstone
407. Storme Ferry
408. Currie
409. Larbert
410. Dolphington
411. Murrayfield
412. Cambus
413. Woodside
414. Cornhill
415. Dufftown
416. Polmont
417. Dreghorn
418. Ringford
419. Twynholm
420. Kirkgunzeon
421. Dalry
422. Prestwick
423. Braemar
424. Guthrie
425. Port Appin
426. George St. Edinburgh
427. Auchinleck
428. Reston
429. Earlston
430. Arrochar
431. Lochawe
432. Auldgirth
433. Ardrishaig
434. Abernethy
435. Alford
436. Auchencairn
437. Lauder
438. Lamington
439. Portaskaig
440. Tarbert Lochfyne
441. Bowmore
442. Port Ellen
443. Wemyss Bay
444. Bonnyrigg
445. Lower Largo
446. Iona
447. Whitburn
448. Strathpeffer
449. Roslin
450. West Linton
451. Culter Cullen

452. David's Mains
453. Corrie, Arran
454. Broxburn
455. Carron
456. Redgorton
457. Armadale Station
458. Fife Sorting Tender
    Fife Sorting Carriage
459. Kincardine
460. Carradale
461. Clachan
462. Tayinloan
463. Moidart
464. Gourock
465. East Wemyss
466. Freuchie
467. Rousay
468. Falkland
469. East Grange Station
470. Fortingal
471. Armadale
472. Blaino
473. Laudale
474. Ratho Station
475. New Galloway Station
476. Longriggend
477. Skinflats
    Bothkennar
478. Guard Bridge
479. Loanhead
480. Dailly
481. Roxburgh
482. Juniper Green
483. Gorebridge
484. Johnshaven
485. Ormiston
486. Yetholm
487. Kettle
488. Lesmahago
489. Polmont Station
490. Balerno
491. Glenbarr
492. Blairmore
493. Rowardennan
494. West Wemyss
495. Tighnabruaich
496. Monifieth
497. Strichen
498. Brucklay
499. Douglas N.B.
500. Kilchrennan
    Kilchrenan
501. Port Sonachan
502. Renton
503. Crianlarich
504. Dalmeny
505. Beattock
506. Lochinver
507. Isle of Whithorn
508. Lilliesleaf
509. Auchmill
    Bucksburn
510. Palnure

511. Oyne
512. Balblair
513. Kinlochbervie
514. Cardross
515. Castlebay
516. Lochboisdale Pier
517. Philipstown
    Philipstoun
518. Inverie
    Knoydart
519. Kinlochewe
520. Friockheim
521. Collieston
522. Cove
    Aberdeen
523. Lumphanan
524. Broughton
525. Old Deer
526. Thankerton
527. Galston
528. Glenboig
529. Tynehead
530. Bishopton
531. East Calder
532. Lhanbryde
533. Addiewell
534. Ardeonaig
535. Ardtalnaig
536. Fearnan
537. Lawers
538. Gullane
539. Cardenden
540. Archiestown
541. Craignure
542. Connel
543. Lochbuie
544. King Edward
545. Onich
546. Staffin
547. Airth Rd. Station
548. Skelmorlie
549. Newmains
550. Stenhousemuir
551. Kilbirnie
552. Lochearnhead Station
    Balquhidder Station
553. Crookham
554. New Mills, Fife
555. Sauchie
556. Bellshill
557. Shiskine
558. Law
559. Caldercruix
560. North Queensferry
561. Auchterless Station
562. Strone
563. Kames
564. Lonmay
565. Eskbank, Dalkeith
566. Avonbridge
567. Skeabost Bridge
568. Denino
569. Tyndrum

570. Cove, Helensburgh
571. Kilcreggan
572. Struan
573. Hollandbush
574. Collessie
575. Aberfoyle
576. Uphall Station
577. Gateside
578. Gartmore Station
579. Cladich
580. Lochwinnoch
581. Acharacle
582. Slamannan
583. Methven
584. Oxton
585. Glendaruel
586. Urray
587. Strathconon
588. Abernethy
589. Aberdour
590. Thornton
591. Tarbolton Station
592. Row
593. Garelochhead
594. Glenfarg
595. Shandon
596. Hollybush
597. Stravithie
598. Riccarton, Kilmarnock
599. Carsaig
600. Croggan
601. Rum
602. Gailes Camp
Irvine
603. Galloway Sorting Tender
Galloway Sorting Carriage
604. St. Margaret's Hope
605. Ruthwell
606. Muthill Station
607. Newport, Fife
608. Cobbinshaw
609. Coalburn
610. Kilninver
611. Orton Station
612. Lismore
613. Chapelton
614. Blackshiels
615. Heriot
616. Leadburn
617. Lamancha
618. Blackhall
619. Cramond
620. Cramond Bridge
621. Fountainhall
622. Crosslee
623. Gordon
624. Winchburgh
625. Uphall
626. Liberton
627. Polton
628. Rosewell
629. Rosslyn Castle
630. Gilmerton

631. Fauldhouse
632. West Calder
633. Macmerry
634. Milton Bridge
635. King's Cross, Arran
636. Rumbling Bridge
637. Fionport
638. Kirkhill
639. Tomintoul
640. Drumoak
641. Craighouse
Jura
642. Howwood
643. Kilbarchan
644. Machany
645. Dunecht
646. Tarves
647. Balloch
648. Conon Bridge
649. Meikleour
650. Newcastleton
651. Ancrum
652. Blairadam Station
653. Kippen Station
654. Whitehouse
655. Achluachrach
Glenborrodale
656. Comrie
657. Blacksboat
658. Mindrim Mill
659. Shiskine
660. Deanston
661. Westfield
662. St. Fillans
663. Springfield
664. Haywood
665. Eddleston
666. Grenadier Steamer
667. Lochmaben
668. Auchendinny
669. Aros
670. Port of Monteith Station
671. Kilconquhar
672. Bridge of Weir
673. Glengarnock
674. Kilmalcolm
675. Cross Gates
676. Ardlui
677. Dalbeallic
Knockando
678. Rannoch Station
679. Roy Bridge
680. Spean Bridge
681. Tulloch
682. Bridge of Orchy
683. Amisfield
684. Kirkmuirhill
685. Kinloch Rannoch
686. Maud
687. Darvel
688. Strathcarron
689. Achanalt
690. Auchnashellach

691. Lochbroom
692. Lochluichart
693. Forsinard
694. Kinbrace
695. Glenfinnan
696. Blackmill Bay
697. Plockton
Berriedale
698. Bank
Latheron
699. Toberonochy
700. Cornaig
701. Hartwood
702. Carron
703. Hurlford
704. Kilchoan
705. Kincardine
706. Longmorn
707. Balvicar
708. Blackburn, Bathgate
709. Marchmont
710. New Lanark
711. Kyle
712. Port Erroll
713. Kinlocheil
714. Crawford
715. Hatton
716. Boddam
717. Raasay
718. Eskbank
Dalkeith
719. Lochailort
720. Arisaig
721. Kettleholm
722. Bonawe Quarries
723. Aberlady
724. Dirleton
725. Achnacarry
726. Aberchirder
727. Cambuslang
728. Newton, Glasgow
729. Shettleston
730. Carstairs
731. Kenmore
732. Craigmillar
733. Rosehearty
734. Strath
735. Findochty
736. Portknockie
737. Langbank
738. Auchenheath
739. Netherburn
740. Quarter
741. Roseneath
742. Clynder
743. Cleland
744. Colonsay
745. Kilmun
746. Sandbank
747. Toward Point
748. Inchbare
749. Bieldside
755. Canna

Ireland

124

125

124 Numbered cancellations in diamond, from 1844 . . . . 2.50
125 Duplex cancellations, from early 1860s 1.00

1. Abbeyleix
2. Adair
   Adare
3. Ahascragh
   Bunratty
4. Ardara
   Cratloe
5. Ardee
6. Ardglass
   Ardrahan
7. Ardrahan
   Abbeyfeale
8. Armagh
9. Ballingarry
10. Arklow
11. Arthurstown
    Armoy
12. Arva
    Ashbourne
13. Ashbourne
    Aghadowey
14. Ashford
15. Athboy
16. Athenry
17. Athleague
    Ardsollus
19. Arva
20. Athy
21. Aughnacloy
22. Aughrim, Gal
    Aughrim, Wick
23. Antrim
24. Askeaton
25. Bagnalstown
    Bagenalstown
26. Baileyborough
    Baily
27. Balbriggan
28. Ballaghaderin
29. Ballina
30. Ballybay
31. Ballinakill
    Ballinamallard
32. Ballinasloe

33. Ballincollig
    Ballybrack
34. Ballinderry
    Ballybofey
35. Ballingarry
    Ballycassidy
36. Ballinrobe
    Ballybrophy
37. Ballycastle
    Ballybunion
38. Ballyclare
39. Ballyconnell
    Ballylongford
40. Ballybrittas
    Ballygawley
41. Ballygawley
    Ballycastle
42. Ballyglass
    Balla
43. Ballyhaise
    Ballyglunin
44. Ballyjamesduff
    Ballyhaunis
45. Ballymahon
46. Ballymena
47. Ballymoe
48. Ballymoney
49. Ballymore
    Ballymore Eustace
50. Ballymote
51. Ballynacargy
    Ballymurry
52. Ballynahinch
53. Ballynamore
    Baltinglass
54. Ballyragget
55. Ballyshannon
56. Ballytore
57. Banagher
58. Banbridge
59. Bandon
60. Bangor
    Barnesmore
61. Bantry

62. Belfast
63. Bellaghy
    Belleek
64. Belmullet
    Beauparc
65. Belturbet
66. Broadford
    Bessbrook
67. Blackwatertown
    Blackrock
68. Blackrock ⬎
    Booterstown
69. Blessington
70. Boyle
71. Booterstown
    Borris
72. Bray
73. Broadway
    Belfast and N. Counties R.P.O.
74. Brookeborough
    Belmullet
75. Broughshane
    Beragh
76. Bruff
    Bangor Erris
77. Buncrana
    Belmont
78. Bunratty
    Beaufort
79. Burrin
    Blarney
80. Borrisakane
    Bruree, Kilmallock
81. Borrisoleigh
    Brittas
82. Borris-in-Ossory
83. Bushmills
    Bundoran
84. Buttevant
85. Baltinglass
    Burton Port
86. Cabineteely
    Cabinteely
87. Cahirciveen

59

88. Cahirconlish
Rathdowney
89. Camp
90. Cahir
91. Caledon
92. Caledon
Caragh
93. Callan
94. Camolin
95. Cappoquin
96. Carlingford
Carbury
97. Carlow
98. Carey's Cross
99. Carna
100. Carn
Carrickmore
101. Carnew
Carrickmines
102. Carrickfergus
103. Carrickmacross
104. Carrick-on-Shannon
105. Carrick-on-Suir
106. Cashel
107. Castlebar
108. Castlebellingham
109. Castlegregory
110. Castleblakeney
111. Castleblayney
112. Castlecomer
Castleconnell
113. Castleconnell
114. Castledawson
115. Castlederg
116. Castledermot
Castleknock
117. Castlefin
118. Castlemartyr
120. Castlepollard
121. Castlerea
122. Castletown
Castletown Bere
123. Castletown Delvin
Castletown Mullingar
Castletown Geoghegan
124. Castletownroche
125. Castlewellan
126. Cavan
127. Celbridge
128. Charleville
129. Church Hill
Clifden
130. Clane
131. Clare
Clanabogan
132. Clare
Claremorris
133. Clashmore
Clara
134. Clifden
Clandeboye
135. Cloghan
136. Clogheen
137. Clogher

Clonee
138. Cloghnakilty
Clonakilty
139. Clonard
Cleggan
140. Clonee
Clonelly
141. Clones
142. Clonmel
143. Clough, Down
Clough, Newry
144. Cloughjordan
Clonsilla
145. Cloyne
Cloughjordan
146. Coachford
Clonbur
147. Coalisland
148. Colehill
Clogher
149. Coleraine
150. Collon
Collooney
151. Collooney
Coachford
152. Cong
Comber
153. Comber
Coole
154. Cookstown
155. Cootehill
156. Cork
157. Cove
Queenstown
158. Carrigart
Courtmacsherry
159. Craughwell
Corofin
160. Creeslough
Craughwell
161. Crookstown
Crossgar
162. Crossakiel
163. Crossdoney
164. Crossmolina
165. Croome
Croom
166. Crumlin
Crossmolina
167. Corofin
Cullybackey
168. Cushendall
169. Dartrey
170. Dangan
Draperstown
171. Delgany
172. Derry
173. Dervock
174. Dingle
175. Donaghadee
Donaghmore
176. Donegal
177. Doneraile
Donabate

178. Down
Downpatrick
179. Drogheda
180. Dromod
Dromore, Tyrone
181. Dromore, Down
Dromod
182. Dromore, West
Dromore Down
183. Drumcree
Drumsna
184. Drumsna
Drumcondra
185. Draperstown
186. Dublin
187. Dundalk
188. Dunfanaghy
189. Dundrum
190. Dundrum
Dublin and Belfast R.P.O.
Dunkineely
191. Drumkeerin
192. Dromara
Dungloe, Don
Dunmore, Tuam
193. Dungannon
194. Dungarvan
195. Dungiven
Dunkettle Station
Glanmire
196. Dunlavin
Dunadry
197. Dunleer
198. Dungloe
199. Dunmurry
200. Dunmanway
201. Dunmore
Dunrymond
202. Dunmore East
Dunshaughlin
203. Dunshaughlin
204. Durrow
205. Edenderry
206. Edgworthstown
207. Elphin
208. Emo
209. Emyvale
210. Enfield
211. Ennis
212. Enniscorthy
213. Enniskerry
214. Enniskillen
215. Ennistimon
216. Eyrecourt
217. Ferbane
Farranfore
218. Fermoy
219. Ferns
220. Fethard, Tip.
221. Fethard, Wexford
222. Fintona
Finglas
223. Fiuemilotown
Fintona

224. Florence Court
    Fintown
225. Flurrybridge
    Fivemiletown
226. Forkhill
227. Foxford
228. Foynes
229. Frankford
230. Frenchpark
231. Freshford
    Geashill
232. Galway
233. Garvagh
    Gilford
234. Geashill
    Glasslough
235. Gilford
    Glasnevin
    Glencolumbkille
236. Glasslough
    Glenealy
237. Glenarm
    Garvagh
238. Glenavy
    Glenties
239. Glin
240. Golden
    Glenhull
241. Golden Ball
242. Gort
243. Gorey
244. Gowran
245. Graig
    Graigue
    Graiguenamanagh
246. Granard
247. Grey Abbey
    Greystones
248. Goresbridge
249. Headford
    Hazelhatch
250. Hillsborough
251. Hollymount
252. Hollywood
    Howth
253. Howth
    Irvinestown
254. Inistiogue
    Inniskeen
255. Innishannon
    Island Bridge
    Inver
256. Johnstown
    Inch, Gorey
257. Kanturk
258. Keady
    Kells, Killarney
259. Kells
260. Kenmare
261. Kilbeggan
    Kesh
262. Kilcock
263. Kilconnell
    Kilbride, Manor

Kilbride, Dublin
264. Kilcullen
    Kilbrittain
265. Kildare
266. Kildorrey
    Killorglin
267. Kildysart
    Kilcar
268. Kilkeel
269. Kilkenny
270. Killala
    Killeshandra
271. Killaloe
272. Killarney
273. Killinardrish
    Killiney
274. Killeagh
    Kilfenora
275. Killucan
276. Killybegs
    Killygordon
277. Killyleigh
278. Killynaule
    Killybegs
279. Killeshandra
    Killylea
280. Killinchy
281. Killough
282. Kilmacrennan
283. Kilmallock
284. Kilrea, Belfast
285. Kilrush
286. Kilworth
287. Kilmacthomas
288. Kingscourt
    Kincasslagh
289. Kingstown
290. Kinsale
291. Kinnegad
    Knockcloghrim
292. Kinnetty
    Rathmore
293. Kircubbin
294. Kish
    Knockcroghery
295. Knock
    Kylemore
296. Knocktopher
    Larne Harbour
297. Kinvara
    Leixlip
298. Lanesborough
    Letter
299. Larne
300. Leighlinbridge
    Laurencetown
301. Leixlip
    Leggs
302. Letterkenny
303. Limerick
304. Lisburn
305. Lismore
306. Lisnaskea
307. Listowel

308. Littleton
    Lixnaw
309. Longford
310. Loughbrickland
    Loughlinstown
    Shankhill
311. Loughgall
    Lough Eske
312. Loughrea
313. Lowtherstown
    Lispole
314. Louth
    Lucan
315. Lucan
    Lahinch
316. Lurgan
317. Macroom
    Lusk
318. Maghera
    Mageney
319. Magherafelt
320. Malahide
321. Mallow
322. Manorhamilton
    Manorcunningham
323. Markethill
    Magheramena
324. Maryborough
325. Maynooth
    Maghera
326. Middleton
    Midleton
327. Millstreet
    Markethill
328. Miltown
    Milltown
329. Miltown Malby
330. Mitchelstown
331. Moate
332. Mohill
    Moira
333. Moira
    Moyvore
334. Monaghan
335. Monasterevan
336. Moneygall
    Monkstown
337. Moneymore
338. Mountmellick
339. Mount Nugent
    Mount Pleasant
340. Mountrath
341. Mount Talbot
    Multyfarnham
342. Moville
    Muckamore
343. Moy
344. Moynalty
    Mulhuddart
345. Mullingar
346. Naas
347. Narin
348. Navan
349. Nenagh

507. Ballinrobe	526. Ballycroy	547. Lisselton Cross
508. Timoleague	527. Ballyglass	Lisselton
509. Bailieborough	528. Tourmakeady	548. Headford, Killarney
510. Kingscourt	529. The Neale	549. Ballincollig
511. Macroom	530. Cong	550. Ballinskelligs
512. Ballinlough	531. Sion Mills	551. Glenbeigh
513. Glenanne	532. Dromahair	552. Valencia Island
514. Limerick Junction	533. Toombeola	553. Waterville
515. Hill of Down	534. Bangor	554. Dunboyne
516. Moycullen	535. Holywood	555. Annascaul
517. Rosscahill	536. Strandtown	556. Blennerville
518. Oughterard	537. Donaghadee	557. Woodenbridge
519. Maam Cross	538. Dundrum, Down	558. Bawnboy
520. Maam	539. Newcastle, Down	559. Ballyconnell
521. Leenane	540. Ardagh	560. Bushmills
522. Rusmuck	541. Six Mile Cross	561. Ardara
Rosmuck	542. Maguiresbridge	562. Bruckless
523. Recess	543. Slane	563. Carrick
524. Cashel, Galway	544. Ardfert	564. Mount Charles
525. Letterfrack	545. Lisdoonvarna	

REMEMBER!

Prices in C.B.P. are minimum values
for a **clear strike on a clean card or cover.**
Have you read the notes
at the beginning?

PUZZLED?

From time to time all collectors find covers which have
curious or unexplained features. Send a photocopy (with SAE
or IRC) and I will send my comments or refer to a specialist in
a particular field. Some of the most interesting – or ones which
still cannot be explained – illustrated in the next
Collect British Postmarks.

8. THE SQUARED CIRCLE

Experimental London Types

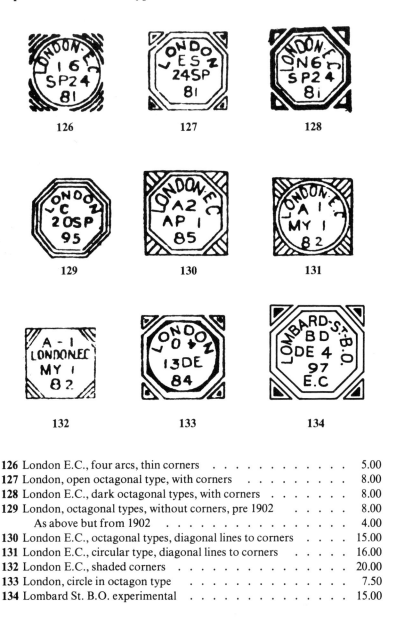

126   127   128

129   130   131

132   133   134

126 London E.C., four arcs, thin corners 5.00
127 London, open octagonal type, with corners 8.00
128 London E.C., dark octagonal types, with corners 8.00
129 London, octagonal types, without corners, pre 1902 . . . . . 8.00
       As above but from 1902 . . . . 4.00
130 London E.C., octagonal types, diagonal lines to corners 15.00
131 London E.C., circular type, diagonal lines to corners 16.00
132 London E.C., shaded corners 20.00
133 London, circle in octagon type 7.50
134 Lombard St. B.O. experimental 15.00

The Regular Issue

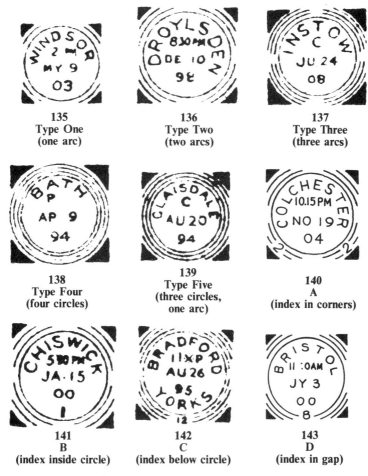

135
Type One
(one arc)

136
Type Two
(two arcs)

137
Type Three
(three arcs)

138
Type Four
(four circles)

139
Type Five
(three circles,
one arc)

140
A
(index in corners)

141
B
(index inside circle)

142
C
(index below circle)

143
D
(index in gap)

(Each type can be found in several sizes)

	Pre-1902	1902–10	1911–20	After 1920
Types One, Two or Three, **135–7**	0.60	0.40	0.50	2.00
Types 1A, 1B, 1C, 1D, 2A, 2B, 2C, 2D, 3A, 3B, 3C, 3D	0.75	0.55	0.75	2.50

Type Four (all dates) **138**   20.00
Type Five (all dates) **139**   15.00

London Head District Offices

Office	Types	Indexes		Office	Types	Indexes
London E.C.	2, 3			London W	1B	66
London E	2A	2, 4, 11, 14, 16, 27			2A	7
	3				2B	47, 48, 52, 56, 61–72, 75, 80, 81
	3A	1–33			2D	33, 51, 53, 55
	3B	1–16			3A	12
London N	1, 2, 3				3B	18, 19, 33–38, 41, 47–50, 52, 55, 57, 60–83
	2A	5, 7, 10, 11, 18			3D	49–51, 53
London N.W.	1, 2, 3			Paddington W	2A	60
	3A	1–4, 6–9, 11, 12, 15, 17, 18, 20, 21, 24, 26			3	
	3B	1			3A	52, 57–67, 70, 72, 100
	3C	1, 2, 13			3B	11, 14, 21, 52, 59, 60, 64, 66
	2A	3, 5, 16, 18, 25		London W.C.	1, 2, 3	
London S.E.	1B	32, 38			2A	21, 22, 26, 29, 30, 35–37
	2A	6			3A	1–5, 15, 18–30
	2B	1, 2, 5, 7, 11, 12, 23, 27, 31, 32, 34, 36				
	3A	8, 9				
	3B	1–9, 11, 12, 18–20, 23, 24, 27–38				
London S.W.	1A	22, 23				
	2A	2, 20, 21, 23, 25, 29				
	2C	1				
	3A	3–7, 11–12, 19–21, 24–33				
	3C	2, 3, 5, 6, 8				
	3D	4				

London Branch Offices

Office	Types	Indexes		Office	Types
Aldgate B.O./E	3			Lombard St. B.O./E.C.	3
	3A	1		Mark Lane E.C.	3
Bedford St. S.O./W.C.	3			Threadneedle St. B.O.	3
	3A	1		Threadneedle St. B.O./E.C.	3
Charing Cross W.C.	1, 2, 3				
	2A	1–5			
London W.C./CX	1, 2, 3				

	Types	Indexes		Types	Indexes
Wimbledon	3		Wood Green/N	3	
Winchmore Hill S.O./N	3			3A	1
	3A	1			

Provincial Offices

	Types	Indexes		Types	Indexes
Aldbourne	3		Bideford	3	
Alford	3		Biggleswade	1, 3	
Alfreton	3		Bildeston	3	
Alton/Hants	2, 3		Billingshurst	3	
Ampthill	1, 3		Billinghurst	3	
			Bilston Deepfields	3	
Andoversford	3		Bingley	3	
Appledore/Devon	3		Birkenhead	3	
Ardleigh	3			3A	4–6, 8
Armley	3			3B	8
Arundel	2. 3		:Liscard/Cheshire	3	
Asbourne	3		:Liscard/Liverpool	3	
Ashford/Kent	3		:New Brighton/Cheshire	3	
Ashley Green	3		:New Brighton/Liverpool	3	
Ashton under Lyne	3		:Oxton/Birkenhead	3	
Aspley Guise	3		:Rock Ferry/Birkenhead	3	
Atherstone	3			3A	1, 2
Atherton	3		:Seacombe/Cheshire	3	
Axminster	1, 2, 3		:Seacombe/Liverpool	3	
Aylsham	3		Birmingham	2, 3	
Aysgarth Station	3			1A	68, 71, 74, 78
Bacup	3			2A	50, 53, 57, 60, 63, 65, 66, 69, 70, 72, 73, 75, 76
Bakewell	3				
Baldock	2, 3				
Barham	3				
Barnet	2, 3				
Barnetby	3			3A	50, 58, 59, 63–5, 67, 70, 72, 76, 88, 90, 98
Barnsley	1, 3				
	3A	1, 2			
Barnstaple	1, 2, 3				
Barrasford	2, 3		Bishops Stortford	2, 3	
Barrow in Furness	2, 3		Blackheath/Staffs	3	
Barry	3		Blackley	2	
Barry Dock B.O./Cardiff	3		Blisworth	3	
Bath	1, 2, 3, 4		Bloxwich	3	
Bawtry	3		Bodmin	1, 2, 3	
Baydon	3		Bognor	2, 3	
Beaworthy	3		Bolton	2, 3	
Beckenham	2			2A	11
Bedford	2, 3			3A	12–14
Beer	3		Boroughbridge	2, 3	
Beer Alston	3		Boscastle	3	
Beeston/Notts	3		Boston	2, 3	
Belper	1, 3		Boughton/Kent	3	
Berkhamsted	3		Bow/North Devon	3	
Berwick	1, 2, 3		Box	3	
Bexley	2, 3		Boxmoor	3	
Bicester	2, 3				

	Types	Indexes
Bracknell	3	
Bradford/Lanc	3	
Bradford	3A	1–3, 5, 6, 8, 9, 13
	3C	8, 9, 11, 12
Bradford, Yorks	3B	7, 10, 11
Bradford/Yorks	3	
	3A	2,4
	3C	8, 9, 12, 13
Braintree	2, 3	
Brandis Corner	1, 2, 3	
Braunton	3	
Brentwood	1, 3, 4	
Bridge	3	
Bridgewater	1, 2, 3	
Bridport	1, 2, 3	
Brierley Hill	1, 2, 3	
Brigg	3	
Brightlingsea	3	
Brighton	3	
Brighton/H.P.O.	2, 3	
:Cannon Place B.O./ Brighton	3	
:College Road B.O./ Brighton	3	
:Kemp Town/ Brighton	3	
:Old Steine/ Brighton	3	
:Western Rd. B.O./ Brighton	3	
Bristol	1A	1
	1B	3, 10, 12
	1D	3, 5, 10
	2, 3	
	2A	7, 9, 11
	2B	1, 10, 12, B.D.J.S.
	2D	1–10
	3B	11
	3D	4
:Clifton/Bristol	2, 3	
:Hotwells/Bristol	3	
Briton Ferry	2	
Bromley, Kent	2, 3	
Brompton	5	
Brough	3	
Broxbourne	3	
Bruton	3	
Bude	3	
Budleigh Salterton	3	
Bulwell	3	
Buntingford	3	
Burgh	2, 3	

	Types	Indexes
Burnham/Somerset	3	
Bury/Lancs	2, 3	
Buryas Bridge	3	
Bury St. Edmonds	3	
Buxton	3	
	3A	1
	3B	1
Cadoxton	3	
Caerphilly	3	
Caistor	3	
Callestick	3	
Callington	3	
Calne/Wilts	1, 2, 3	
Calstock	3	
Camborne	3	
Camelford	2, 3	
Canterbury	1, 2, 3	
Cardiff	2, 3	
	2A	5, 7
	3A	5, 6
:Bute Docks/Cardiff	3	
Carmarthen	1, 3	
Castleton	5	
Chacewater	3	
Chard	3	
Charlton Kings	3	
Charmouth	3	
Chartham	3	
Chatham	2, 3	
Cheadle/Cheshire	3	
Chelmsford	3	
Cheltenham	3	
	3A	G, J
:Pittville/ Cheltenham	3	
:Townsend Rd/ Cheltenham	3	
Chepstow	3	
Chester	3	
Chester/Station office	1, 2, 3	
	3A	5
Chesterfield	2, 3	
Chichester	3	
Chichester/ Station Office	3	
Chigwell Road	3	
Chilham	3	
Chippenham	2, 3	
Chislehurst	3	
Chorley	3	
Chorlton Cum Hardy	2, 3	
Church Stretton	3	
Cirencester	3	
Clacton on Sea	3	

	Types	Indexes
Colchester	2, 3	
	2A	2
	3A	1, 2
Colyford	3	
Colyton	3	
Conway	1, 3	
Copplestone	3	
Cornholme	3	
Cornwall R.S.T.	3	
Coventry	2, 3	
Cowbridge	3	
Cowes	2, 3	
Cradley/Staff	3	
Cradley Heath	3	
Crediton	3	
Crewe	3	
	3A	2
Crewe Station	3	
	3A	3
Criccieth	1, 2, 3	
Crickhowell	3	
Cromer	3	
Croydon	2	
Cullompton	3	
Cury Cross Lanes	3	
Dagenham	3	
Darlington	3	
	3A	1, 2, 3
Darwen	2, 3	
Dawley/Salop	3	
Dawlish	1, 3	
Deal	1, 2, 3	
Deepfields	3	
Denton/Lanc	3	
Derby	3A	4, 5, 8
Dereham	2, 3	
Devizes	2, 3	
Devoran	3	
Devonport	2, 3	
Didcot	3	
Dinas	3	
Diss	3	
Doncaster	1, 2, 3	
Dorchester	2, 3	
Douglas/Isle of Man	2, 3	
Dover	2, 3	
Downham	1, 2, 3	
Droitwich	2, 3	
Droylsden	2, 3	
Dunmow	3	
Dunstable	3	
Dunster	3	
Eastwood/Yorks	3	

	Types	Indexes
Eastbourne	1, 2, 3	
	3A	4
Eccles	2, 3	
Egloskerry	3	
Eltham	3	
Ely	1, 3	
Enfield	3	
Epping	2, 3	
Esher	1, 2, 3	
Etchingham	3	
Evesham	1, 2, 3	
Exbourne	3	
Exeter	1, 2, 3	
Exmouth	2, 3	
Eye	3	
Fakenham	3	
Fallowfield	3	
Falmouth	2, 3	
Farnborough Road	5	
Farnborough Station	3	
Farnham	2, 3	
Faverhsam	1, 2, 3	
Felixstowe	3	
Filey	2, 3	
Finghall	2, 3	
Fladbury	2, 3, 5	
Folkestone	1, 2, 3	
:Tontine St. B.O./ Folkestone	3	
Foots Cray	2, 3	
Fowey	3	
Frowe	3	
Gainsborough	2, 3	
Gamlingay	3	
Ganton	5	
Glaisdale	5	
Glossop	3	
Gloucester	2, 3	
	2A	1, 7
	3A	4
	3D	4
Gloucester Station	2, 3	
Godalming	3	
Gomersall	3	
Gorton	3	
Gorton Brook	3	
Grampound Road	1, 3	
Gravesend	2, 3	
Great Somerford	3	
Great Yarmouth	2, 3	
Greenstreet/Kent	3	
Grimsby	2, 3	
Grimsby & Lincoln Sorting Tender	3	

	Types	Indexes		Types	Indexes
Guernsey	2, 3		Hornchurch	3	
Guildford	1, 2, 3		Horndean	2, 3	
Hadleigh	3		Houghton-le-Spring	3	
Hailsham	1, 2, 3		Hounslow	2, 3	
Halesworth	2, 3		Hoylake	3	
Halifax	1A	4	Hull	2, 3	
	2A	4		1A	3
	2, 3			1D	2
Halstead	3			3A	3
Halstead/Essex	3			3D	2
Halstead/Kent	3		Hunmanby	3	
Handcross	2, 3		Huntingdon	1, 3	
Hanley	1, 2, 3		Huttoft	3	
Harleston	2, 3		Hyde	2, 3	
Harlow	3		Ilford	2, 3	
Harrogate	1, 2, 3		Ilfracombe	2, 3	
Harwich	2, 3		Ilminster	2, 3	
Hastings	2, 3		Ingatestone	3	
:Gensing Station Rd/			Instow	3	
Hastings	3		Ipswich	2, 3	
Hatfield/Herts	3			2A	4
Hatherleigh	2, 3			3A	3, 4
Haverfordwest	3			3B	1
Haverhill	2, 3			3C	2
Hawkhurst	1, 2, 3		:St. John's/Ipswich	3	
Haxby	3		Isleworth	3	
Hay	3		Ivybridge	2, 3	
Hayes/Middx	3		Jersey	1, 2, 3	
Haywards Heath	3		Kelvedon	3	
Heamoor	3		Kettering	1, 3	
Heathfield	3		Kilmington	3	
Hebden Bridge	2, 3		Kineton	3	
Heckington	3		Kingsbridge	1, 2, 3	
Helston	3		King's Lynn	1, 2, 3	
Hereford	3		Kingston-on-Thames	1, 2, 3	
Hertford	3		Kirkby Stephen	3	
Hetton le Hole	3		Kirkham	3	
Hexham	3		Kirkham Abbey	3, 5	
Heytesbury	3		Kiveton Park	3	
Heywood	2, 3		Knockholt	3	
Higham Ferrers	2, 3		Lakenheath	5	
Highampton	2		Lambourn	2, 3	
Highbridge	3		Langport	2, 3	
Hingham	3		Launceston	3	
Hinstock	3		Leamington	2, 3	
Hitchin	2, 3		Leamington Spa	2, 3, 4	
Hockcliffe	3			1A	4
Hoddesdon	3			2A	1–3
Holbeach	3			3A	3, 5
Holbeton	3		Ledbury	3	
Holsworthy	3		Leeds	2, 3	
Holt/Norfolk	2, 3			2A	1, 4, 8,
Honiton	2, 3				A.C.L.
Hoo	3			3A	8, B

	Types	Indexes		Types	Indexes
:Call Lane/Leeds	3		:Walton Rd. Sub P.O./		
:Chapeltown Rd/Leeds	2, 3		Liverpool	3	
:Holbeck B.O./Leeds	3			3A	1, 2
:Hyde Park Corner/Leeds			:Waterloo/Liverpool	2, 3	
	2, 3		:Wavertree/Liverpool	3	
:Market Street/Leeds	3		:West Derby/Liverpool	3	
:Marsh Lane B.O./Leeds	2, 3		(see also Birkenhead)		
:Marsh Lane S.O./Leeds	2		Liverpool & London T.P.O.		
Leicester	1A	1		3	
	2A	1–5, 8	Liverton	1, 2	
	3		Llwynypia	3	
	3A	1, 3–9	Longfield	3	
Leigh/Lanc	2, 3		Longridge	3	
Lelant	3		Long Rock	3	
Levenshulme	2, 3		Long Stratton	3	
Lewdown	3		Looe	2, 3	
Lewes	2, 3		Loughborough	2, 3	
Lewes/Station office	3		Louth/Linc	3	
Leyland	3		Lower Walmer/Deal	3	
Lifton	2, 3		Lower Sheringham	3	
Lincoln	2		Luton	3	
Lincoln/S.C.	3		Lyme	3	
Lincoln/S.T.	3		Lymington	1, 2, 3	
Lindfield	3		Lynmouth	3	
Liskeard	1, 2, 3		Lynton	3	
Littleborough	3		Mablethorpe	3	
Liverpool	1, 2, 3		Macclesfield	2	
	1A	33	:Chestergate B.O./		
	2A	27, 32, 35,	Macclesfield	3	
		36	Maidenhead	1, 2, 3	
	3B	2, 4	Maldon	3	
Liverpool/E.1	3		Malmesbury	3	
Liverpool N	3		Malvern	2, 3	
Liverpool	3	ND2, ND3,	Manchester	1, 2, 3	
		ND6, SD20,	Manchester/S.W.	3	
		SD21	Manchester/		
		(District	Station Office	3	
		initials	:Barlow Moor Rd/		
		over date)	Manchester	1	
:Aigburth/Liverpool	3		:Pendleton D.O./		
:Blundellsands/			Salford	3	
Liverpool	3			3A	2
:Bootle/Liverpool	3		Manningtree	3	
:Bootle-cum-Linacre/			Marazion	3	
Liverpool	3		March	3	
:Exchange/Liverpool	1, 2, 3		Margate	3	
:Liverpool/LX	2		:NorthumberlandRd/		
:Liverpool	1, 2, 3	(LX	Margate	3	
		over date)	Market Harborough	2, 3	
:Garston/Liverpool	3		Market Rasen	1, 3	
:Lark Lane/Liverpool	2, 3		Marlborough	3, 5	
:Old Swan/Liverpool	3		Marlow	3	
:Rice Lane/Liverpool	2, 3		Martock	3	
:Seaforth/Liverpool	3		Matlock Bath	3	

	Types	Indexes		Types	Indexes
Mawgan	3		Ongar	2, 3	
Melbourne	3		Openshaw	3	
Melton Constable	3		Orleton	3	
Merthyr Vale	3		Orpington	2, 3	
Mevagissey	3		Ossett	1, 3	
Middleton/Lanc	3		Ottery St. Mary	2, 3	
Midhurst	3		Oundle	3	
Milborne Port	3		Padstow	2, 3	
Milford/Surrey	3		Par Station	2, 3	
Minehead	3		Patricroft	3	
Morchard Bishop	3		Peel/Isle of Man	5	
Morpeth	3		Penarth	2, 3	
Morthoe	3		Pendlebury	3	
Mossley	3		Penryn	3	
Mounts	3		Penzance	2, 3	
Narberth	3		Perranarworthal	3	
Narborough/Norfolk	3		Perranporth	3	
Navigation	3		Perranwell Station	3	
Newbridge/Cornwall	3		Pershore	2, 3	
Newcastle on Tyne	1B	S	Peterborough	2, 3, 5	
	2, 3			3A	3
	2B	A	Peterborough/Parcel Post	3	
	3B	1–3, 6, B, C, D, E, F	Petersfield	1, 2, 3	
			Plymouth	2, 3	
Newent	3			3A	1
Newhaven	3			3C	1
Newhaven/Sussex	3		:Stonehouse/Devon	3	
Newington/Kent	2/3		:Stonehouse B.O./Plymouth		
Newmarket	1, 3			3	
Newnham	2, 3		Plympton	3	
Newnham/Glos	2, 3		Polegate	2, 3	
Newport/Mon	1, 3		Pontefract	1, 2, 3	
Newquay/Cornwall	3		Pontlottyn	3	
Newton Abbot	3		Pontyclown	3	
Newton le Willows/Yorks			Pontyclun	3	
	3		Pontypridd	3	
Newtown/Mony	3		Portscatho	3	
New Tredegar	3		Portsmouth	1, 2, 3	
Neyland	3			1A	2
Normanton	3		:Landport/Portsmouth	3	
Northampton	2, 3		:Portsea/Portsmouth	3	
North Shields	2, 3		Port Talbot	2, 3	
North Tawton	3		:Taibach/Port Talbot	3	
North Walsham	2, 3		Poulton Le Fylde	3	
Norwich	3		Preston	3	
	3A	12, 13		3A	2
	3C	A		3D	2
	3D	K	Princetown	2, 3	
Nottingham	3		Radcliffe	3	
	3A	5, 12	Rainham/Essex	3	
	3D	4	Rainham/Kent	2, 3	
Old Brentford	3		Ramsbottom	3	
Oldbury	1, 2, 3		Ramsey/Isle of Man	3	
Old Hill	3		Ramsgate	1, 2, 3	

	Types	Indexes		Types	Indexes
Rawtenstall	2, 3		Sheffield	1B	12
Rayleigh	3			2A	4, 10
Reading	1, 2, 3			2B	13
Redruth	2, 3			3	
Retford	3			3A	2, 4, 10,
Richmond/Surrey	1, 2, 3				11, 14
Rillington	5			3B	12, 13
Ringwood	1, 2, 3		Sheffield N	3	
Robertsbridge	3			3A	1, 2
Rochdale	3		Sheffield/S.D.O.	3	
	3A	1		3A	1, 2
Rochester	1, 2, 3		Sheffield/W.D.O.	3	
Romford	1, 2, 3			3A	1, 2
Ross	3		Sherborne	2, 3	
Rowley Regis	3		Shipley/Yorks	2, 3	
Royston/Cambs	2, 3		Shrewsbury	2, 3	
Royston/Herts	3		Sidcup	2, 3	
Ruan Minor	3		Sidmouth	2, 3	
Rugby	1, 2, 3		Sittingbourne	2, 3	
Rugby Station	2, 3		:Milton/Sittingbourne	3	
Ryde	2, 3		Skegness	3	
St. Annes-on-the-Sea	3		Slough	2, 3	
St. Austell	1, 2, 3		Snodland	2, 3	
St. Buryan	3		Soham	3	
St. Columb	2, 3		Somerton/Somerset	3	
St. Germans/Cornwall	2, 3		Southampton	1, 2, 3	
St. Ives/Cornwall	2, 3		:Oxford St. B.O./		
St. Ives/Hunts	3		Southampton	2, 3	
St. Just	3		Southend/Essex	3	
St. Keverne	3		Southend on Sea	2, 3	
St. Mabyn	3		South Molton	2, 3	
St. Martin/Cornwall	3		South Petherton	2, 3	
St. Mary Cray	3		Southport	2, 3	
St. Mawes	3		:Birkdale B.O./		
St. Neots	3		Southport	3	
St. Tudy	3		South Shields	3	
Sale	3		South Stoke	3	
Saltash	2, 3		Southwick/Sussex	2, 3	
Sandown	1, 3		Spalding	3	
Sandwich	3		Spennymoor	3	
Sandy	3		Spilsby	3	
Saxmundham	3		Spondon	2, 3	
Scarborough	1, 3		Staines	3	
	2A	1	Stantonbury	3	
	2C	1	Staplehurst	3	
Scorrier	3		Stevenage	3	
Seaford	2, 3		Stockport	2, 3	
Sedgley	3			2A	1
Selby	3		Stoke on Trent	2, 3	
Sennen	3			1A	5
Sevenoaks	2, 3		Stonham	3	
Shaftesbury	1, 3		Stony Stratford	2, 3	
Shanklin	2, 3		Stratton/North Devon	2, 3	
			Strensall	3, 5	

	Types	Indexes		Types	Indexes
Stretford	3		Welburn	5	
Stroud/Glos	1, 2, 3		Wellington/Som	2, 3	
Sturry	2, 3		Wellington College Stn.	3	
Sudbury/Suffolk	2, 3		Wells/Somerset	3	
Sutton/Linc	3		Wells/Norfolk	2, 3	
Sutton in Ashfield	3		Welwyn	3	
Swaffham	2, 3		Wem	3	
Swanley Junction	1, 2, 3		West Bromwich	1, 2, 3	
Swansea	3		Westbury/Wilts	2, 3	
Tadcaster	1, 2, 3		West Hartlepool	2A	1
Taunton	1, 2, 3			3	
Tavistock	2, 3		West Kirby	3	
Teignmouth	3		Weston Super Mare	2, 3	
	3D	1, 2	Wetterby	3	
Tenby	3		Weybridge	3	
Terrington	3, 5		Weymouth	2, 3	
Tetbury	2, 3		Whitford/Devon	3	
Tewkesbury	3		Wickwar	3	
The Lizard	2, 3		Wigan	3	
Thetford	2, 3		Williton	2, 3	
Thrapston	2, 3		Wilmslow	3	
Tideswell	3		Winchester	1, 2, 3	
Tintagel	3		Windsor	1, 2, 3	
Tipton Green	3		Winksworth	1, 2, 3	
Tredegar	2, 3		Witham	3	
Treen	3		Witham/Essex	2, 3	
Tregony	3		Withington	3	
Treharris	3		Woburn	3	
Trowbridge	2, 3		Woburn Sands	3	
Truro	2, 3		Woking	1, 2, 3	
Tunbridge	3		Wokingham	1, 2	
Tunbridge Wells	3		Wolverhampton	1A	11
:Calverley/Tunbridge				2, 3	
Wells	3			2A	2, 11
:Mount Ephraim/			Wolverton/Bucks	1, 2	
Tunbridge Wells	3		Woodford & South		
Twyford/Berks	5		Woodford/Essex	3	
Tyldesley	3			3A	2
Upminster	3		Woodford Green	3	
Uppingham	3		Woolpit	3	
Wadebridge	1, 2, 3		Woolwich	3	
Wakefield	3			3B	2
Walmer	3			3C	6
Walmer Road	2, 3		Worcester	2, 3	
Walsall	3		Worksop	3	
Walsden	3		Worthing	3	
Walton-on-Naze	3		Worthing Station B.O./		
Ware	1, 2, 3		Worthing	3	
Wargrave/Berks	3		Wrexham	2, 3	
Warrington	3			2A	2
Washaway	3		Wrington	3	
Washford	3		Wroxall	2, 3	
Waterford	3		York	1, 2, 3	
Wednesbury	3				

9. GENERAL PURPOSE HANDSTAMPS

Single Circles

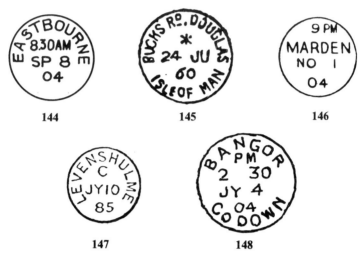

144   145   146

147   148

144 Single circles as back stamps, usually black or blue, from 1857 .   1.50
      As above but cancelling stamps, coded or timed, before 1900 .   5.00
      As above but after 1900 . . . .   0.50
145 Modern single circles used in counter work 0.10
146 Single circle with name of office horizontally across circle . . .   1.75
147 'Thimble' or very small diameter single circle 0.75
148 Larger Irish type of single circle 0.50

149   150

149 Rubbers, thicker letters in black, blue-black or violet . (if clear)   3.00
150   As above but head office across circle . . . . . . (if clear)   5.00
      Modern soft packet stamps 0.10

Skeletons (or 'Travelling'. Composed of pieces of loose type held together in a frame. Used for various temporary purposes. Prices are for complete clear strikes.)

151   152

151 Office name in arc, cross beneath, unframed, seriffed or
    non-seriffed letters 1840s. 55.00
    As above but index number instead of cross, 1840s. 50.00
152 Circular 34 mm, year in full, seriffed or non seriffed letters,
    1840–50s. 40.00

153   154   155

153 Circular, year in two figures, non seriffed, late Victorian and
    Edwardian 5.00
    As above but county name at base 5.00
    As above but county name following town name at top . . . 6.00
154 As above but sub office name at top and town name at base . 7.00
    As above but sub office name at top with town and county at
    base 7.00
155 As above but with spelling or other errors 8.50

156	157	158

156 Small skeletons 6.00
157 Rubber skeletons . . . . (if clear) 15.00
158 Circular 28 mm, day month and year in one line, office name
    at top only, from 1914 . . . . 5.00
    As above but county name at base 5.00
    As above but sub-office name at top, town name at base . . . 5.50
    As above but sub-office name at top, town and country at base 5.50

Double Circles

159	160	161

159 Scottish type with 1844 office numbers between pairs of arcs,
    from 1883 . . . . 1.50
    As above but larger 0.75
160   As above with English Office numbers, from 1885

75	Birmingham	. . 2.00	K34	Haswell	. . . . . 5.00
466	Liverpool	. . . . 2.50	K35	Murton Colliery	. . 7.00
			K36	South Hetton	. . . 4.00

161   As above with blank space in Irish stamps 0.50
    As above with cross or stamp number between pairs of arcs,
    English, Scottish and Irish 0.50

162	163	164

162 With one pair of thick arcs broken by cross 0.10
With one pair of thick arcs broken by stamp number 0.15
With one pair of thick arcs broken by identifying letter 0.50
163 With one pair of thick arcs broken by post-town, county or
district office 0.15
With one pair of thick arcs broken by six pointed star 1.00
With one pair of thick arcs broken by eight pointed star 2.00
With one unbroken thick arc 0.50
With pair of very short thick arcs and cross 0.50
164 With pair of thin arcs broken by post-town, county, etc 0.10
With one unbroken thin arc 0.50

Scrolls (or 'Hooded' or 'Crested' Circles)

165	166	167	168

165 London or London E.C. on Victorian mail, cancelling stamps . 0.75
As above but Edwardian period 2.00
As above but receiving marks, usually from abroad 0.75
166 Liverpool, on Victorian mail, cancelling stamps 6.00
As above but Edwardian period 3.00
Liverpool S 3.00
V. Liverpool S., (Victoria St.) 50.00
E. Lowhill D., (Liverpool) 8.00

167 Cork 6.00
Waterford 35.00
Limerick 10.00
Londonderry 35.00

Used for late Fees:
Threadneedle St. B.O. E.C. 10.00
Leadenhall St. 10.00
Liverpool E.C. 10.00
Ludgate Circus E.C. 25.00
Fleet St. E.C. 10.00
Eastcheap Station B.O. E.C. 10.00
47 Cannon St. 15.00
Throgmorton Avenue B.O. E.C. 15.00
Fenchurch St. B.O. E.C. 15.00
Mark Lane E.C. 15.00

Registered:
London and Queensborough S.T. 20.00
Empire Games Village, (Barry, 1958) 20.00
Army Post Office 5.00
Paddington W.2 . . . . 5.00
168 London W.C. 5.00

Parcel Post:
Euston 10.00
London Bridge Parcel Post Depot 10.00
Stamford Mercury with 742 numeral 10.00
London E.C. with miniature 1844 numeral 50.00

(see also Stations and Royalty)

Paid Handstamps (in red)

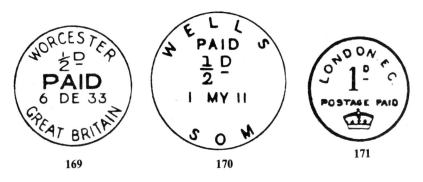

169   170   171

169 Single circle types with Great Britain and £ S D amount 0.50

As above but with 1st or 2nd 0.05

170 Skeleton Paid marks 10.00

171 London E.C./1D/Postage Paid, (Wilkinson Machine), January

25 or August 31, 1912 . . . . 15.00

As above but other dates 100.00

Double oval parcel post paid handstamps 0.15

Some other types

172

173

174

172 Double circles cancelling stamps, Edwardian. (cut down

machine?) 2.00

173 Very large double circles of London, some with unbroken thick

arc 1.75

174 Continental type double circle ('Hammer'), London or London

E.C. coded 1–6 . . . . 40.00

175

176

177

178

175 Single circle London mis-sort stamps 1.00

176 Single arc types as backstamp 2.00

As above but as cancellation, Edwardian 5.00

177 Double circle Victorian backstamps, red or black 0.75

178 Square types of backstamp in red or black 1.50

10. MACHINE CANCELLATIONS

Pearson Hill Experimental Machines, 1857–58

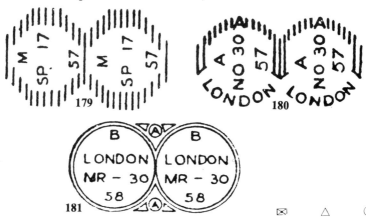

179

180

181

	⊠	△	○
179 Without London, First Trial, 1857	4000.00	500.00	200.00
180 With London, coded A or M, Second Trial, 1857–8	300.00	30.00	20.00
181 Opera Glass Type, Third Trial, 1858	2000.00	250.00	100.00

Charles Rideout, from 1858

182

183

182	Machine Number one, coded HS	75.00
183	Machine Number Two, coded CR	75.00

Pearson Hill, from 1858

184

185

184 Parallel Motion Machines, London, numbered 1–6, 87, 90–92, 97, 100–101 . . . . 1.00
185 Parallel Motion Machines, London District offices 1.00
Pivot Machines, London 0.75
Pivot Machines, Provincial 0.75

Azemar, 1869–73

186

Datestamp at lower left, April 1869 . . . . 150.00
186 Bars in four, five or six sections (order varies), datestamp aligned   75.00

Sloper's Patent, 1870–74

Stamped Postcard perforated by single hole 15.00
As above but series of holes in shape of arrow 30.00
As above but series of holes in shape of orb 120.00

Hoster, 1882–93

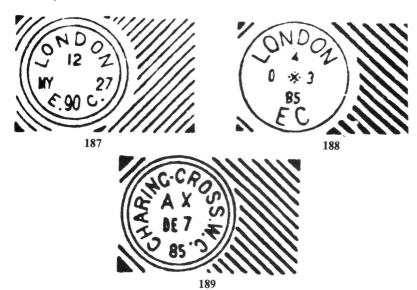

187

188

189

Single circle datestamp, fourteen downward bars, no
   corners at left 20.00
187 As above but corners at left 15.00
As above but two bars broken by figures 15.00
As above, two bars broken by figures and asterisk each side of
   year 25.00
Double circle datestamp, London/E.C., downward bars 10.00
As above but London only 10.00

188 As above but eighteen upward bars, London/E.C. 10.00

189 Double circle, Charing Cross W.C. 200.00

Single circle, London/N.P.B 200.00

Double circle, Bedford St. B.O. W.C. 250.00

Ethridge, September 1886 – April 1887

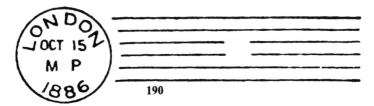

190 Single circle datestamp, six straight bars with central space . . . 200.00

Hey Dolphin, 1893–1933 (or Internationals, or Fliers)

191 Single circle circle datestamp, seven straight bars with 1
(Sept. 1893 trial) 75.00

192 Single circle datestamp, seven undulating bars with I and C
(1902–3, 11 trials) 18.00

Single circle datestamp, five undulating bars (1915–20 working
trials) 3.00

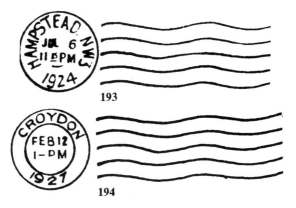

193 As above but regular issue (from 1921) 0.50
194 Double circle datestamp without county name, five undulating
      bars (from 1923) 0.40
      As above but with county name (from 1928) 0.30

Imperial Mail Marking, 1897–98

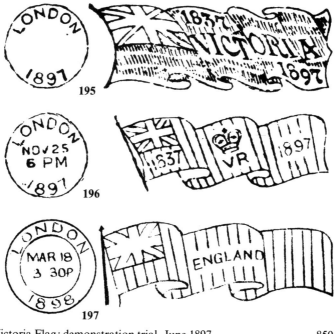

195 Victoria Flag; demonstration trial, June 1897 . . . . 850.00
196 VR Flag; demonstration trial, November 1897 . . . . 850.00
197 England Flag; used on four days in March 1898 . . . . 600.00

Bickerdike, 1897–1907

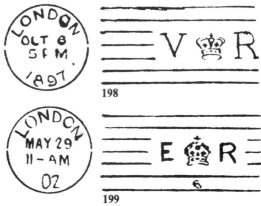

198

199

198 Single circle datestamp, seven straight bars with tall seriffed VR . 100.00
As above but smaller non-seriffed VR 100.00
As above but numbers 1–6 beneath crown 5.00
As above but Liverpool; 1 or 2 beneath crown 15.00
199 Single circle datestamp, seven straight bars with ER, numbers
1–6 beneath crown 3.00
As above but without code numbers 1.00
As above but Liverpool; 1 or 2 beneath crown 12.00

Boston, 1898–1908

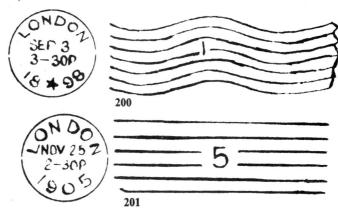

200

201

200 Single circle datestamp with star, seven undulating bars with 1,
joined. (August – September 1898) 100.00
As above but without star or 1, bars not joined (1899–1904) . 6.00
As above but with six straight bars shaped to datestamp, codes
1–6 . . . . 3.00
As above but four bars, codes 2 or 3 . . . . 4.00

201   As above but bars straight by datestamp, codes 1–6 . . . . .   1.00

    Liverpool, Code 3 or 4, seven undulating bars 15.00

Columbia, 1901–1921

202

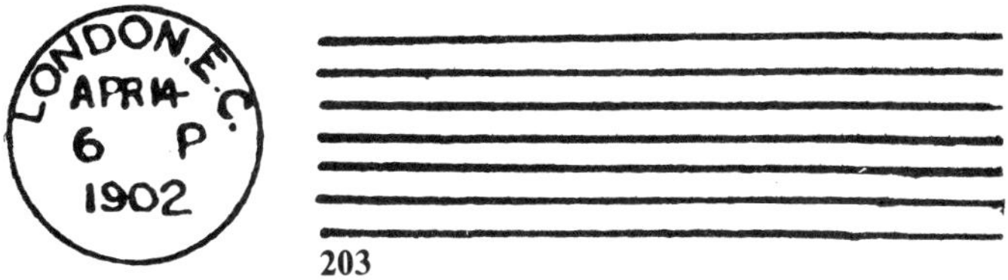

203

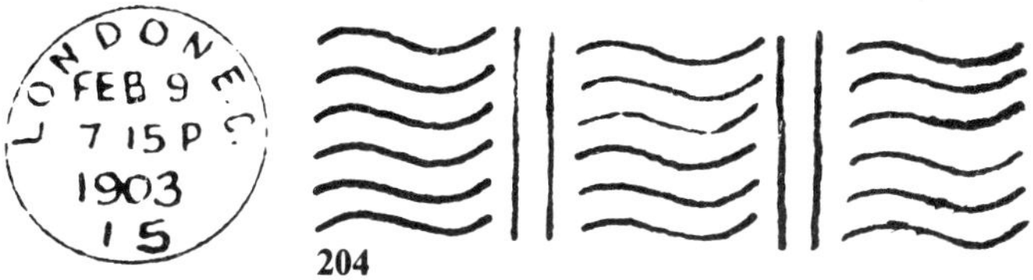

204

205

202 London E.C., single arc datestamp with seven straight bars . . 10.00

203 Single circle datestamp, London EC, SE, SW, WC, W or MP,

    seven straight bars 1.00

    As above but London EC coded 1, 2, 3, 15 or 58 . . . . . .   1.25

204 London E.C. circular datestamps with three groups of wavy

    bars 2.50

    As above E.C. or M.P., with 3 in central bars and extra pair of

    bars above and below . . . . (if clear)   3.00

205 Circular datestamp, district initials EC, WC, W, SW or E,

    between bars 1.50

LONDON

MAR 7 1 ^

6.   PM

206

LONDON.EC

3.30 PM

JAN15 06

207

LONDON. E.

415 —PM   No. 18.

DEC17'04

208

EDINBURGH

5. 15 PM

MAR 22 14   209

Three line London datestamp, three pairs of straight bars, single
    impression 5.00

    As above but continuous impression 8.00

206 Three line London datestamp, six or seven straight bars 0.50

207   As above but London District datestamps 0.60

    As above but provincial datestamps 0.70

208 Three line London District datestamp, with or without bar above
    and below, six straight bars with machine number at left:
    London E (18), NW (19 and 20), SE (15 and 19), SW (14),
    WC (16 and 19), W (17), EC (1), Paddington (19 and 21)   . .   0.75

    As above but provincial machines: Aberdeen (1), Birmingham
    (1), Bristol (1), Cardiff (1), Dublin (1), Edinburgh (1),
    Glasgow (1), Hull (1), Leeds (1), Liverpool (1 and 2),
    Manchester (1 and 2), Newcastle-upon-Tyne (1),
    Nottingham (1) 0.75

    Three line London or provincial datestamp coded A-E, with
    straight bars 0.50

209 Three line London or provincial datestamp with five wavy bars   .   0.60

    London District triangular dies (eg SE, M.T.P. 1 or 2, SW) with
    bars 3.00

    London or provincial paid dies with cancelling bars, struck in red   2.50

Krag, from 1905 (all continuous impression unless stated otherwise)

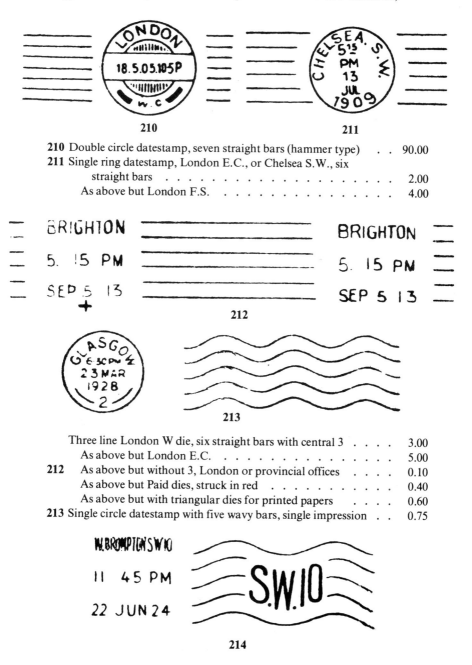

210 Double circle datestamp, seven straight bars (hammer type) . . 90.00
211 Single ring datestamp, London E.C., or Chelsea S.W., six
straight bars 2.00
As above but London F.S. 4.00

Three line London W die, six straight bars with central 3 . . . . 3.00
As above but London E.C. 5.00
212 As above but without 3, London or provincial offices 0.10
As above but Paid dies, struck in red 0.40
As above but with triangular dies for printed papers 0.60
213 Single circle datestamp with five wavy bars, single impression . . 0.75

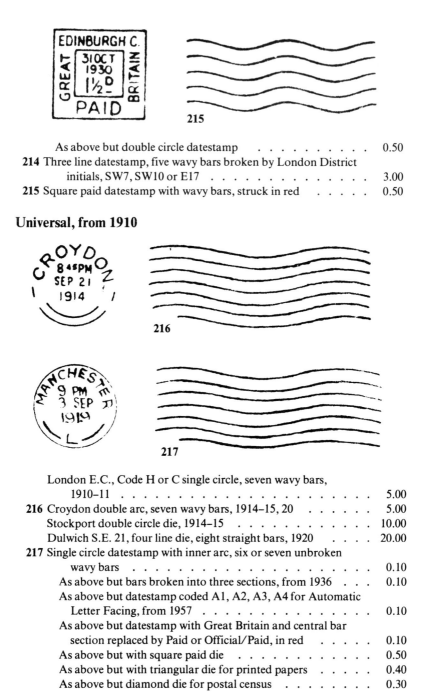

215

As above but double circle datestamp 0.50
214 Three line datestamp, five wavy bars broken by London District
    initials, SW7, SW10 or E17 . . . . 3.00
215 Square paid datestamp with wavy bars, struck in red 0.50

Universal, from 1910

216

217

London E.C., Code H or C single circle, seven wavy bars,
    1910–11 . . . . 5.00
216 Croydon double arc, seven wavy bars, 1914–15, 20 . . . . . . 5.00
Stockport double circle die, 1914–15 . . . . 10.00
Dulwich S.E. 21, four line die, eight straight bars, 1920 . . . . 20.00
217 Single circle datestamp with inner arc, six or seven unbroken
    wavy bars 0.10
As above but bars broken into three sections, from 1936 . . . 0.10
As above but datestamp coded A1, A2, A3, A4 for Automatic
    Letter Facing, from 1957 . . . . 0.10
As above but datestamp with Great Britain and central bar
    section replaced by Paid or Official/Paid, in red 0.10
As above but with square paid die 0.50
As above but with triangular die for printed papers 0.40
As above but diamond die for postal census 0.30

Time Mail Marking Machine Company, 1912–13

218 Cricklewood single circle with seven straight bars, 1912 . . . . 150.00
219 St. John's Wood single circle with seven straight bars, central
    date, 1913 . . . . 150.00

Alma or Bee, 1912–1922

220 London E.C., three line datestamp, six short bars, continuous
    impression, 1912–14 . . . . 5.00
    London E.C., SW.1, S.E. 18, or Southend. Similar to wavy line,
    Krags but smaller letters, 1915–22 . . . . 0.75

Standard, 1930–37

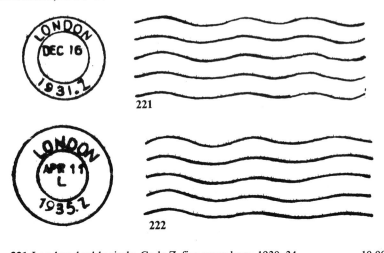

221

222

221 London double circle, Code Z, five wavy bars, 1930–34 . . . . 10.00
222 As above but larger die, 1935–37 . . . . 15.00

Magazine cancelling Machines (Roddis' Mangles), from 1957

Identical to wavy line Krag, continuous impression, struck in red   0.25

Totometer, from 1957

223

223 Large oval, for stamping wrappers, in red 0.50

11. MACHINE POSTMARKS WITH SLOGANS

The following selection is taken from the excellent handbook by C. R. H. Parsons, C. G. Peachey and G. R. Pearson whose numbers are used with permission. All Slogans appeared to the right of datestamp. The number of dies, if more than one, is given in brackets but in the early period is often only approximate. Slogans used continuously into the next year will only be listed under the year of introduction. Full details of design and periods of use are given in the handbook.

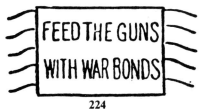

224	225

1917

1	War Bonds Now, single	(60)	1.00
2	War Bonds Now, cont	(100)	0.80
3	War Bonds Now, Alma	(8)	1.50

1918

A4	War Bonds, single	(3)	19.00
4	War Bonds, lines r & l	(30)	0.60
5	War Bonds, lines r	(20)	1.00
6	Feed the Guns, single **224**	(40)	1.50
7	Feed the Guns, cont	(130)	0.65
7A	Feed the Guns, Alma	(6)	1.50

1922

8	BIF 1922	(5)	2.50
9	Cable Canada, boxed	(20)	1.00
10	Cable Canada, unboxed		20.00
11	Cable Canada, Triangle LE		12.00
12	Post Early box, single	(25)	0.50
13	Post Early box, cont	(2)	5.00
14	Empire Exhib., single	(22)	0.50
15	Empire Exhib., cont	(12)	0.70
16	BIF 1923	(10)	1.60

1923

17	Ulster Pavilion, single	(2)	9.00
18	Ulster Pavilion, cont	(3)	15.00

1924

19	BIF 1924	(12)	2.00
A20	Empire Exhib., single		4.00
20	Empire Exhib., Wembley		4.00
21	Pageant of Empire	(30)	1.50

1925

22	Empire Exhib	(30)	0.50
23	Ulster Pavilion	(2)	10.00
24	Empire Exhib, Wembley	(4)	5.00
24A	Govt. Pavilion		7.50
25	Join the Fellowship	(5)	1.50
26	London Defended	(25)	1.30
27	Torchlight Tattoo, Sept	(25)	1.30
28	T.T. – 10th Oct	(10)	5.00
29	T.T. Dates removed	(10)	15.00
30	T.T. dots, lines, etc	(29)	5.00
31	British Goods, large **225**	(200)	0.20
32	British Goods, small	(15)	0.60
33	British Goods, cont		24.00
A34	British Made Goods	(5)	20.00
34	Christmas – FOR –	(100)	0.75
35	BIF 1926	(12)	1.25

1926

36	British Goods, framed	(2)	4.00
37	King's Roll **226**	(50)	1.50
38	Say it by Telephone	(125)	0.75
39	Christmas – FOR –	(100)	0.60
40	BIF 1927	(12)	1.00

1927

41	Christmas – FOR –	(100)	0.60
42	BIF 1928	(12)	1.00

1928

43	Christmas – FOR –	(100)	0.55
44	BIF 1929	(12)	1.00

1929

45	Newcastle Exhib	(30)	0.60
46	Christmas – FOR –	(100)	0.75

226

227

1930			
47	BIF	(12)	1.00
48	Christmas –FOR–)	(150)	0.75
49	Christmas FOR)		0.75
1931			
50	BIF	(12)	1.50
51	BIF Cotton	(30)	2.00
52	Every Home a Phone	(25)	0.20
52a	— Tel. Exhib		5.00
53	Telephone Habit	(25)	0.25
54	Quicker to Telephone	(25)	0.20
55	Shop by phone, dot dash	(25)	5.00
56	Shop by phone, solid	(25)	0.20
57	Best investment	(25)	0.25
A57	— L removed		3.00
58	Life Easier	(25)	0.20
59	Sound Investment	(25)	0.20
60	Time and Money	(25)	0.20
61	Trade follows	(25)	0.20
62	You are wanted	(25)	0.20
63	Christmas –FOR–)	(150)	0.55
64	Christmas FOR)		0.45
1932			
65	BIF 1932	(18)	0.65
66	BIF Textiles	(20)	0.85
67	Christmas –FOR–)	(150)	0.55
68	Christmas FOR)		0.45
69	BIF, thin 1933	(12)	1.00
70	BIF, thick 1933	(10)	1.50
71	BIF 1933, Textiles	(20)	1.00
1933			
72	Christmas –FOR–)	(150)	0.60
73	Christmas FOR)		0.45
74	BIF 1934, 22 mm	(30)	1.00
75	BIF 1934, 19 mm	(3)	3.50
76	BIF Textiles, 22 mm	(15)	3.00
77	BIF Textiles, 19 mm	(8)	3.50
1934			
77Ba	Tel. Exhib		5.00
78	Mt. Pleasant		55.00
79	Christmas –FOR–)	(150)	0.80
80	Christmas FOR)		0.40
81	BIF Eng. & H.	(35)	1.00
82	BIF Textiles, 22 mm	(15)	1.25
83	BIF Textiles, 19 mm	(8)	3.50

1935			
84	Christmas –FOR–)	(150)	1.20
85	Christmas FOR)		0.60
86	BIF 1936	(35)	1.00
87	BIF Textiles, 22 mm	(15)	1.50
88	BIF Textiles, 19 mm	(8)	3.00
1936			
A89	Telephone Habit, G.P.O. Exhib		6.50
89	Christmas –FOR–)	(150)	0.90
90	Christmas FOR)		0.50
91	BIF 1937	(50)	0.75
92	Yng. People Exhib		6.00
1937			
93	Post Early sunburst **227**	(200)	0.10
94	Post Early, Box, Leith	(1)	17.50
95	As above GPO Exhib		2.50
96	Christmas –FOR–)	(150)	2.00
97	Christmas FOR)		0.40
98	BIF 1938	(50)	1.00
1938			
99	Post Early sunburst **227**	(?)	0.20
A100	Post Early box G.P.O. Exhib		2.50
100	Glasgow Exhib		0.10
100a	— Exhib. P.O.		0.55
101	— Pavilion		2.50
102	Christmas –FOR–)	(150)	2.50
103	Christmas FOR)		0.25
104	BIF 1939	(50)	0.75
1939			
A105	Post Early box, G.P.O. ex.		5.00
105	Every home a phone, red		16.00
106	Post Early sunburst **227**	(?)	0.15
107	Road Users	(100)	0.50
108	Grow more food	(75)	0.50
109	Christmas –FOR–)	(100)	7.50
110	Christmas FOR)		0.25

228

229

	1940		
A111	Every home a phone		14.00
111	Post Early Sunburst	(?)	0.10
112	Grow more food	(50)	0.50
113	Kitchen Front	(50)	0.50
114	Save waste paper	(50)	0.40
115	Christmas –FOR–	(3)	5.00
116	Christmas FOR	(100)	0.30
	1941		
117	Post Early Sunburst	(?)	0.20
118	Kitchen Front		4.00
119	Save waste paper	(50)	0.50
120	Grow more food	(50)	0.50
121	Christmas FOR	(75)	0.50
	1942		
122	Post Early Sunburst	(?)	0.25
123	Christmas FOR	(50)	0.50
A124	Telephone Habit		14.00
	1943		
124	Post Early Sunburst	(22)	0.40
125	Christmas FOR	(50)	0.50
	1944		
126	Post Early Sunburst	(11)	0.40
127	Christmas FOR	(50)	0.50
	1945		
128	Post Early Sunburst	(8)	0.65
129	Victory Europe **228**	(400)	0.10
130	Victory Japan **228**	(400)	0.10
131	Christmas FOR	(50)	0.30
132	Christmas Holly	(100)	0.30
133	United Nations	(100)	1.00
	1946		
134	National Savings	(350)	0.30
135	Don't Waste Bread	(350)	0.30
136	Death off road	(350)	0.30
137	Britain can make it	(350)	0.50
138	Christmas FOR	(40)	0.75
139	Christmas Holly	(350)	0.25

	1947		
140	BIF 1947	(50)	0.50
141	Staggered Holidays	(350)	0.30
142	Blood Donors	(350)	0.30
143	Forces Career	(350)	0.30
144	Britain for Holidays	(50)	0.50
145	Silver Lining	(350)	0.30
146	Royal Wedding **229**	(400)	0.10
147	Christmas FOR	(40)	0.75
148	Christmas Holly)	(350)	0.30
149	— Rough Holly)		0.35
	1948		
150	BIF 1948	(50)	0.50
151	Hand on the Land **230**	(350)	0.30
152	Blood Donors	(350)	0.30
153	Nursing	(350)	0.25
154	As 151 but June		4.50
155	Edinburgh Festival	(30)	0.60
156	Eisteddfod **231**	(12)	2.00
157	Olympic Games	(2)	0.65
158	Blood Donors	(350)	0.35
159	Save waste paper	(350)	0.30
160	Christmas FOR	(30)	1.00
161	Christmas Holly)	(350)	0.20
162	— Rough Holly)		0.55
	1949		
163	Volunteer Forces	(350)	0.30
164	BIF 1949	(50)	0.50
165	Mind how you go	(350)	0.30
166	Edinburgh Festival	(31)	0.85
167	British Air Lines	(350)	0.30
168	Scottish Ind.	(30)	0.85
169	Colonial month	(100)	0.30
170	Food Gifts	(50)	0.50
171	Savings Week	(300)	0.20
172	Blood Donors	(350)	0.30
173	Christmas FOR		0.80
174	Christmas Holly)	(350)	0.20
175	— Rough Holly)		0.65

LEND A HAND ON THE LAND

230

ROYAL NATIONAL EISTEDDFOD OF WALES 31 JULY – 7 AUG BRIDGEND · GLAM

231

1950		
176 BIF 1950	(50)	0.50
177 Road Users	(350)	0.20
178 Stamp Exhib.	(50)	0.30
179 Edinburgh Fest.	(31)	0.90
180 Christmas FOR		7.50
181 Christmas Holly	(350)	0.30
182 — Rough Holly		5.00
1951		
183 Voters List	(350)	0.35
184 BIF 1951	(50)	0.30
185 Blood Donors	(350)	0.20
186 Festival Britain	(40)	0.30
187 — S.E.1		0.45
188 Civil Defence	(350)	0.30
189 Christmas Holly	(350)	0.30

1952		
190 BIF 1952	(50)	0.30
191 Voters List	(300)	0.30
192 Postage for Europe	(350)	0.12
193 Christmas Rough Holly		7.50
194 — Holly)	(350)	0.25
195 — Dark Holly)		0.20
1953		
196 Voters List	(350)	0.30
197 BIF 1953	(50)	0.30
198 Eisteddfod		10.00
199 Coronation	(921)	0.30
200 Postage for Europe	(350)	0.25
201 Blood Donors	(350)	0.20
202 Check Address	(350)	0.20
203 Holly)	(350)	0.25
204 Dark Holly)		0.20

Slogan with circular paid Die, in red . . . Three times Normal
Slogan with square paid Die, in red . . . . . Twice Normal
Slogan with diamond census die . . . . Twice Normal
Slogan with triangular die . . . . Four times Normal

During the present reign the number of Slogans used has been very greatly expanded. More than three thousand general slogans have now been used and a further two thousand local Publicity Slogans. From 1963 many Slogans appeared transposed, i.e., to the left of the datestamp. Full details of all Slogans are given in the Handbooks of C. R. H. Parsons, C. G. Peachey and G. R. Pearson.

PUZZLED?

From time to time all collectors find covers which have curious or unexplained features. Send a photocopy (with SAE or IRC) and I will send my comments or refer to a specialist in a particular field. Some of the most interesting – or ones which still cannot be explained – illustrated in the next *Collect British Postmarks.*

12. SPECIAL EVENT POSTMARKS

Full details of the design and period of use are given in the excellent handbook by George Pearson whose numbers are used here with permission. Cancellations marked — in the price column may not exist, those marked ? cannot be priced at present.

232

233

234

235

1862
1	Int. Exhib. Duplex	90.00
2	Int. Exhib. S/C **232**	100.00
3	I.E/W. **233**	90.00

1879
4	Agric. Exhibition	?

1883
5	Manch. Exhibition	—
6	Fisheries Exhibition	90.00

1884
7	Health Exhibition	90.00

1885
8	Inventions Exhibition	90.00

1886
9	Liverpool Exhibition	—
10	Col. & Ind. Exhibition **234**	90.00

1887
11	Saltaire Exhibition	—
12	U.S. Exhibition	90.00
13	Manchester Exhibition	90.00

1888
14	Glasgow Exhibition	80.00
15	Italian Exhibition	100.00

1890
16	French Exhibition	—
17	Military Exhibition	90.00
18	1840 Jub. numbered	10.00
19	— unnumbered	10.00
20	Edinburgh Exhibition	85.00
21	1840 Jub. large circle	9.00
22	— smaller circle	12.00
23	— G crown R shield	10.00
24	— Museum **235**	10.00
25	— Tube Post	11.00
26	— Tube Post Reply	11.00
27	BA/E	20.00

1891
28	German Exhibition	20.00
29	Naval Exhibition	20.00
30	Naval Exhib. B.O.	85.00

1892
31	Hort. Exhibition	80.00
32	Warwk. Show	75.00

1893
33	Agric. Show	—
34	Eddystone	20.00
35	Bristol Exhibition	85.00

1894
36	Cambridge Show	50.00

1895
37	Taunton Show	70.00
38	Darlington Show	70.00

236	**237**	**238**

1899		
39	Windsor Show	—
40	Maidstone Show	70.00

1900		
41	Bradford B.A.	70.00

1901		
42	Glasgow Exhib. D/C	8.50
A43	— S/C	50.00
43	Brit. Assn. G. W.	60.00
44	Int. Eng. Cong.	—

1902		
45	Wolv. Exhibition	50.00
46	Cork Exhibition	40.00
47	Bot. Gdns	?
48	Br. Ass. B.E.	40.00

1903		
49	Henley Regatta	?
50	Brit. Assn. Southport	40.00
A51	Plymouth Exhib.	40.00

1904		
A52	Brit. Assn. Cambridge **236**	?

1905		
52	Plymouth Exhibition	40.00

1907		
53	Dublin Exhibition	5.00

1908		
54	Edinburgh Exhibition	8.00
55	Fr-Brit. Exhib. **237**	1.00
56	Shep. Bush Exhibition	25.00
57	Sh. Bush Ex. B.O.	?
58	Ballymaclinton	1.40

1909		
59	Phil Congress	6.00
60	Int. Imp. Exhibition	5.00
A61	— Machine	45.00
61	Ballymaclinton	4.00
62	— packets	?
63	Sh. Bush Stadium	—
64	Scottish Village	12.00

1910		
65	Jap-Brit. Exhibition	4.00
66	— Machine	12.00
67	Agric. Show	?
A68	Spalding Show	?
68	Lanark	45.00

1911		
69	Glasgow Exhibition	9.00
70	Empire Fest. 1–6	8.50
71	Empire Fest. 7–8	30.00
72	Hort. Ex	?
73	Phil. Congress	12.00
74	Coronation Exhibition	6.00
75	Norwich Show	?
76	St. Andrews	?
77	Inverness	—
78	Health Congress	—
79	Aerial Post, London **238**	10.00
80	— Windsor	16.00

1912		
81	Phil Congress	5.00
82	Hort. Exhibition	14.00
83	Radio Conference	—
84	Royal Society	35.00
85	Sh. Bush Exhibition	10.00
86	Stamp Exhibition	2.00

239

240

241

1913		
87	Phil Congress	12.00
88	Liverpool Exhibition	?
89	Aylesbury	—
A90	Burnley Show	?
· 90	Med. Congress	35.00
91	Gt. Int. Exhibition	—
	1914	
92	Sh. Bush Exhibition	10.00
93	Bristol Exhibition **239**	35.00
A93	U.M.C. Conference	35.00
	1917	
94	Hort Exhibition	—
95	Dublin	40.00
	1919	
A96	R34	?
	1920	
96	Phil Congress	7.00
97	Cowes	25.00
	1921	
98	Harrogate	7.00
	1922	
99	Bath	6.00
	1923	
100	London Exhib	1.50
	1924	
101	Glasgow Cong	13.00
102	Wembley Exhib. Slogan	2.50
103	— in red	15.00
104	— with lion **240**	3.50
105	— with red	10.00

106	— with 2★	10.00
107	— Registered **241**	15.00
108	— Engineering	10.00
109	— Engineering Parcel	20.00
110	— Industry	12.00
111	— Industry Parcel	20.00
	1925	
112	Wembley Exhib Slogan	3.50
113	— in red	16.00
114	— P.O. Exhib Slogan	7.00
115	— Govt. Pav.	5.00
116	— Exhib	6.00
117	— Exhib in red	15.00
118	— with 2★	14.00
A119	— Packet 2★	12.00
119	— Registered	15.00
120	— Exhib. Pkt.	15.00
121	— Exhib. Parcels	20.00
122	— Industry	15.00
123	— Industry Parcel	20.00
A124	— Stadium	—
B124	— Conf. H	—
124	Phil. Congress	5.00
125	Railway	—
126	Chester Show	20.00
	1926	
127	Bournemouth Show	20.00
128	Phil Congress	4.00
129	Reading Show	17.00
130	Harrogate Show	25.00
131	Burnley Show	20.00
	1927	
132	Phil. Congress	4.00
133	Newport Show	25.00
134	Bolton Show	25.00

242   243   244

1928		
135	B.I.F. B'ham	8.00
136	Phil. Congress **242**	4.00
137	Nott. Show	20.00
138	Glasgow Conf	12.00
139	Stamp Exhib	0.80
140	— Reg.	3.00

1929		
141	B.I.F. B'ham	8.00
142	Exhib. Newcastle **243**	8.00
143	— Parcel	18.00
144	PUC **244**	5.00
145	— Reg.	20.00
146	— packets	15.00
147	Phil. Cong	3.00
148	Harrogate Show A	15.00
149	— parcel	19.00
150	Harrogate Show B	15.00
151	— parcel	19.00
152	Alloa Show	20.00
153	Arrowe Park Scout Camp	40.00

1930		
154	Naval Conference	15.00
155	B.I.F. B'ham	8.00
156	Phil. Congress	4.00
157	Sanitary Congress	20.00
158A	Manchester Show A	18.00
158B	— Show B	18.00
159	— Parcels	18.00
160	Dumfries Show	15.00
161	Esperanto	12.00
162	S.A.T.	28.00
163	Bristol Conference	8.50
164	Indian Conference	12.50

1931		
165	B.I.F. B'ham	5.00
166	Bristol Show	18.00
167	Portsmouth Show	18.00
168	St. Columb	18.00
169	Chippenham	18.00
170	Edinburgh HS	12.00
171	Crawley	22.00
172	Lincoln	18.00
173	Leicester	3.00
174	Warwick Show	11.00
175	— parcel	18.00
176	Canterbury	18.00
177	Huddersfield	18.00
178	Bristol	8.00
179	Indian Conf, Oct	14.00
180	Calshot	8.00
181	Indian Conf, Dec.	18.00
182	Burma	15.00

1932		
183	B.I.F. B'ham	8.00
184	Telephone Exhibition	3.50
185	Chelsea	18.00
186	Yeovil	22.00
187	Sutton Coldfield	8.00
188	Phil. Congress	2.50
189	Inverness	15.00
190	Southampton	18.00

| 245 | 246 | 247 |

	1933		
191	Telephone Exhibition	3.50	
192	B.I.F. B'ham	5.00	
193	Chelsea	18.00	
A194	Bath Show	20.00	
194	Bournemouth	20.00	
195	Phil. Congress	2.50	
196	Worcester	20.00	
197	Econ. Conference	3.50	
198	— S/c	11.00	
199	— parcel	18.00	
200	— packets	18.00	
201	Nfk Show	22.00	
202	Derby Show	?	

	1934	
203	B.I.F. B'ham	3.50
204	Air Exhibition **245**	1.00
205	Phil. Congress	2.50
206	Chelsea	14.00
207	Salisbury	22.00
208	Hereford	22.00
209	Peterborough	18.00
210	Ipswich	15.00
211	— parcel	18.00
212	Bradford	?
213	Bolton	18.00
214	Aberdeen **246**	13.00
215	Mildenhall **247**	4.00
216	Mt. Pleasant	55.00

	1935	
217	Telephone Exhibition	3.00
218	Rotary Margate	28.00
219	B.I.F. B'ham	4.00
220	Chelsea	15.00
221	Taunton	20.00
222	Edinburgh CS	10.00
223	Weymouth	20.00
224	Gloucester	20.00
225	Bath	1.20
226	Aberdeen	15.00
227	Peterborough	20.00
228	Newcastle	?
229	Bristol	8.00
230	Burnley	?
231	T.U.C. Margate	18.00

	1936	
232	B.I.F. B'ham	3.50
233	— Reg.	3.50
234	Chelsea	3.50
A235	Telephone Exhibition	2.50
235	Phil. Congress	1.25
236	Worcester	15.00
237	Melrose	8.00
238	Worthing	15.00
239	Peterborough	15.00
240	Bristol	15.00
241	Edgcumbe	50.00
A242	Bath	?
242	SAT	6.00
A243	Darlington	50.00
243	Blackpool	6.00
244	Stamp Exhibition	0.75
245	Young People	5.00

248 **249** **250**

	1937	
A246	G.P.O. Exhib	3.50
246	B.I.F. B'ham	3.50
247	— Reg.	2.50
A248	Newark	15.00
B248	Paignton	?
248	Chelsea	3.00
249	Shrewsbury	8.00
250	Phil. Congress	0.80
A250	Wadebridge	15.00
A251	Fakenham	15.00
251	Alloa	5.00
A252	Peterborough	15.00
252	Henley	7.00
253	Wolverhampton	8.50
254	— parcels	10.50
A255	Canterbury	15.00
B255	Warwick	15.00
C255	Monmouth	15.00
D255	G.P.O. Exhib	3.00
E255	Birmingham Dog	15.00

	1938	
255	G.P.O. Exhibition	2.50
256	B.I.F. B'ham	2.50
257	— Reg	3.50
258	N.U.T. Margate	18.00
259	Glasgow Exhib slogan	0.75
260	— machine	2.50
261	— handstamps 1–4	2.00
262	— handstamps 5–6 **248**	1.80
263	— parcels	5.00
264	— packets	2.50
265	— pavilion slog.	2.50
266	U.P.W. Margate	15.00
267	Oddfellows	15.00
268	Chelsea	2.00
269	Edinburgh C.S.	8.00
270	Bournemouth	6.00
271	Phil. Congress	0.70
272	Dumfries	5.00
273	Esperanto	6.00
274	I.L.O.	14.00
275	Birmingham Dog	14.00

	1939	
276	G.P.O. Exhibition	5.00
277	B.I.F. B'ham	4.00
278	— Reg.	4.00
279	Chelsea	2.50
280	Edinburgh C.S.	6.00
281	Portsmouth	15.00
282	Phil. Congress	0.80
283	Edin. Show	8.00
284	Windsor	6.00
285	Henley	6.00
286	Dundee	8.00

	1940	
287	Phil. Congress	0.75
288	Stamp Centenary	0.75
A289	Pavilion B'mouth	?
289	Red Cross	0.75
290	Edinburgh C.S.	5.50

	1941	
291	Edinburgh C.S.	6.00
292	Edinburgh T.U.C.	8.00
293	C of S. Edinburgh	7.00
294	Edin. C of S.	4.00

	1943	
295	Edinburgh C.S.	3.50

	1944	
296	Edinburgh C.S.	4.00

	1945	
297	Edinburgh C.S.	3.00
298	C.C.I.F.	18.00

	1946	
299	Phil. Congress	0.50
300	Edinburgh C.S.	4.00

	1947	
301	B.I.F. B'ham **249**	2.00
302	— Reg **250**	1.50
303	Edinburgh C.S.	3.00
304	Chelsea	2.00
A305	Wimbledon	6.00
305	Dundee	3.00
A306	Lincoln	?
306	Phil. Congress	0.50

251 252 253

1948		
307 B.I.F. B'ham		2.00
308 — Reg.		2.00
309 Edinburgh C.S.		2.00
310 Phil. Congress		0.40
311 Chelsea		3.50
312 Gloucester		?
313 Wimbledon		3.00
314 Inverness		4.00
A315 York		14.00
315 Olym. Games		0.70
B315 Wembley		1.25
1949		
A316 B.I.F. B'ham		2.00
316 B.I.F. B'ham 1–3		2.00
317 — Reg		2.00
318 Phil. Congress		0.40
319 Chelsea		2.20
320 Edinburgh C.S.		3.00
321 Wimbledon		2.50
322 Dundee		3.00
323 Shrewsbury		7.00
324 Esperanto		8.50
A325 Brit. Association		8.50
1950		
325 Stamp Exhib 6–13 **251**		0.25
326 — Reg		1.75
327 — narrow		2.25
328 Phil. Congress		0.35
329 B.I.F. B'ham		3.00
330 — 1–2		3.00
331 — Reg		2.50
332 Chelsea **252**		2.00
333 Edinburgh C.S.		2.00
334 Gloucester		2.00
335 Paisley		2.00
336 Wimbledon		1.00
337 Oxford		2.00
A338 Manrelns		11.00

338 GATT		2.50
339 — Reg		3.75
1951		
340 B.I.F. B'ham		2.50
341 — 1–3		1.30
342 — Reg		1.85
343 Fest. Brit. m/c		0.45
344 — handst.		0.55
345 — parcels		11.00
A346 — parcel label		3.50
346 Wimbledon		2.00
347 Chelsea		1.25
348 Edinburgh C.S.		2.00
349 Phil. Cong		0.35
350 Aberdeen		2.00
351 Wimbledon		1.50
352 Cambridge		3.50
353 Henley **253**		4.50
354 B.A.A.S.		3.50
355 Int. Air Tpt		8.00
356 S.B.A.C. EX		8.00
357 — Hants		5.00
358 — Hts		?
1952		
359 B.I.F. B'ham		2.00
360 — 1–2		2.00
361 — Reg		3.00
362 — parcels		4.00
363 Chelsea		1.20
364 Edinburgh C.S.		1.20
365 Phil. Cong		0.40
366 P.H. Exhib		0.40
A367 Redruth		11.00
367 Kelso		2.00
368 Wimbledon		1.20
369 Newton Abbot		2.00
370 Dental Cong		2.50
371 S.B.A.C.		2.50
372 B.A.A.S.		2.50

During the present reign the use of Special Event Postmarks has been very considerably expanded and about four thousand have now been used. Full details are given by George Pearson.

13. RAILWAY POSTMARKS

257

256

259

Stations

255

258

254

Stations	254 Double Arc	Numeral	255 Duplex	256 Squared Circle	257 Scottish Double Circle	258 English Double Circle	259 Single Circle	Others (and notes)
Aberdeen						1.50		
Addlestone							7.00	
Airth Road					4.00			(Scottish Numeral 547)
Angmering		?	20.00				1.00	(Numeral G73)
Annbank						2.50	1.00	
Armadale					4.00			(Scottish Numeral 457)
Ashford			10.00			1.00	2.00	(Numeral 31)

Ashington						5.00	
Ash Vale					3.50	1.00	
Atherstone							Undated parcel type: £10
Auchterless				4.00		1.00	(Scottish Numeral 561)
Aysgarth				5.00		4.00	
Balcombe						?	
Balfron					1.00	1.50	
Ballygarry						1.00	
Balquhidder				3.00			(Scottish Numeral 552)
Barnham						3.50	
Bath						1.50	
Beaconsfield						2.50	
Bedlington					1.50		
Belvedere					1.50	2.00	
Berwick	40.00	20.00	15.00		1.00	4.00	(Numeral 66)
Bexhill	?		15.00		?		(Numeral K27)
Bickley	?		12.50				Skeleton: £50. (Numeral B12)
Birmingham New St							
Blair-Adam				?			(Scottish Numeral 652)
Blantyre						?	
Bletchley	45.00	20.00	15.00		4.00	4.00	Single arc: £55. (Numeral 025)
Bogside				3.00			
Bootle		?	9.00		1.00	0.50	(Numeral K58)
Bosham				1.00		2.00	Skeleton: £10
Bournemouth Central						1.00	
Bow							
Bradford							Scroll: £20
Braidwood					4.00		
Brampton						1.00	
Brayton	?				?		(Numeral K38)

	254		255	256	257	258	259	
	Double Arc	Numeral	Duplex	Squared Circle	Scottish Double Circle	English Double Circle	Single Circle	Others (and notes)
Bridlington						0.50		Krag: £2. Slogan: £5
Brighton								Oval Reg.: £20
Bristol	35.00							
Broad Clyst						1.00	5.00	Skeleton: £12. (Rubber single circle)
Broadstairs			10.00			0.50	0.60	(Numeral 737)
Buckhurst Hill							1.75	Skeleton: £5
Byfleet							4.00	
Caerwys						1.50		
Cardiff							?	
Carlton							2.00	
Carstairs					4.00	1.00		(Scottish Numeral 70)
Castle Cary							2.00	
Castle Eden	60.00	30.00					5.00	Single arc: £60. Numeral D70
Caterham		25.00	25.00					(Numeral C70)
Chester			10.00	2.00				(Numeral 180)
Chichester			10.00	4.00		2.00		(Numeral 190)
Chislehurst							2.50	
Clapham, Lancaster							4.00	(Rubber single circle)
Craigellachie			15.00		25.00		10.00	(Scottish Numeral 86)
Crewe	40.00	?	10.00	3.00		1.00	1.00	(Numeral 047)
Crowthorne							0.50	
Croy, Glasgow						3.00		
Cumberland						1.00		
Dess, Aberdeen							3.00	
Dover			12.00				3.00	(Numeral 258)
Drymen, Glasgow						1.50		
Dunkettle RSO		?					7.50	(Irish Numeral 195)

Station								Notes
Eaglescliffe							10.00	(Scottish Numeral 469)
East Grange								
Euston						1.00	7.00	
Euston Square	30.00	10.00						(Numeral 964)
Exeter	?							
Farnborough	50.00	35.00	10.00	10.00				(Numeral 023)
Fawley		?		?				(Numeral K28)
Fimber							4.00	
Flaxton, York	60.00						2.00	
Fort George		25.00			?		10.00	(Scottish Numeral 14)
Freshwater IOW			2.50			1.50	2.00	Skeleton : £7. (Numeral H06)
Gartmore					10.00			(Scottish Numeral 578)
Gartness							12.00	
Gloucester	25.00	12.00		10.00	7.00		4.00	(Numeral 312 and E94)
Godstone		?	30.00					(Numeral 874)
Gorseinon		?						(Numeral G42)
Greenisland							20.00	
Hampstead Heath							?	
Harperley		?					2.50	
Harrow		?	?					(Numeral 909)
Hastings			10.00			1.00		(Numeral 342)
Heathfield		30.00	15.00					(Numeral H54)
Henlow						3.50		
High Peak							4.00	
Holyhead								
Horley		?	17.00					(Numeral H37)
Horsham			12.00					(Numeral 381)
Ilkeston Junction							2.00	
Ipswich							1.50	
Killearn							3.00	

107

	254 Double Arc	Numeral	255 Duplex	256 Squared Circle	257 Scottish Double Circle	258 English Double Circle	259 Single Circle	Others (and notes)
Kippen					4.00	2.50		(Scottish Numeral 653)
Kirby, Liverpool							1.75	
Knapton, York							5.00	(Rubber single circle)
Knebworth, Stevenage						3.50		Skeleton : £10
Knowle								
Laindon							3.00	
Lancing							10.00	
Leeds								Scroll : £25
Leith Central							1.00	
Lewes			10.00			5.00		(Numeral 451)
Limerick R.S.O.		?		7.00			4.00	(Irish Numeral 485)
Lintz Green		?	25.00					(Numeral F77)
Liverpool							1.00	Scroll : £20
Liverpool, Lime St							4.00	(Rubber single circle)
Liverpool St.							1.50	
Livingstone						1.50		
Llandudno Junction						1.00	2.50	Skeleton : £5
Lochearnhead					4.00			(Scottish Numeral 552)
Lockington							2.00	
Lostock							?	
Lowthorpe							3.00	
Maghull, Liverpool							0.50	
Maidstone			12.00				?	(Numeral 493)
Manchester				?				Scroll : £20
Manchester, London Rd						5.00	3.50	(Rubber single circle)
Martin Mill, Dover						1.00	2.00	Rubber Skeleton : £50
Meopham, Gravesend							2.00	Skeleton : £15

Place							Notes
Micheldever	45.00	20.00	8.00		1.50	1.50	Skeleton : £10. (Numeral 22)
Middleton						1.50	
Milford Junction	45.00	30.00	30.00				Single arc : £40 (Numeral 015)
Mintlaw				3.00	1.00	10.00	(DC without number)
Misterton					0.50		
Moorgate St.						20.00	
Murthly		?		?		?	(Scottish Numeral 405)
Murthill				10.00		10.00	(Scottish Numeral 606)
Newcastle-on-Tyne		20.00					(Numeral A16)
New Galloway			?	4.00		4.00	(Scottish Numeral 475)
New Killearn						?	
Nigg		25.00		4.00	1.00	1.00	(Scottish Numeral 271)
Normanton			6.00	6.00		1.50	(Numeral 048)
Northampton Castle						?	
Nunburnholme York						2.00	
Old Killearn						?	
Orpington					2.00	4.00	(Rubber single circle)
Orton				6.00		1.00	(Scottish Numeral 611)
Paddington	30.00	?	?		2.00	1.00	(Numeral 049)
Par	17.50	?		6.00	2.00	1.00	Skeleton : £10. (Numeral B04)
Park, Birkenhead						1.00	
Penmaenmawr					?		
Penybont						1.50	
Perranwell			7.00				
Peterborough North					2.50		
Petts Wood						?	
Pevensey						1.50	
Pilmoor, York						2.00	
Pluckley, Ashford					2.00	1.00	
Plumpton						8.00	

	254		255	256	257	258	259	
	Double Arc	Numeral	Duplex	Squared Circle	Scottish Double Circle	English Double Circle	Single Circle	Others (and notes)
Plymouth							?	
Polmont					4.00			(Scottish Numeral 489)
Portadown							2.00	
Portarlington							5.00	
Port of Monteith					4.00			(Scottish Numerals 288 and 670)
Portslade							?	
Prudhoe							?	
Putney							?	
Queensbury, Edgware							1.00	
Rannoch					3.00	0.50		(Scottish Numeral 678)
Rathen							3.00	
Ratho					4.00		1.75	(Scottish Numeral 474)
Redhill			12.00			2.50		(Numeral A21)
Robin Hood's Bay				5.00		1.00	1.00	Skeleton: ?
Rugby			8.00			1.00		Skeleton: £12. (Numeral 659)
Stafford							1.00	
St. Budeaux						3.50		
St. Leonards-on-Sea			10.00			2.50		(Numeral 342)
Semley							3.00	
Sheffield Park, Lewes							4.00	(Rubber single circle)
Sherburn							30.00	(undated)
Shortlands, Bromley							?	
Sleights, Whitby						2.00	2.00	
Southampton							8.00	
South Kensington							1.00	
Southwick						?		
Stafford			12.50			1.50		(Numeral 730)

Station							Notes
Stoke-upon-Trent	35.00						
Stoke Newington							
Strabane						3.00	
						?	
Straffan		25.00				1.50	(Irish Numeral 415)
Sunningdale, Ascot						1.00	
Sutton						?	
Swanley Junction				5.00	1.50		
Swindon	?		8.00		2.00		Skeleton: £10
							Skeleton: £10. (Numeral 881)
Tarbolton					3.00		(Scottish Numeral 591)
Thorntonhall						2.00	
Thornton Heath					3.50		
Tilbury						1.75	
Timperley, Altrincham						2.00	
Tipton Grn, York						?	
Tonbridge			9.00		2.00		Skeleton: £10. (Numeral 818)
Udny				3.00	2.00		(Scottish Numeral 333)
Uphall				2.50			(Scottish Numeral 576)
Victoria S.W.1						1.00	
Wadhurst			11.00				(Numeral J82)
Warling						10.00	
Washington	?		9.00		2.00	2.50	(Numeral B43)
Waterloo							Skeleton: ?
Wellington College	25.00	?		5.00	2.00		Skeleton: £15. (Numeral 109)
Weybridge	25.00		15.00				(Numeral B87)
Whitehead, Belfast						6.50	(Rubber single circle)
Wingate	?		15.00			?	(Numeral H49)
Woking	30.00		12.50				(Numeral C66)
Woodland						2.00	
Worthing			10.00	8.00		4.00	

Some stations used several sub-types. Prices are for cheapest. Full details are given by D. Gowen

111

Railway Sub Offices

260	261

260 R.S.O. Single circles 1.00
261 R.S.O. Double circles 0.50
    R.S.O. Parcel types 6.50
    R.S.O. Skeleton cancellations 10.00
    R.S.O. Rubber types 5.00

TRAVELLING POST OFFICES

(Full details of operation, sub-types etc. are given in H. S. Wilson. Dates given here are often only approximate.)

Aberdeen and Elgin S.C. (1885–1916)

North of Scotland/Sorting Carriage, single circle, from 1885 . . 25.00
Aberdeen & Elgin S.C., single circle, from 1904 . . . . 12.00
A. & E.S.C., across double circle 15.00

Aberwystwyth-Shrewsbury S.C. see Shrewsbury – Aberystwyth S.C.
Ayr-Carlisle R.S.C. or S.C. see Carlisle – Ayr S.C.

Bangor and Crewe T.P.O. (1855–1979)

262

Missent to B & N/Railway – P.O., unframed, 1855 . . . . . . ?
Missent to B & N/Railway Post Office, unframed, 1855 . . . . 100.00
Mst – B & N/R.P.O. Forwd, unframed, 1856 . . . . ?
Mst – to – Bangor/R.P.O. Up-Mail, unframed, from 1856 . . . 80.00
    As above but Down, from 1856 . . . . 80.00
Bangor & Leeds R.P.O/Forward, boxed, from 1859 . . . . . 50.00
B & L, Star Stamps, from 1862 . . . . 25.00
Received open and resealed/at the B & L R.P.O., from 1866 . . 30.00

112

Bangor & Leeds/T.P.O. Forward, boxed 25.00
Bangor & Leeds T.P.O., single circle, from 1869 . . . . . . 25.00
Bangor & Leeds T.P.O./From the West, single circle, from 1869 . 25.00
Bangor & Leeds T.P.O./From the East, single circle, from 1869 . 25.00
Normanton & Stalybridge T.P.O./From East, single circle, from
1875 . . . . 25.00
Normanton & Stalybridge T.P.O./From West, single circle, from
1875 . . . . 25.00
Normanton & Stalybridge/R.S.C., Single circle for parcels, from
1885 . . . . 30.00
Bangor & Crewe T.P.O./From East, single circle, from 1875 . . 10.00
Bangor & Crewe T.P.O./From West, single circle, from 1875 . . 10.00
Bangor-Crewe T.P.O., single circle, from 1930 . . . . 5.00
Crewe-Bangor T.P.O., single circle, from 1930 . . . . 5.00
Bangor-Crewe T.P.O., double circle with thick arc, from 1954 . 2.50
Crewe-Bangor T.P.O., double circle with thick arc, from 1954 . 2.50
As above but with AM 3.50
Bangor-Crewe T.P.O., double circle with thin arcs, from 1957 . 1.00
Crewe-Bangor T.P.O., double circle with thin arcs, from 1957 . 1.00
262 Chester & Crewe/Parcel T.P.O., single circle, from 1885 . . . . 30.00
Bangor & Crewe/Parcel S.C., single circle, from 1885 . . . . . 30.00
Bangor & Crewe T.P.O./Parcel S.C., single circle, from 1893 . . 30.00
Posted without Late fee, boxed, lower case letters, 1933 . . . . 3.50
Posted without Late fee/1d to Pay, boxed, lower case letters,
1930 . . . . 3.00
As above but upper case letters, 1970 . . . . 1.75

Bangor-Leeds R.P.O. or T.P.O. see Bangor-Crewe T.P.O.
B. & E. R.P.O. see Plymouth-Bristol T.P.O.
Birmingham-Bristol T.P.O. see Bristol-Derby T.P.O.

Birmingham and Crewe Sorting Carriage, (1884–1967)

Birmingham & Staff – S.T/Night Down, single circle, from 1844 . 25.00
Birmingham & Staff – S.T/Night Up, single circle, from 1884 . . 25.00
Birmingham & Crewe S.C., single circle, from 1885 . . . . . . 20.00
Birmingham & Crewe S.C., small single circle, from 1893 . . . 20.00
Crewe-Birmingham/S.C., single circle, from 1930 . . . . . . 7.00
Birmingham-Crewe/S.C., single circle, from 1930 . . . . . . 7.00
Crewe-Birmingham T.P.O., single circle, 1930's 4.00
Birmingham-Crewe T.P.O., single circle, 1930's 4.00
Crewe-Birmingham T.P.O., double circle with thin arcs, from 1957 2.00
Birmingham-Crewe T.P.O., double circle with thin arcs, from 1957 2.00
Birmingham & Crewe/Parcel Mail, single circle, from 1894 . . 25.00
Posted without Late fee, boxed, lower case letters, 1884 . . . . 5.00
Posted without Late fee/1d to Pay, boxed, 1930 . . . . . . 3.00
As above but upper case letters, 1959 . . . . 1.75

Birmingham-Staffs S.T. see Birmingham-Crewe S.C.

B. & L. and B. & L. R.P.O. see Bangor-Crewe T.P.O.

B. & N. Railway see Bangor-Crewe T.P.O.

Bridlington Sorting Carriage (1892–1916)

Hull/Sorting Tender, single circle with BQ (Bridlington Quay),
from 1892 . . . . 35.00

Bridlington Sorting Carriage, single circle, from 1913 . . . . . 20.00

Brighton and Hastings Sorting Carriage (1876–1916)

Hastings & Brighton S.C. Up, single circle, from 1876 . . . . . 25.00

Hastings & Brighton S.C. Down, single circle, from 1876 . . . 25.00

Brighton & Hastings/Sorting Carriage Up, single circle, from
1895 . . . . 20.00

Brighton & Hastings/Sorting Carriage, Down, single circle, from
1895 . . . . 20.00

Brighton S.C. see London-Brighton S.C.

Bristol-Birmingham T.P.O. see Bristol-Derby T.P.O.

Bristol to Derby T.P.O. (from 1910)

Gloucester & Bristol T.P.O./Going South, single circle, from
1910 . . . . 15.00

Gloucester & Bristol T.P.O./Going North, single circle, from
1910 . . . . 15.00

Bristol – Gloucester T.P.O., single circle, from 1930 . . . . . . 5.00

Gloucester – Bristol T.P.O., single circle, from 1930 . . . . . . 5.00

Bristol – Derby T.P.O., double circle with one solid arc, from
1949 . . . . 1.00

Derby – Bristol T.P.O., double circle with one solid arc, from
1949 . . . . 5.00

Bristol – Birmingham T.P.O., single circle, from 1938 . . . . . 4.00

Birmingham – Bristol T.P.O., single circle, from 1938 . . . . . 4.00

Bristol – Derby T.P.O., double circle with thin arcs, from 1965 . 1.00

Derby – Bristol T.P.O., double circle with thin arcs, from 1965 . 1.00

Bristol – Derby/T.P.O., double circle with AM and thin arcs,
from 1966 . . . . 4.00

Bristol – Derby T.P.O./AM, double circle with thick arc, from
1962 . . . . 3.00

Bristol – Derby/AM/T.P.O., double circle with thin arcs, from
1965 . . . . 1.00

Bristol – Derby/T.P.O., double circle without arcs, from 1978 . 0.50

Derby – Bristol/T.P.O., double circle with thin arcs, from 1978 . 0.50

Bristol – Derby/AM/T.P.O., double circle without arcs 1.00

Posted without late fee, boxed 1.00

Posted without late fee, 1d to pay, boxed 1.00

Bristol and Exeter Day T.P.O. (1875–1917)
Bristol & Exeter T.P.O./Day Mail, single circle, from 1875 . . . 25.00

Bristol-Exeter Ry P.O. see Plymouth-Bristol T.P.O.
Bristol-Gloucester T.P.O. see Bristol-Derby T.P.O.
Bristol-London T.P.O. see London-Bristol S.C.
Bristol-Newton Abbot T.P.O. see Plymouth-Bristol T.P.O.
Bristol-Penzance T.P.O. see Plymouth-Bristol T.P.O.
Bristol-Plymouth T.P.O. see Plymouth-Bristol T.P.O.
Bristol-Shrewsbury-Normanton T.P.O. see Shrewsbury-York T.P.O.
Bristol-Shrewsbury-York T.P.O. see Shrewsbury-York T.P.O.

Bristol Sorting Carriage (1895–1914)
Bristol S.T., single circle from 1902 . . . . 25.00
Bristol/S.C., single circle, from 1905 . . . . 20.00
Bristol, single circle, 1880 . . . . 20.00

Caledonian T.P.O. (from 1848)

263

Missent to/Caledonian R.W.P.O., unframed, issued 1848 . . . 100.00
CR, various sizes, in red or black, from 1848 . . . . 12.50
MST – Caledonian/R.P.O. – Night, from 1857 . . . . 80.00
London/CR across single circle, red or black, 1865 . . . . . . 25.00
CR/PO across large skeleton type, 1867 . . . . 30.00
263 CR/F in small circle, from 1859 . . . . 20.00
C/R.P.O./FO in small circle, from 1865 . . . . 20.00
C.R./P.O. in small circle, from 1865 . . . . 20.00
Caledonian T.P.O./Day Down, dated unframed circular, from
1869 . . . . 15.00
Caledonian T.P.O./Day Up, as above, from 1869 . . . . . . 15.00
Caledonian T.P.O./Night Up, single circle, from 1872 . . . . . 2.00
Caledonian T.P.O./Night Down, single circle, from 1872 . . . 2.00
Caledonian T.P.O./Day Up, single circle, from 1873 . . . . . 2.00
Caledonian T.P.O./Day Down, single circle, from 1873 . . . . 2.00
Caledonian T.P.O. Day Up/1 or 2, double circle with thin arcs,
from 1958 . . . . 0.50
Caledonain T.P.O. Day Down/1 or 2, as above, from 1958 . . . 0.50
Caledonian T.P.O. Day Up/G.W., single circle, from 1935 . . . 3.00
Caledonian T.P.O. Day Up/E, as above, from 1935 . . . . . . 3.00
Caledonian T.P.O. Up G.W. Sect, double circle with thin arcs
from 1959 . . . . 0.50

Caledonian T.P.O. Up/E.H. Sect, as above, from 1959 . . . . 1.50
Caledonian T.P.O. Up/E.H. section, double circle with short
    thin arcs, from 1968 . . . . 0.50
Posted without/Late fee, boxed 3.00
Posted without late fee/1d to pay, boxed 2.50
1D/8–12/To pay/Posted in/T.P.O./Late fee/Not paid, boxed . 1.00
    As above but with route number 30–1 . . . . 1.00
More to/Pay/Late fee/unpaid, boxed 1.00
'P' in star, from 1877 . . . . 12.00

Cambridge District Sorting Carriage (1863–69)
Duplex: Cambridge/Dist. Sorting, Carriage, with L & C/D.S.C.,
    in numeral portion . . . . ?
C.D./S.C., circular . . . . ?

Cardiff-Crewe T.P.O. (from 1920)
Crewe Cardiff/Rly. S.C., double circle with short thick arcs, from
    1920 . . . . 7.50
Cardiff Crewe/Rly. S.C., double circle with short thick arcs, from
    1920 . . . . 7.50
Cardiff-Crewe/T.P.O., single circle, from 1934 . . . . 5.00
Crewe-Cardiff/T.P.O., single circle, from 1934 . . . . 5.00
Crewe-Cardiff T.P.O., single circle, from 1947 . . . . 0.60
Cardiff-Crewe T.P.O., single circle, from 1947 . . . . 0.60
Posted without Late Fee, boxed, 1933 . . . . 3.00
1d/10–15/To pay/posted in/T.P.O./Late Fee/Not paid, boxed,
    1965 . . . . 1.00
Crewe-Cardiff/T.P.O., double circle thin arcs, with AM, from
    1965 . . . . 1.00
Crewe-Cardiff/AM/T.P.O., single circle from 1963 . . . . . . 3.00

Cardiff-York T.P.O. see Shrewsbury-York T.P.O.

Carlisle and Ayr S.C. (1874–1969)
Carlisle & Ayr/Sorting Tender, single circle 20.00
Carlisle & Ayr S.T., single circle, from 1902 . . . . 20.00
Carlisle & Ayr Sorting Carriage, single circle, from 1904 . . . . 8.00
Ayr – Carlisle/R.S.C., single circle, from 1921 . . . . 5.00
Carlisle – Ayr R.S.C., single circle, from 1921 . . . . 5.00
Ayr – Carlisle S.C., single circle, from 1937 . . . . 4.00
Carlisle – Ayr S.C. double circle with thin arc, from 1957 . . . 1.50
Ayr – Carlisle S.C., as above, from 1957 . . . . 1.50
Carlisle – Ayr S.C., single circle with AM, 1964 . . . . 4.50
Posted without/Late fee, boxed 2.00
Posted without Late fee/1d to pay, boxed 2.50

Carlisle-Edinburgh S.C. see Edinburgh-Carlisle S.C.

Carmarthen and Newcastle Emlyn Sorting Carriage (1877–1904)

D25, numeral in upright oval, from 1877 . . . . 40.00
Duplex: Llandyssil/Sorting Tender, with numeral D25, from
1877 . . . . 30.00
Llandyssil/Sorting Tender, single circle, from 1877 . . . . . . 25.00
Llandyssil Sorting Tender, single circle, from 1889 . . . . . . 20.00
Carmarthen & Newcastle Emlyn S.C., single circle, from 1895 . 20.00
Llandyssil S.T., across double circles, rubber parcel stamp, from
1891 . . . . 25.00

Carnforth-Whitehaven T.P.O. see Whitehaven-Huddersfield T.P.O.
C.D.S.C. see Cambridge District Sorting Carriage.
Chester-Crewe T.P.O. see Bangor-Crewe T.P.O.
Chester-Holyhead R.W.P.O. see London-Holyhead T.P.O.
C. & G. R.P.O. see Glasgow-Carlisle S.C.
Continental Night Mail see London-Dover S.C.

Cornwall Sorting Tender (1859–95)

Cornwall Railway, single circle, from 1859 . . . . 30.00
Cornwall T.P.O., single circle, issued 1871 . . . . —
Cornwall/R.S. Tender, single circle, from 1871 . . . . 25.00
Cornwall R.S.T., squared circle, from 1880 . . . . 25.00
Cornwall R.S.T., single circle, from 1886 . . . . 23.00

C.R. see Caledonian T.P.O.
Crewe-Bangor T.P.O. see Bangor-Crewe T.P.O.
Crewe-Birmingham S.C. and T.P.O. see Birmingham-Crewe S.C.
Crewe-Cardiff S.C. and T.P.O. see Cardiff-Crewe T.P.O.
Crewe-Glasgow R.S.C. and S.C. see Glasgow-Carlisle S.C.

Crewe to Liverpool Sorting Carriage (1885–1939)

264

Crewe to Liverpool/S.C., single circle, 1897 . . . . 18.00
264 Crewe to Liverpool S.C./1, single circle, 1904 . . . . 15.00

Crewe-Manchester S.C. see Manchester-Crewe S.C.
Crewe-Peterborough T.P.O. see Peterborough-Crewe T.P.O.

Dartmoor Railway Sorting Tender (1873)
Duplex: Dartmoor/R.S.T., with numeral C18, issued 1873 . . .   ?

Derby-Bristol T.P.O. see Bristol-Derby T.P.O.
Dingwall-Perth R.S.C. see Highland T.P.O.
Doncaster-London T.P.O. see London-Leeds S.C.
Dover-London F.D.M. see London-Dover French Day Mail
Dover-London O.D.M. see London-Dover Ostend Day Mail
Dover-London R.S.C. see London-Dover S.C.

Down Special T.P.O. (from 1923)

Posted without late fee
1ᵈ to pay.

265

266

Down Special/T.P.O., double circle with short thick arcs, from
    1923 . . . .   5.00
Down Special/T.P.O., single circle, from late 1920's 4.00
Down Special/T.P.O., double circle with long thick arcs from
    1930's 3.00
265 Down Special/T.P.O., double circle with thin arcs, from 1950   .   2.00
Down Special T.P.O./1 or 2, double circle with thin arcs, from
    1957 . . . .   0.50
    As above but 2, from 1957 . . . .   0.50
Down Special T.P.O./1, single circle, from 1957 . . . .   3.00
    As above but 2, from 1957 . . . .   3.00
Down Special T.P.O./A, double circle with thin arcs, from 1959   1.00
    As above with AM (used only 4 Sept 1964) 5.00
Down Special/T.P.O. No 1, rubber stamps 3.50
266 Posted without late fee/1d to pay, boxed, lower case letters . . .   3.50
    As above but in upper case letters, 1960 . . . .   2.50
1d/41–2/To pay/posted in/T.P.O./Late fee/Not Paid, boxed,
    1961 . . . .   1.75
    As above but 1d/17–2, boxed, 1960 . . . .   1.75
Charge marks with route numbers deleted, 1968 . . . .   1.00
Charge marks with 1d deleted, 1969 . . . .   0.75

Down Special T.P.O. see also North Western T.P.O.

Edinburgh and Carstairs S.T. (1877–1914)

Edinr & Carstairs Sorting Tender, unframed circular with D or U,
from 1877 . . . . 20.00
As above but duplex, with numeral 131 . . . . 30.00

Edinburgh and Newcastle S.C. (1866–1922)

Edinr & Newcastle Sorting Tender, circular unframed, from 1866   20.00
Edinr & Newcastle/Sorting Tender, single circle, from 1886   . . 15.00
Edinr & Newcastle/Sorting Carriage, single circle, from 1904   . . 8.00
Edinr & Newcastle Sorting Carriage, single circle, from 1908   . . 6.00
Edinr & Newcastle S.T. Day Mail, circular unframed, from 1883   10.00

Edinburgh S.T. see Edinburgh-Berwick S.T.

Edinburgh-York T.P.O. (from 1853)

Missent-to-York/& Newcastle-Ry, unframed, issued 1853   . . .   —
York & Newcastle R.P.O., boxed, issued 1862   . . . . 70.00
York & Newcastle T.P.O./Going South, single circle, from 1875   25.00
York & Newcastle T.P.O./Going North, single circle, from 1875   25.00
North Eastern T.P.O. Up, single circle, from 1895   . . . . . . 7.00
North Eastern T.P.O. Down, single circle from 1895   . . . . . 7.00
North Eastern T.P.O. Going South, single circle, from 1908   . . 6.00
North Eastern T.P.O. Going North, single circle, from 1908   . . 6.00
North East T.P.O./Going South, skeleton, 1911   . . . . 25.00
Edinburgh – York S.C., single circle, from 1926   . . . . 6.00
Edinburgh – York T.P.O., single circle, from 1930   . . . . . . 4.00
Edinburgh – York T.P.O., double circle with thin arcs, from 1958   1.50
Edinburgh – York/T.P.O., double circle with thin arcs, from 1971   0.50
Posted without Late fee, boxed, from 1921   . . . . 2.50
1D/30–1/To pay/posted in/T.P.O./Late fee/Not paid, boxed,
from 1966   . . . . 1.00
D/More to pay/late fee/unpaid, boxed 1.00

E.G.W. see London-Exeter T.P.O.
E.M.R. see Midland T.P.O.
E.N.R. see Great Northern R.P.O.
E.S.E. see South Eastern T.P.O.
Euston Station Irish Mail see London-Holyhead T.P.O.

Exeter and Torrington Sorting Carriage (1906–17)

Exeter Torrington SC/Up, Skeleton, 1906 . . . . 25.00
Exeter & Torrington S.C./Up, single circle, from 1906 . . . . . 8.00
Exeter & Torrington S.C./Down, single circle, from 1906   . . . 20.00

F.D.M. see London-Dover French Day Mail

East Anglian T.P.O. (from 1869)

267 268

267 Sorting Tender/Norwich, single circle, from 1869 . . . . 25.00
Norwich/Sorting Tender, single circle, from 1876 . . . . 25.00
Norwich Sorting Tender/Up, single circle, from 1878 . . . . . 7.00
Norwich Sorting Tender/Down, single circle, from 1878 . . . . 15.00
Norwich Sorting Carriage/Down, single circle, from 1909 . . . 6.00
Norwich S.C./Up, skeleton, 1909 . . . . 50.00
Norwich Sorting Carriage/Up, single circle, from 1909 . . . . 6.00
268 East Anglian T.P.O. Up, single circle, from 1929 . . . . . . 4.00
East Anglian T.P.O. Down, single circle, from 1929 . . . . . . 4.00
East Anglian T.P.O. Up (Kings Lynn section), single circle, 1929 7.50
East Anglian T.P.O. Down (Kings Lynn section), single circle,
1929 . . . . 7.50
East Anglian T.P.O., Up, double circle thick single arc, 1948 . . 4.00
East Anglian T.P.O. Down, double circle thick single arc, 1948 . 4.00
East Anglian T.P.O. Up/K.L. section, double circle short thick
arcs, 1948 . . . . 6.00
East Anglian T.P.O. Down/K.L. section, double circle short
thick arcs, 1948 . . . . 6.00
E.A.T.P.O. Down/Peterborough section, double circle thin arcs,
from 1949 . . . . 3.00
East Anglian T.P.O. Down/1 or 2, double circle thin arcs, from
1958 . . . . 0.50
East Anglian T.P.O. Up/1 or 2, double circle thin arcs, from 1958 0.50
East Anglian T.P.O. Dn – Pe Section/1 or 2, double circle thin
arcs, from 1958 . . . . 0.50
East Anglian T.P.O. Up – Pe Section/1 or 2, double circle thin
arcs, from 1958 . . . . 0.50
East Anglian T.P.O. Down/AM/3 as above 1.00
East Anglian T.P.O. Up/AM, double circle with thin arc . . . 1.00
East Anglian T.P.O. Down P.E. Sect./AM/3 double circle, short
thin arcs 1.00
1D/L.05, unframed, from 1906 . . . . 10.00
1D/015, unframed 10.00
Posted without late fee, boxed, from 1890 . . . . 5.00

Edinburgh-Berwick S.T. (1866–85)

Edinburgh/S.T., single circle, from 1866 . . . . 30.00
Edinr & Berwick/Sorting Tender, from 1873 . . . . 20.00

Edinburgh and Carlisle S.C. (from 1859)

269

270

Early single circle types with EDINR across circle, from 1859 . . 35.00
Edinr M or M2 in top arc of single circle, from 1859 . . . . . . 25.00
269 Edinr – Carlisle Sorting Tender, unframed circular, from 1874 . 10.00
270 Edinr & Carlisle/S.T., double circle, from 1890 . . . . 10.00
Carlisle – Edinburgh/Sorting Carriage, single circle, from 1924 . 3.00
Carlisle – Edinburgh S.C. double circle with thin arc, from 1957 1.75
    As above but wider spaced lettering and shorter arc, from 1971 0.50
Duplex type with numeral 131, from 1871 . . . . 20.00
Up Special/T.P.O., double circle E plug, short thick arcs, from
    1922 . . . . 4.00
Up Special T.P.O./E.H. Sec., single circle, from 1930 . . . . . 3.00
Up Special T.P.O./Edinburgh Sect., double circle short thin arcs,
    from 1951 . . . . 2.50
Carlisle – Edinburgh S.C., single circle, from 1954 . . . . . . 3.00
Carlisle – Edinburgh T.P.O. (EH), double circle with thin arc,
    from 1959 . . . . 0.50
Posted without/Late fee, boxed 3.00
To Pay/Posted in/T.P.O./Late fee/Not paid, boxed 1.00
Late fee/Paid, boxed 2.50

Fife Sorting Carriage (1884–1917)

271

Fife Sorting Tender Down/458, double circle, from 1884 . . . 35.00
271 Fife Sorting Tender Up/458, double circle, from 1884 . . . . . 20.00
Fife S.C./Night Down, double circle 30.00

F.N.M. see London-Dover S.C.

Galloway T.P.O. (1866–1940)

Galloway Sorting Tender, single circle, from 1866 . . . . . . 10.00
Galloway/Sorting Tender, single circle, from 1876 . . . . . . 15.00
Galloway Sorting Tender/603, double circle, from 1891 . . . . 10.00
Galloway Sorting Carriage, single circle, from 1904 . . . . . . 7.00
Galloway T.P.O./Up Day, double circle with thick arcs, from
1930 . . . . 6.00
Galloway T.P.O./Down Night, as above from 1930 . . . . . . 6.00
1d 5.00
Posted without Late fee, boxed 3.00

Glasgow and Carlisle S.C. (from 1865)

272

Small circle with C & G/R.P.O., from 1865 . . . . 30.00
Glasgow/Sorting Tender, single circle, from 1876 . . . . . . 10.00
Glasgow & Carlisle S.C./Down Postal, single circle, from 1904 . 6.00
Preston – Glasgow R.S.C., single circle, from 1914 . . . . . . 5.00
Crewe – Glasgow R.S.C./No 1, single circle, from 1926 . . . . 5.00
Crewe – Glasgow R.S.C./No 2, single circle, from 1926 . . . . 5.00
Crewe – Glasgow S.C./single circle, from 1937 . . . . 4.00
Crewe – Glasgow S.C./1, double circle with thin arcs, from 1957 0.50
Crewe – Glasgow S.C./2, double circle with thin arcs, from 1957 0.50
As above with AM, 1964 . . . . 4.00
Glasgow – Carlisle Sorting Tender, unframed circular, duplex,
numeral 159, from 1871 . . . . 20.00
Glasgow – Carlisle/Sorting Tender, duplex, numeral 159, from
1873 . . . . 20.00
Glasgow – Carlisle/Sorting Tender, single circle, from 1885 . . 12.00
Glasgow & Carlisle/Sorting Tender, from 1890 . . . . 8.00
Glasgow & Carlisle S.C./Up Limited, from 1904 . . . . . . 7.00
Glasgow. Preston R.S.C./Up Limited, from 1914 . . . . . . 6.00
Glasgow & Carlisle/Sorting Tender, duplex with numeral 159,
from 1887 . . . . 20.00
Glasgow & Carlisle S.C./Up Postal, single circle from 1904 . . 6.00
Glasgow. Preston R.S.C./Up Special, single circle, from 1916 . 5.00
Up Special/T.P.O., double circle short medium arcs, from 1917 5.00
Up Special G.T.P.O., single circle, from 1924 . . . . 5.00
272 Up Special G./T.P.O., single circle, from 1931 . . . . 4.00

Up Special T.P.O./Glasgow Sect, double circle with short thin
arcs, from 1951 . . . . 2.00
Up Special T.P.O. – GW. Sect/1 or 2, as above, from 1957 . . . 0.50
Up Special G/T.P.O., skeleton 1926 or 1934 . . . . 25.00
Registered/Glasgow Sorting Tender, single circle, from 1884 . . 35.00
Glasgow Sorting Tender/Registered, oval with crown, from 1880 40.00
Posted without Late fee, boxed 5.00
1d/17–2/To pay/Posted in/T.P.O./Late fee/Not paid, boxed . 1.00
As above but without trip numbers 1.00
32–1/To pay/Posted in/T.P.O./Late fee/Not paid, boxed . . . 1.00
Late Fee/Paid, boxed 2.50
Found Open and Resealed/In/Glasgow Sorting Tender, boxed . 10.00
As above but Glasgow and Carlisle S.T. 10.00
Star stamp with G.W. 25.00

Glasgow Gk S.T. see Greenock S.T.
Glasgow-Preston R.S.C. see Glasgow-Carlisle S.C.
Glasgow Sorting Tender see Glasgow-Carlisle S.C.
Gloucester-Bristol T.P.O. see Bristol-Derby T.P.O.
Gloucester-Tamworth R.W.P.O. see Midland T.P.O.
G.N.R. see Great Northern R.P.O.
G.N.S.C. see Great Northern and Day S.C.

Grand Junction Railway
Missent to/Railway/Post Office, unframed,
from 1838 . . . . ?

Great Northern R.P.O. (1838–65)

273

Missent to/London & Birmingham/Railway office, unframed
from 1838 . . . . 300.00
Missent to/G.N.R. Post Office unframed, from 1838 . . . . . 200.00
Missent to/G.N. Railway Post Office/Day unframed, from 1839 200.00
273 E/NR, circled, night mail, from 1844 . . . . 60.00
M/NR, circled, day mail in red from 1844 . . . . 60.00
Missent to/G.N. Railway Post Office/Night, unframed from 1851 100.00

Great Northern see also North Eastern T.P.O.

Great Northern Sorting Carriage, Day (1877–1922)

Great Northern S.T., single circle, from 1877 . . . . 25.00
G.N./S.C., boxed 25.00
Great Northern S.C./Down Day Mail, single circle, from 1902 . 15.00

Great Northern T.P.O. Midday Mail (1885–1914)

Gt Northern/T.P.O./Midday Mail Down, Single circle, from
1885 . . . . 25.00
Gt Northern/T.P.O./Midday Mail Up, Single circle, from 1885 25.00

Great Western District Sorting Carriage (1859–69)

Gt Western/District S.C., unframed, from 1859 . . . . ?
Received open and resealed/at the G.W.D.S.C., issued 1866 . . —

Great Western Sunday Sorting Tender (1850)

G.W.S.T., boxed 1850 . . . . ?

Great Western T.P.O. (from 1895)

274

Great Western T.P.O./Down Night, single circle, from 1895 . . 5.00
Great Western T.P.O./Up Night, single circle, from 1895 . . . 5.00
Great Western T.P.O. Parcels/Down Night, single circle, from
1895 . . . . 12.00
Great Western T.P.O. Parcels/Up Night, single circle, from 1895 12.00
Great Western T.P.O./Night Down, single circle, from 1897 . . 10.00
274 Great Western T.P.O./Going West, single circle, from 1907 . . 7.00
Great Western T.P.O./Going East, single circle, from 1907 . . . 7.00
Great Western T.P.O.W./Going East, single circle, from 1916 . 7.00
Great Western T.P.O./Going East, double circle thick short arcs,
1929 . . . . 5.00
Great Western T.P.O./Up, single circle, from 1931 . . . . . . 5.00
Great Western T.P.O./Down, single circle, from 1931 . . . . . 5.00
Great Western T.P.O./Up, double circle thin arcs, from 1950 . . 2.50
Great Western T.P.O./Down, double circle thin arcs, from 1950 2.50

Great Western T.P.O. Up/1 or 2, double circle thin arcs, from
1957 . . . . 0.50
Great Western T.P.O. Down/1 or 2, double circle thin arcs, from
1957 . . . . 0.50
Great Western T.P.O. Up/1 or 2, single circle, from 1957 . . . 2.00
Great Western T.P.O. Down/1 or 2, single circle, from 1957 . . 2.00
Great Western T.P.O./AM/Up, double circle with thin arcs . . 1.00
Great Western T.P.O. Down/AM/2 as above 1.00
Posted without late fee/1d to pay, boxed, 1958 . . . . 2.00
1d/21–22/1/To pay/posted in/T.P.O./late fee/not paid, boxed
1959 . . . . 1.00
As above but 2 . . . . 1.00
As above but route number 41-1, 1968 . . . . 1.00

Greenock S.T. (1872–79)
Glasgow Gk St, small single circle, from 1872 . . . . 30.00
Greenock Sorting Tender, small single circle, from 1873 . . . . 25.00

Grimsby and Lincoln Sorting Carriage (1885–1915)
Grimsby & Lincoln. Sorting Tender, squared circle, from 1885 . 25.00
Grimsby & Lincoln. Sorting Tender, single circle, from 1885 . . 15.00
Posted without Late fee, boxed, from 1885 . . . . 12.00
Grimsby & Lincoln. Sorting carriage, single circle, from 1897 . . 12.00
Grimsby & Lincoln. S.C., double circle, long medium arcs and
cross from 1905 . . . . 10.00

Grimsby and Peterborough Sorting Carriage (1900–17)

275

Grimsby & Peterboro/Stg. Tender, double circle short thick arcs,
from 1900 . . . . 18.00
Grimsby & Peterboro/Stg. Tender, single circle, from 1900 . . . 15.00
275 Grimsby & Peterborough/Stg. Carriage, double circle medium
arcs, from 1905 . . . . 10.00
Grimsby & Peterborough/Stg. Carriage, single circle, from 1905 12.00
Grimsby Peterboro/SC, skeleton, 1910 . . . . 25.00
1D/K. 97, unframed, 1910 . . . . 12.00

Gt Northern Railway see London-Leeds S.C.
Gt Northern T.P.O. see London, York, Edinburgh T.P.O.
Gt Western R.W.P.O. see London-Exeter T.P.O.
G.W. see Glasgow-Carlisle S.C.

Halifax Sorting Tender (1871-79)

276

276 Halifax/S.T., single circle, from 1871 . . . . 30.00

Hastings-Brighton S.C. see Brighton-Hastings S.C.
Helmsdale-Dingwall R.S.C. see Highland T.P.O.

Highland T.P.O. (1870-1978)

277

277 Highland S.T., duplex with numeral 391, from 1870 . . . . . 25.00
Highd Sorting Carriage/Night Mail, single circle, from 1873 . . 10.00
Highd Sorting Carriage/Day Mail, single circle, from 1873 . . . 10.00
Highland S.C. Night Mail, single circle, from 1890 . . . . . . 20.00
Highland S.C./Night Mail No 1, single circle, from 1898 . . . . 10.00
Highland S.C./Night Mail*, single circle, from 1900 . . . . . 6.00
Highland S.C./Night Mail, single circle, from 1910 . . . . . . 5.00
Dingwall – Perth R.S.C., single circle, from 1917 . . . . 7.00
Perth – Helmsdale/R.S.C., single circle, from 1923 . . . . . . 12.00
Helmsdale – Dingwall/R.S.C., single circle, from 1923 . . . . 12.00
Dingwall – Perth/R.S.C., single circle, from 1923 . . . . 12.00
Highland T.P.O./Down, double circle thick arcs, from 1930 . . 4.00
Highland T.P.O. Up/Northern section, double circle, short thick
arcs from 1930 . . . . 4.00
Highland T.P.O. Up/Northern section, double circle, no arcs
from 1930 . . . . 4.00

Highland T.P.O. Up/Southern Section, double circle, short thick
    arcs, from 1930 . . . . 4.00
Highland T.P.O. Down/1, double circle with thin arcs, from 1958   1.00
    As above but Down/2, double circle with thin arcs, from 1958   4.00
Highland T.P.O. (NS)/2, as above from 1958 . . . . 1.50
Highland T.P.O. (SS)/1 or 2, as above, from 1958 . . . . . . 1.50
Highland T.P.O./Up, as above, from 1967 . . . . 1.00
Highd Sortg Carriage/Day Mail, single circle, from 1906 . . . 6.00
Highd Sortg Carriage/Parcels, single circle, 1894 . . . . 10.00
Highland S.C., across double circle 8.00
H.P.S.C., across double circle 8.00
Posted without Late fee/1d to Pay, upper case letters, boxed . . 6.00
    As above but lower case letters 3.50
    As above with charge removed 2.00

Holyhead-London T.P.O. see London-Holyhead T.P.O.
H.P.S.C. see Highland T.P.O.

Huddersfield-Whitehaven T.P.O. see Whitehaven-Huddersfield T.P.O.

Hull Sorting Carriage (1867–1917)

278

279

S.T./Hull/date, in circle, from 1867 . . . . 25.00
A/Hull-ST/date, duplex, with numeral 383, from 1869 . . . . 25.00
Hull/Sorting Tender, single circles numbered 1, 2 or 3, from 1872 20.00
278 Hull/Sorting Tender, duplex with numeral 383, from 1872 . . . 23.00
Hull Sorting Tender, duplex with numeral 383, from 1878 . . . 20.00
Hull Sorting Tender, single circle with 4, 1900 . . . . 18.00
279 Hull Sorting Carriage, double circle, medium arcs and cross, from
    1904 . . . . 5.00
Hull Sorting Carriage, single circle, from 1904 . . . . 7.00
Hull-Leeds Rly Sorting Carriage, double circle medium arcs and
    cross, from 1914 . . . . 8.00
Leeds-Hull Rly Sorting Carriage, single circle, from 1914 . . . 8.00
Hull/S.T., across double circles, rubber 12.00
Hull S.T., across double circles, rubber, from 1889 . . . . . . 12.00

Hull Sorting Tender B.Q. see Bridlington S.C.

Ipswich Sorting Carriage (from 1858)

I.S.T., boxed	50.00
Ipswich/Dist.-Sortg.-carriage, unframed, from 1858	50.00
Ipswich/Sorting Tender, single circle, from 1872	30.00
Ipswich Sorting Tender, single circle, from 1876	15.00
Ipswich Sorting Tender/Night/Down, single circle 1903	15.00
Ipswich Sorting Tender/Night/Up, single circle, 1903	15.00
Ipswich Sorting Tender/Day/Down, single circle, 1903	15.00
Ipswich Sorting Tender/Day/Up, single circle, 1903	15.00
Ipswich Sorting Carriage/Night Up, single circle, from 1907 . .	10.00
Ipswich Sorting Carriage/Night Down, single circle, from 1907 .	10.00
Ipswich Sorting Carriage/Down/Day, single circle, from 1907 .	10.00
Ipswich Sorting Carriage/Up/Day, single circle, from 1907 . .	10.00
Ipswich Sorting Carriage/Day, single circle, from 1923	7.00
Ipswich – London/T.P.O. Day, Skeleton, 1929	25.00
London – Ipswich/T.P.O. Day, Skeleton, 1929	25.00
Ipswich – London/T.P.O. Day, single circle, from 1929	6.00
London – Ipswich/T.P.O. Day, single circle, from 1929	6.00
Norwich – London T.P.O./Day, single circle, from 1931	4.00
London – Norwich T.P.O./Day, single circle, from 1931	4.00
Norwich – London T.P.O., double circle with thin arcs, from 1967	0.50
Posted without late fee/1d to pay, boxed, lower case letters . . .	2.00
As above but upper case letters	1.00

L. & B.S.C. see London-Bristol S.C.
L. & C.D.S.C. see Cambridge District S.C.
L. & C.S.C. see London-Crewe S.C.
L. & D.D.M. see London-Dover French Day Mail
L. & D.S.C. see London-Derby S.C.
Leeds-London S.C. and T.P.O. see London-Leeds S.C.
L. & E., L. & E.R.P.O. and L. & E. T.P.O. see London-Exeter T.P.O.
L. & H.R.P.O. see London-Holyhead T.P.O.

Lincoln Sorting Carriage (1867–1940)

280

281

Lincoln – S.T., boxed . . . . ?
Lincoln S.T., single circle, from 1868 . . . . 30.00
Lincoln Sorting Tender, single circle, from 1874 . . . . . . 20.00
Lincoln/Tender, single circle, from 1876 . . . . 17.50
280 Duplex, Lincoln Sorting Tender, numeral 458, from 1881 . . . 13.00
Lincoln Tender, single circle, from 1890 . . . . 12.00
Lincoln/S.T., squared circle, from 1892 . . . . 9.00
Lincoln/S.C., squared circle, from 1904 . . . . 6.00
Lincoln Sorting carriage, single circle, from 1904 . . . . . . 7.00
Lincoln/Sorting carriage, single circle, issued 1908 . . . . . . 6.00
Lincoln Sorting carriage, single circle, from 1909 . . . . . . 6.00
281 Lincoln Sorting CGE/West, Skeleton 1914 . . . . 25.00
Lincoln Sorting Carriage, double circle thick arcs and cross, west,
from 1914 . . . . 7.50
As above but East, from 1914 . . . . 7.50
Tamworth-Lincoln S.C., single circle, from 1926 . . . . . . 5.00
Lincoln-Tamworth S.C., Single circle, from 1926 . . . . 5.00
Lincoln/Tender, across double circles, rubber, for parcels, from
1892 . . . . 6.00
Lincoln Sorting Carriage, rubber single circle, from 1908 . . . 5.00
Lincoln/Sorting Carriage, across double circles, from 1911 . . 5.00
Of the nature/of a letter/458. ST, boxed from 1887 . . . . . . 8.00
More to pay/above – oz/45 & S.T. boxed, from 1887 . . . . 8.00
Closed contrary/to regulations/1. oz, boxed from 1911 . . . . 8.00
Liable to letter rate/1. oz, boxed, from 1911 . . . . 8.00
Oval Registration Stamps, 1930's 10.00

Lincoln-Tamworth S.C. see Lincoln S.C.

Liverpool and Huddersfield T.P.O. (1920–65)

282

282 Liverpool-Huddersfield/Rly S.C., double circle with short thick
arcs, from 1920 . . . . 10.00
Liverpool-Huddersfield T.P.O., single circle, from 1930 . . . 6.00
L-H T.P.O./1, double circle with thin arcs, from 1958 . . . . 2.00
L-H T.P.O./2, double circle with thin arcs, from 1958 . . . . 2.00
Posted without late fee/1d to pay, boxed 3.00
1d/26–1/To pay/posted in/T.P.O./Late Fee/Not paid, boxed . 2.00
As above but 26-2 . . . . 2.00

Liverpool and London T.P.O. (1863–1918)

Duplex, N.W.R.P Office/Liverpool, with numeral 466, from 1863   30.00
Liverpool & London/N. Western T.P.O., single circle, from 1878   20.00
Liverpool & London/T.P.O., squared circle, from 1881 . . . . 50.00
Liverpool & London T.P.O., single circle, from 1881 . . . . . 12.00

Llandyssil S.T. see Carmarthen-Newcastle Emlyn S.C.
L. & L.S.T. see London-Leeds S.C.
L. & N.W. T.P.O. see North Western T.P.O.
London-Birmingham Railway Office see Great Northern R.P.O.

London and Brighton Sorting Carriage, Day (1885–1910)

Brighton/S.C., single circle, from 1885 . . . . 25.00
Brighton S.C./L, single circle, from 1895 . . . . 25.00
London & Brighton S.C./Day Down, single circle, from 1898 . 20.00
London & Brighton S.C./Day Up, single circle, 1905 . . . . . 20.00
Posted without Late fee, boxed 3.00

London and Brighton Sorting Carriage, Night (1870–1910)

L & B Sorting Carriage/Down, single circle, issued 1870 . . . . —
L & B Sorting Carriage/Up, single circle, issued 1870 . . . . . —
London & Brighton Sorting Carriage/Up, single circle, from 1881   25.00
London & Brighton S.C./Up, small circle, from 1900 . . . . . 20.00

London and Bristol Sorting Carriage (1868–1940)

283

London & Bristol S.T., single circle, from 1877 . . . . 25.00
L & B/S.C., boxed from 1884 . . . . 25.00
London & Bristol S.C./Down Day Mail, from 1902 . . . . 15.00
283 London – Bristol T.P.O., single circle, from 1930 . . . . 10.00
Bristol – London T.P.O., single circle, from 1930 . . . . 10.00

London C.R. see Caledonian T.P.O.

London and Crewe Sorting Carriage (1877–1918)

London & Crewe S.T., single circle, from 1877 . . . . 25.00
L & C/S.C., boxed, from 1884 . . . . 30.00
London & Crewe S.C./Up Day Mail, single circle, from 1902 . . 12.00
London & Crewe S.C./Down Day Mail, single circle, from 1902   12.00

London and Derby Sorting Carriage (1877–1918)

St Pancras & Derby S.T., single circle, from 1877 . . . . 35.00
As above but 'thimble', from 1877 . . . . 20.00
L & D/S.C., boxed, from 1896 . . . . 28.00
Posted without Late fee, boxed, from 1896 . . . . 12.50
London & Derby S.C./Going North, single circle, from 1908 . . 18.00
London & Derby S.C./Going South, single circle, from 1908 . . 10.00

London-Doncaster S.T. see London-Leeds S.C.

London and Dover Sorting Carriage, Continental Night Mail (1884–1923)

London & Dover T.P.O./Night Mail, single circle, from 1884 . 20.00
London & Dover S.C./Night Mail Up, single circle, from 1906 . 15.00
London & Dover S.C./Night Mail Down, single circle, from 1906 15.00
Duplex: Continental Night Mail, C.S./2 in numeral portion, from
1879 . . . . : . 20.00
Duplex: Continental Night Mail, C.X./1 in numeral portion,
from 1879 . . . . 30.00
Continental Night Mail/C.S., double circle medium arcs, from
1895 . . . . 18.00
Continental Night Mail/C.X., double circle medium arcs, from
1895 . . . . 25.00
Registered/F.N.M./London, oval, from 1871 . . . . 15.00
London – Dover/R.S.C., double circle, thick arcs, from 1922 . . 7.50
Dover – London/R.S.C., double circle, thick arcs, from 1922 . . 7.50

London and Dover Sorting Carriage, French Day Mail (1860–1918)

London/F.D.M., single circle, from 1860 . . . . 30.00
C68 in upright oval, numeral type, from 1865 . . . . 28.00
Dover to London/F.D.M., single circle, from 1880 . . . . . . 28.00
London & Dover S.C./Day Mail Up, single circle, from 1906 . . 15.00
London & Dover S.C./Day Mail Down, single circle, from 1906 15.00
Registered/F.D.M./London, oval from 1871 . . . . 15.00
Registered/Day Mail Down/London & Dover S.C., oval, 1916 . 10.00
Registered/Day Mail Up London & Dover S.C., oval 1916 . . . 10.00
T/C72, hexagonal charge stamps, with 5, 10, 15, or 25, from 1907 10.00
As above but T/C68, additionally 20, 30 or 40, from 1907 . . 10.00
Express Fee paid 3D/L & D.D.M., boxed 15.00

London and Dover Sorting Carriage, Ostend Day Mail (1887)

Dover to London/O.D.M., single circle, issued 1887 . . . . . ?

London and Exeter T.P.O. (1847–95)

Missent To/Gt Western R.W.P.O., unframed, from 1847 . . . 75.00
E/GW, circular, from 1855 . . . . 40.00

Mst – L & E.R.P.O., unframed with 1 or 2 or without a number
above from 1856 . . . . 75.00
Missent – to/London & Exeter – R.P.O., unframed, from 1856 . 75.00
Mst – L & E/R.P.O. Forwd, unframed, from 1856 . . . . . . —
London & Exeter R.P.O./Forward, unframed, from 1862 . . . —
L & E, star stamps, from 1862 . . . . 40.00
L & E/R.P.O., circular, from 1863 . . . . 40.00
Received open and resealed/at the L & E.R.P.O., unframed,
issued 1866 . . . . —
L & E/R.P.O., star stamps, from 1869 . . . . 35.00
L & E.T.P.O./From the West, single circle, from 1870 . . . . . 30.00
L & E.T.P.O./From the East, single circle, from 1870 . . . . . 30.00
GO1, number cancellation, 3 barred upright oval, from 1873 . . 25.00
L & E/TPO/E, in double framed diamond, from 1873 . . . . 28.00
Duplex, L & E. T.P.O., with P/S in numeral portion, from 1879 28.00
L & E. T.P.O./From the West, single circle, from 1888 . . . . 20.00
L & E. T.P.O./From the East, single circle, from 1888 . . . . . 20.00
L & E. T.P.O./Parcel Mail, single circle, from 1888 . . . . . . 30.00

London F.D.M. see London-Dover S.C. French Day Mail

London and Folkestone Sorting Carriage (1890–1915)
London & Queenboro S.T., single circle, from 1890 . . . . . . 25.00
London & Queensborough S.T., single circle, from 1905 . . . . 20.00
As above but also 'Registered' in scroll above, from 1898 . . 30.00
London & Folkestone S.C., with 'Registered' in scroll above,
single circle, from 1911 . . . . 25.00
London & Folkestone S.C., single circle, from 1911 . . . . . . 20.00

London and Holyhead Day T.P.O. (1854–1939)
Missent to/Chester & Holyhead/R.W.P.O., unframed from 1854 80.00
London & Holyhead R.P.O./Irish Mail Day, unframed from 1860 80.00
Four pointed star, from 1860 . . . . 25.00
Euston Station/Irish Mail, single circle, from 1860 . . . . . . 30.00
B34 numeral cancellation, from 1865 . . . . 30.00
London & Holyhead R.P.O./Irish Mail Day, boxed, from 1860 . 35.00
Received open and resealed/at the L & H.R.P.O., unboxed, from
1866 . . . . 35.00
London & Holyhead T.P.O./Day, single circle, from 1870 . . . 25.00
1/RPO/M, in circle, struck in red, from 1871 . . . . 25.00
London & Holyhead T.P.O./Day Up single circle from 1881 . . 7.50
London & Holyhead T.P.O./Day Down, single circle, from 1881 7.50
London-Holyhead T.P.O./Day Up, single circle, from 1929 . . 5.00
London-Holyhead T.P.O./Day Down, single circle, from 1929 . 5.00
London-Holyhead T.P.O./Day, single circle, from 1934 . . . . 5.00
Holyhead-London T.P.O./Day, single circle, from 1934 . . . . 5.00

London and Holyhead Night T.P.O. (1860-1940)

London & Holyhead R.P.O./Irish Mail Night, unframed, from 1860	50.00
Four pointed star, from 1860	20.00
Received open and resealed/at the L & H.R.P.O., unframed from 1866	30.00
London & Holyhead R.P.O./Irish Mail Night, unframed, 1860's	30.00
London & Holyhead R.P.O./Irish Mail Night, framed, from 1868	25.00
London & Holyhead T.P.O./Night, from 1870	25.00
1/RPO/E, circular, from 1871	25.00
London & Holyhead T.P.O./Night Up, single circle, from 1871	7.50
London & Holyhead T.P.O./Night Down, single circle, from 1871	7.50
London-Holyhead T.P.O./Night Up, single circle, from 1929	5.00
London-Holyhead T.P.O./Night Down, single circle, from 1929	5.00
London-Holyhead T.P.O./Night, single circle, from 1934	5.00
Holyhead-London T.P.O./Night, single circle, from 1934	5.00

London and Holyhead T.P.O. (Canadian and USA Mails) (1895-1908)

London & Holyhead/T.P.O./United States Mail, single circle, from 1895	20.00
London & Holyhead/T.P.O./Canadian Mail, single circle, from 1895	20.00
London Supplementary/Canadian Mail, single circle, from 1895	20.00
K.48, numeral, from 1895	17.50
London-Holyhead/US/T.P.O., double circle, short medium arcs, from 1911	20.00
London & Holyhead/T.P.O./United States mail, rubber single circle, issued 1910	20.00
T with L & H beneath, unframed, from 1895	15.00
T in frame with L & H beneath frame, from 1910	15.00

London-Ipswich T.P.O. see Ipswich Sorting Carriage

London and Leeds Sorting Carriage (1854-1940)

Gt Northern Railway, unframed, in red, from 1854	60.00
Gt Northern Railway, unframed, in red, from 1856	60.00
London & Doncaster S.T., single circle, from 1891	15.00
London and Leeds/S.T., single circle, from 1901	15.00
L & L/S.T., boxed, from 1901	20.00
London & Leeds S.C./Down Day Mail, single circle, from 1902	10.00
London & Leeds S.C./Up Day Mail single circle, from 1902	10.00
London – Leeds (Day)/Rly S.C., double circle short thick arcs, from 1922	10.00

Leeds – London (Day)/Rly S.C., double circle short thick arcs,
from 1922 . . . . 10.00
London – Leeds/T.P.O., double circle thick arcs, from 1930 . . 8.50
Leeds – London/T.P.O., double circle thick arcs, from 1930 . . 8.50
Doncaster – London/T.P.O., single circle, from 1932 . . . . . 8.50
Posted without Late fee, unframed, from 1933 . . . . 3.50

London and Newhaven Sorting Carriage (1923–39)
London – Newhaven/R.S.C., single circle, from 1923 . . . . . 10.00
Newhaven London/R.S.C., single circle, from 1923 . . . . . . 10.00
Newhaven – London S.C., single circle, from 1929 . . . . . . 10.00
London – Newhaven S.C., single circle, from 1929 . . . . . . 10.00

London-Norwich T.P.O. see Ipswich Sorting Carriage
London-Queenboro S.T. see London-Folkestone S.C.
London Supplementary Canadian Mail see London-Holyhead T.P.O.

London, York, Edinburgh T.P.O. (from 1909)
Gt Northern/Night Mail Down, single circle, from 1909 . . . . 9.00
Gt Northern/T.P.O./Night Mail Down, single circle, from 1917 8.00
London – York – Edinburgh/Rly S.C., double circle short thick
arcs, from 1922 . . . . 8.00
London – York – Edinburgh/T.P.O., skeleton, 1930 . . . . . 25.00
London – York – Edinburgh/T.P.O., single circle, from 1930 . . 6.00
London – York – Edinburgh T.P.O., single circle, from 1930 . . 6.00
London – York – Edinburgh T.P.O., double circle short thick arc,
1957 . . . . 2.50
London – York – Edinburgh T.P.O./1 or 2, double circle thin
arcs, from 1958 . . . . 0.50
London – York – Edinburgh T.P.O., E, double circle thin arcs,
1958 . . . . 1.00
London – York – Edinburgh/T.P.O., E, double circle thin arcs,
1971 . . . . 0.50
Posted without late fee, unframed, 1930 . . . . 3.00
As above but boxed, 1931 . . . . 2.00
1D/27–31/1/To pay/posted in/T.P.O./Late fee/Not paid,
boxed, 1960 . . . . 1.00
As above but 2, 1961 . . . . 1.00
As above but route number 30-1 and no stamp number, 1961 1.00
As above but route number 30-2 and no stamp number, 1962 1.00
D/More to/pay/Late fee/unpaid, boxed 0.75

L. & S.W.R.P.O. see South Western T.P.O.

Manchester and Crewe Sorting Carriage (1864-1939)

A/Manchester/S.T., single circle with town across circle from
1864 . . . . 30.00
Manchester/S.T., single circle, from 1880 . . . . 20.00
Manchester & Crewe S.C./1, medium arcs, double circle, from
1908 . . . . 10.00
As above but 2 . . . . 10.00
Crewe & Manchester S.C./2, short thick arcs, double circle . . 5.00
Crewe-Manchester S.C./1, short thick arcs, double circle, from
1934 . . . . 3.50

Manchester to Glasgow Sorting Carriage (1951-1977)

Manchester-Glasgow S.C., double circle with thin arcs, from 1951   4.00
Manchester-Glasgow S.C./1, double circle with thin arcs, from
1957 . . . . 2.00
As above but 2, from 1957 . . . . 2.00
1d/41-1/To pay/posted in/T.P.O./Late Fee/Not paid, boxed,
1966 . . . . 4.00
As above but no route numbers, from 1968 . . . . 2.50

Manchester S.T. see Manchester-Crewe S.C.

Midland District Sorting Carriage (1858-1869)

Midland/District. S.C. unframed, 1858 . . . .   ?
Received open and resealed/at the Midland D.S.C., unframed
1866 . . . .   ?

Midland Railway Post Office, Day (1853-1873)

Missent – to/R & L.R.P.O., unframed, from 1853 . . . . . . 65.00
Midland R.P.O. day, boxed, from 1862 . . . . 35.00
Mid Ry/Day, Star stamps, from 1862 . . . . 35.00
Day Mail Going North/Mid T.P.O., from 1869 . . . . 30.00
Day Mail Going South/Mid T.P.O., from 1869 . . . . 30.00

Midland T.P.O. (from 1845)

Missent to Rugby/and Newcastle RWPO, unframed, from 1845   70.00
Missent to Gloster/and Tamworth/R.W.P.O., unframed,
issued 1850 . . . . 70.00
E/MR, in circle, from 1851 . . . . 20.00
Missent – to/Midland R.P.O. Up, unframed, black or blue, from
1855 . . . . 40.00
Missent – to/Midland R.P.O. Down, unframed, from 1855 . . . 40.00
Mst – Midland/R.P.O. Forwd, unframed, issued 1856 . . . . .   —
Mid Ry/Night, star stamp, from 1862 . . . . 25.00
Received open and resealed/at the Midland R.P.O., unframed,
from 1866 . . . . 30.00

Nt. Mail, Going North/Mid TPO, single circle, from 1869 . . . 20.00
Nt. Mail Going South/Mid TPO, single circle, from 1869 . . . 20.00
Midland T.P.O., single circle, from 1870 . . . . 20.00
Midland T.P.O./From South, single circle, from 1879 . . . . . 10.00
Midland T.P.O./From North, single circle, from 1879 . . . . . 10.00
Mid T.P.O./From the North, single circle, from 1880 . . . . . 15.00
Mid T.P.O./From the South, single circle, from 1880 . . . . . 15.00
Midland T.P.O./Going North, double circle, short medium arcs,
   from 1913 . . . . 8.00
Midland T.P.O./Going South, double circle, short medium arcs,
   from 1913 . . . . 8.00
Midland T.P.O./Going South, single circle, from 1921 . . . . 4.00
Midland T.P.O./Going North, single circle, from 1921 . . . . 4.00
Midland T.P.O./Going South, double circle thin arcs, from 1954 1.50
Midland T.P.O. Going North, double circle thin arcs, from 1954 1.50
Midland T.P.O. G.G. South/1 or 2, single circle, 1959 . . . . . 1.50
Midland T.P.O. G.G. North/1 or 2, single circle, 1959 . . . . . 1.50
Midland T.P.O. G.G. South/1 or 2, double circle thin arcs, 1958 0.50
Midland T.P.O. G.G. North/1 or 2, double circle thin arcs, 1958 0.50
Midland T.P.O./G.G. South, double circle thin arcs with AM,
   from 1966 . . . . 1.00
Posted without Late fee, unboxed 1.00
Posted without late fee/1d to pay, boxed 1.00

M.N.R. see Great Northern R.P.O.

Newcastle on Tyne Sorting Tender (1893–1914)
Newcastle on Tyne/Sorting Tender, single circle, from 1893 . . 25.00
Newcastle on Tyne/Sorting Carriage, single circle, from 1909 . . 20.00

Newcastle-London R.S.C. and S.C. see London-Newhaven S.C.
Normanton-Stalybridge T.P.O. and R.S.C. see Bangor-Crewe T.P.O.

North Eastern T.P.O. Night Down (from 1926)
North Eastern T.P.O./Night Down, single circle, from 1926 . . 8.00
N.E.T.P.O./Night Down, single circle, from 1934 . . . . . . 2.00
Posted without Late fee, boxed, 1934 . . . . 2.50
1D/30-1/To pay/posted in/T.P.O./Late fee/Not paid, boxed,
   1959 . . . . 1.00
As above but 27-31 and stamp No 1, 1963 . . . . 1.00
As above but without route or stamp numbers 1.00

North Eastern T.P.O. Night Up (from 1909)
Gt Northern/Night Mail, single circle, from 1909 . . . . . . 9.00
Gt Northern/Night Mail Up, single circle, from 1910 . . . . 8.00

Newcastle London/Rly S.C., double circle thick arcs, from 1922   8.00
North Eastern T.P.O./Night Up, single circle, from 1926   . . . 8.00
N.E.T.P.O./Night Up, double circle with short thick arcs, from
    1934 . . . . 5.00
North Eastern T.P.O. Nt Up/1 or 2, double circle thin arcs, from
    1958 . . . . 0.50
N.E.T.P.O./Night Up, single circle with AM, from 1961 . . . . 1.00
North Eastern T.P.O. Nt Down/1 or 2, double circle with thin
    arcs, from
    1958 . . . . 0.50
North Eastern T.P.O. Nt Down/E, double circle with thin arcs,
    from 1958 . . . . 1.50
North Eastern T.P.O. Nt Down/E, double circle with thin arc,
    from 1971 . . . . 0.50

North East and North Eastern T.P.O. see also Edinburgh-York T.P.O.
North of Scotland S.C. see Aberdeen-Elgin S.C.
North West T.P.O. see Up Special T.P.O.

North Western T.P.O. Day Mail (1856–1922)

Mst – Day – N.W/R.P.O. FORWD, unframed, from 1856 . . . 70.00
NWRY/Day, in star, from 1862 . . . . 25.00
North West T.P.O./Day Up, Unframed dated circular, from 1870 35.00
North West T.P.O./Day Down, unframed dated circular, from
    1870 . . . . 35.00
North Western T.P.O./Day Up, single circle, from 1873 . . . 25.00
North Western T.P.O./Day Down, single circle, from 1873 . . 20.00
NW/TPO/M, in double diamond frame, from 1873 . . . . 30.00
North West T.P.O./Day Up, single circle, from 1877 . . . . 10.00
North West T.P.O./Day Down, single circle, from 1877 . . . 8.50

North Western T.P.O. Mid-day Mail (1883–1915)

L & N.W.T.P.O./Mid day/Down, scroll over single circle, from
    1883 . . . . 25.00
L & N.W.T.P.O./Mid day/Up, scroll over single circle, from 1883 25.00
L & N.W.T.P.O./Mid day Mail down, single circle, from 1884 . 10.00
L & N.W.T.P.O./Mid day Mail Up, single circle, from 1884 . . 10.00

North Western T.P.O. Night Down (1856–1920)

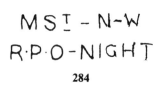

284

285

Mst – Nt – N.W/R.P.O. Forward, unframed from 1856	70.00
Mst – Nt – N.W/R.P.O. Warrington Fd, unframed from 1856	70.00
Mst – Nt – N.W/R.P.O. Carlisle. Fd, unframed from 1856	70.00
284 Mst – N.W/R.P.O. – Night, unframed from 1856	70.00
Mst, N.W.R.P.O/Night, unframed from 1856	70.00
NW/R.P.O./E, circled, from 1858	30.00
Mst – Nt – N.W/R.P.O. Forwd, from 1860	30.00
NWRY/Night, in star, from 1862	25.00
Received open and resealed/at the L & N.W.R.P.O. unframed from 1866	30.00
North West T.P.O./Night. Down, unframed dated circular, from 1870	35.00
NW/TPO/E, in double diamond frame, from 1873	30.00
285 North Westn T.P.O./Night Down, from 1878	20.00
North West T.P.O./Night Down, from 1879	20.00
Down Special T.P.O., single circle issued 1897	10.00
Down Special/T.P.O., issued 1910	8.00
North Westn T.P.O./Night Down 1920	6.00
Down Special T.P.O./ (parcels), from 1909	10.00
N.W.S.T., boxed in hexagon for Sunday Sorting Tender	?
Missent to/D.S.C./North Western, boxed, from 1857	?
North Western/Dist-Sor-Care, boxed from 1862	50.00
Received open and resealed/at the L & N.W.D.S.C., unframed from 1865	?

North Western T.P.O. 10 pm Mail (from 1885)

10 pm. NW Night Mail, single circle, from 1886	20.00
North Western T.P.O./Night Down, double circle, short thick arcs, 1929	5.00
As above but N.T.P.O., from 1948	5.00
North Western T.P.O./Night Down, single circle, from 1932	4.00
North Western T.P.O./Night Down, double circle with thin arcs, from 1956	1.00
North Western T.P.O. Nt Down/1 or 2, double circle thin arcs, from 1958	0.50
As above but AM, Index 2 or 2A	5.00

North Western T.P.O. Nt. Down/AM 1.00
Posted without late fee/1d to pay, boxed, lower case letters, 1948   2.50
   As above but upper case letters, 1950's 1.75
   1d/32-1/To pay/Posted in/T.P.O./Late fee/not paid, boxed,
      1962 . . . . 1.75
   As above but 32-2, 1959 . . . . 1.75

Norwich-London T.P.O. see Ipswich Sorting Carriage
Norwich Sorting Tender and Carriage see East Anglian T.P.O.
N.W.R.P.O. and N.W. Ry see North Western T.P.O.

Perth and Aberdeen S.C. (1871–1885?)

Duplex type Perth & Aberdeen/Sort Carr with numeral 402 . . 45.00

Perth-Helmsdale R.S.C. see Highland T.P.O.

Peterborough – Crewe T.P.O. (from 1966)

Peterborough-Crewe T.P.O., double circle with thin arcs, from
   1966 . . . . 0.50
Crewe-Peterborough T.P.O., double circle with thin arcs, from
   1966 . . . . 0.50
   As above with AM 1.00
Peterborough-Crewe T.P.O./ (Linc. Sect.), as above, from 1966   0.50
Crewe-Peterborough/ (Linc. Sect.), as above, from 1966 . . . . 0.50
   As above with AM 1.00
1d/to pay/posted in/T.P.O./Late Fee/Not paid, from 1966 . . 1.00

Peterborough and Ely Sorting Carriage (1858–1916)

286

Peterboro'/Dist – S.C., unframed, from 1858 . . . . 65.00
286 Sorting Tender/Peterborough, single circle, from 1869 . . . . 30.00
Peterborough/Sorting Tender, single circle, from 1880 . . . . 20.00
Peterborough and Ely/Sorting Carriage, single circle, from 1908   16.00

Plymouth to Bristol T.P.O. (1860–1972)

Bristol & Exeter Ry. P.O., single circle, from 1860	30.00
Bristol & Exeter/R.P.O., boxed, issued 1862	—
Received open and resealed/at the B & E.R.P.O., unboxed, issued 1866	—
B & E/R.P.O., star stamp, from 1867	25.00
North Mail Going East/B & E.T.P.O., single circle, issued 1869	20.00
North Mail Going West/B & E.T.P.O., single circle, issued 1869	20.00
Bristol & Newton Abbot T.P.O./Going West, single circle, from 1872	20.00
Bristol & Newton Abbot T.P.O./Going East, single circle, from 1872	20.00
Bristol & Newton Abbot/T.P.O., single circle, from 1872	20.00
Bristol & Penzance T.P.O. Down, single circle, from 1896	15.00
Bristol & Penzance T.P.O. Up, single circle, from 1896	15.00
Bristol & Penzance T.P.O./Up, single circle, from 1897	10.00
Bristol & Penzance T.P.O./Down, single circle, from 1897	10.00
Bristol Plymouth T.P.O., single circle, from 1930	5.00
Plymouth Bristol T.P.O., single circle, from 1930	5.00
Bristol-Plymouth T.P.O., double circle thin arcs, from 1957	1.00
Plymouth-Bristol T.P.O., double circle thin arcs, from 1957	1.00
Posted without late fee/1d to pay, boxed	2.50
D/More to/pay/Late fee/unpaid, boxed	2.00

Plymouth and Bristol Foreign Mails T.P.O. (1869–1915)

287

B16, numeral in horizontal oval	30.00
287 Plymouth to Bristol T.P.O., single circle, from 1874	20.00
Plymouth to/Bristol T.P.O., single circle, from 1875	20.00
Plymouth & Bristol S.T., from 1900	15.00
B16, numeral in upright oval, from 1875	18.00
1D/B16, also 2D, 3D, 4D, 5D, 8D, unframed	10.00

Plymouth and Exeter Night Mail Tender (1880–94)

Duplex, Plymouth & Exeter/N.M.T., with numeral C24, from 1880	25.00
Duplex, Plymouth & Exeter/N.M. Tender, with numeral C.24 from 1888	25.00
Plymouth & Exeter/N.M. Tender, single circle, 1894	20.00

Portsmouth Sorting Carriage (1865–1923)

288

POR/S.C., star stamp, from 1865 . . . . 30.00
Portsmouth/Sorting Carriage, single circle, from 1873 . . . . 20.00
288 Portsmouth Sorting Carriage, single circle, from 1884 . . . . . 10.00
Portsmouth Sorting Carriage/P.P., single circle, from 1899 . . 15.00

Preston-Glasgow R.S.C. see Glasgow-Carlisle S.C.
Preston-Whitehaven T.P.O. see Whitehaven-Huddersfield T.P.O.
R. & L.R.P.O. see Midland Railway Post Office
Rugby-Newcastle R.W.P.O. see Midland T.P.O.
S.E.D.S.C. see South Eastern T.P.O.
S.E. Ry. P.O. see South Eastern T.P.O.

Shrewsbury and Aberystwyth Sorting Carriage
(1883–1917, 1919–1939)

Shrewbury & Aberystwith S.C., single circle, from 1883 . . . . 28.00
Shrewsbury & Aberystwyth S.C., single circle, from 1900 . . . 12.50
Shrewsbury & Aberystwyth S.C. Up, double circle thick arcs and
    cross, from 1919 . . . . 11.00
Shrewsbury & Aberystwyth S.C. Down, double circle thick arcs
    and cross, from 1919 . . . . 11.00
Shrewsbury & Aberystwyth S.O.C., single circle, from 1920 . . 13.00
Aberystwyth-Shrewsbury S.C., single circle, from 1930 . . . . 7.00
Shrewsbury-Aberystwyth S.C., single circle, from 1930 . . . . 7.00

Shrewsbury-Crewe S.C. see Shrewsbury-York T.P.O.

Shrewsbury and Hereford Sorting Carriage (1885–1902)

Shrewsbury & Hereford S.C., single circle, from 1885 . . . . . 15.00

Shrewsbury-Normanton T.P.O. see Shrewsbury-York T.P.O.

Shrewsbury and Tamworth T.P.O. (1858-1902, 1914-17)

Shrewsbury & Tamworth/Sorting Tender, unframed, from 1858 ?
Shrewsbury & Tamworth/R.P.O., boxed, from 1862 . . . . . 60.00
S. & T.R.P.O., boxed, from 1866 . . . . ?
S. & T.R.P.O. FD, boxed from 1866 . . . . 60.00
Four pointed star, probably for missent mail, from 1866 . . . . 28.00
Received open and resealed/at the S. & T.R.P.O., unframed,
from 1866 . . . . 30.00
Shrewsbury & Tamworth/T.P.O., boxed, from 1868 . . . . . 35.00
Shrewsbury & Tamworth/T.P.O., single circle, from 1872 . . . 25.00
Shrewsbury & Tamworth T.P.O., single circle, from 1878 . . . 20.00
Shrewsbury & Tamworth/S.C., single circle from 1883 . . . . 20.00
Tamworth-Shrewsbury/R.S.C., single circle, 1914 . . . . . . 15.00
Shrewsbury-Tamworth/R.S.C., single circle, 1914 . . . . . . 15.00

Shrewsbury and York T.P.O. (from 1892)

Shrewsbury & Crewe S.C., single circle, from 1892 . . . . . . 30.00
Shrewsbury & Normanton T.P.O./From West, single circle, from
1893 . . . . 30.00
Shrewsbury & Normanton T.P.O./From East, single circle, from
1893 . . . . 30.00
Posted without Late fee/K70, boxed 15.00
Bristol Shrewsbury & Normanton Parcels/From East, single
circle, from 1895 . . . . 25.00
Bristol Shrewsbury & Normanton Parcels/From West, single
circle, from 1895 . . . . 25.00
Bristol Shrewsbury & Normanton/From East, single circle from
1895 . . . . 15.00
Bristol Shrewsbury & Normanton/From West, single circle from
1895 . . . . 15.00
Bristol Shrewsbury & York T.P.O./From West, single circle,
from 1902 . . . . 12.00
Bristol Shrewsbury & York T.P.O./From East, single circle, from
1902 . . . . 12.00
Cardiff & York T.P.O./Going West, single circle, from 1910 . . 10.00
Cardiff & York T.P.O./Going East, single circle, from 1910 . . 10.00
York Shrewsbury/Rly. S.C., double circle, short thick arcs, from
1920 . . . . 10.00
Shrewsbury-York T.P.O., single circle, from 1930 . . . . . . 5.00
York-Shrewsbury T.P.O., single circle, from 1930 . . . . . . 5.00
Shrewsbury-York T.P.O./1 or 2, double circle with thin arcs . . 0.50
York-Shrewsbury T.P.O./1 or 2, double circle with thin arcs . . 0.50
Shrewsbury-York T.P.O./AM/(-), as above, from 1971 . . . . 1.00
York-Shrewsbury T.P.O./AM, as above, from 1972 . . . . . 1.00
Shrewsbury-York T.P.O., single circle without star, from 1971 . 1.00
Shrewsbury-York/T.P.O., as above, from 1979 . . . . 1.00

York-Shrewsbury/T.P.O., as above, from 1979 . . . . 1.00
Posted without Late Fee/1d to Pay, boxed, 1930 . . . . 3.75
1d/36–43/1/To pay/posted in/T.P.O./Late Fee/Not paid,
    boxed from 1968 . . . . 1.00
As above but 2., from 1968 . . . . 1.00

South Eastern T.P.O. (1853–1977)

South E Ry, unframed, black, red or orange, from 1853 . . . . 60.00
South Eastern/Dist. Sorting Carriage, boxed, from 1859 . . . 60.00
Received open and resealed/at the S.E.D.S.C., unframed . . . —
E/S.E., circular 25.00
Duplex: S.E. Ry. P.O./London Bridge, with SE/R.P.O. in
    numeral section, from 1863 . . . . 25.00
As above but Cannon St, from 1866 . . . . 25.00
S.E./R.P.O., circular, from 1863 . . . . 25.00
S.E. T.P.O., circular plated, from 1869 . . . . 25.00
S.E.T.P.O., single circle, from 1893 . . . . 20.00
South Eastern/Down/T.P.O., double circle, medium arcs, from
    1920 . . . . 6.00
South Eastern/Up/T.P.O., double circle, medium arcs, from 1920 6.00
South Eastern T.P.O./Down, double circle thin arcs, from 1936 4.00
South Eastern T.P.O./Up, double circle thin arcs, from 1936 . . 4.00
South Eastern T.P.O./Down, single circle, 1950s 3.00
South Eastern T.P.O./Up, single circle, 1950s 3.00
South Eastern T.P.O./1, double circle thin arcs, Up or Down,
    from 1957 . . . . 1.50
South Eastern T.P.O./2, double circle thin arcs, Up or Down,
    from 1957 . . . . 1.50
South Eastern T.P.O./Up, double circle thin arcs, with AM from
    1962 . . . . 2.00
South Eastern T.P.O./AM/Down, single circle 2.00
South Eastern T.P.O./AM/Down, double circle with thin arcs,
    from 1963 . . . . 4.00
South Eastern T.P.O./Up, double circle with thin arcs, from 1971 1.00
South Eastern T.P.O./Down, as above 1.00
Posted without late fee/1d to Pay, boxed, 1957 . . . . 2.00
1D/34–35/1/To pay/posted in/T.P.O./Late fee/not paid,
    boxed, 1959 . . . . 1.00
As above but 2, 1959 . . . . 1.00
As above but without stamp or route numbers, 1968 . . . . 1.00
D/More to/pay/late fee/unpaid, boxed 1.00

South Wales Night T.P.O. (from 1869)

South Wales T.P.O., single circle, from 1869 . . . . 30.00
South Wales – Sorting Tender/Down, single circle, from 1873 . 25.00
South Wales – Sorting Tender/Up, single circle, from 1873 . . . 25.00
South Wales S.C./Night Down, single circle, from 1886 . . . . 15.00
South Wales S.C./Night Up, single circle, from 1887 . . . . . 15.00
South Wales S.C./Night Mail, single circle, 1890 . . . . 15.00
South Wales S.C./Night Mail Up, single circle, 1909 . . . . . 15.00
South Wales T.P.O./Night Mail, single circle, 1899 . . . . . . 12.00
South Wales T.P.O./Night Mail East, single circle, from 1906 . 10.00
South Wales T.P.O./Night Mail Going East, single circle, from
1910 . . . . 10.00
South Wales T.P.O./Night Mail Going West, single circle, from
1910 . . . . 10.00
South Wales T.P.O./Up, single circle, from 1931 . . . . 5.00
South Wales T.P.O./Down, single circle, from 1931 . . . . . 5.00
South Wales T.P.O. Up, double circle with thick arc, 1955 . . . 1.00
South Wales T.P.O. Down, double circle with thick arc, 1955 . . 1.00
South Wales T.P.O./Up, double circle with thin arcs, from 1957 0.50
South Wales T.P.O./Down, double circle with thin arcs, from
1957 . . . . 0.50
As above with AM 3.00
1d/Late Fee, unframed, 1931 . . . . 7.50
Posted without late fee, boxed, 1931 . . . . 3.50
More to/pay/Late Fee/Unpaid, boxed 1.00

South Wales North Mail T.P.O. (1884–1923)

South Wales. Sorting Carriage/North Mail Up, single circle,
from 1884 . . . . 12.50
South Wales. Sorting Carriage/North Mail Down, single circle,
from 1884 . . . . 12.50
South Wales S.C./North Mail Down, 1902 . . . . 15.00
South Wales T.P.O./North Mail East, 1908 . . . . —
South Wales T.P.O./North Mail Going East, single circle, from
1910 . . . . 10.00
South Wales T.P.O./North Mail Going West, single circle, from
1910 . . . . 10.00
South Wales S.C./North Mail, across two circles, rubber, from
1866 . . . . 18.00
As above but across circle with six bars from 1890 . . . . . 18.00

South Western Day T.P.O. (1890–1940)

South Western T.P.O./Day Mail Down, single circle, from 1890 12.50
South Western T.P.O./Day Mail Up, single circle, from 1890 . . 12.50
Posted without Late fee, unframed 3.00

South Western Night T.P.O. (from 1856)

South W. Ry, unframed, 1856	60.00
S.W.S.T., boxed, 1860	60.00
South Western/District – S.C., unframed, from 1860	60.00
South Western/Dis: SOR: CAR:, boxed, from 1864	60.00
Received open and resealed/at the S.W.D.S.C., unframed, issued 1866	—
South Western/R.P.O., boxed, from 1863	45.00
L & S.W./R.P.O., circular, from 1863	45.00
Duplex: South Western/R.P.O., with S.W./R.P.O. in numeral portion, issued 1873	—
Duplex: S.W.R. Way P.O./Waterloo Stn, with S.W./R.P.O. in numeral portion, issued 1873	—
Received open and resealed/at the S.W.R.P.O., unframed, issued 1866	—
S. West/T.P.O., star stamp, issued 1869	—
South Western T.P.O., single circle, from 1873	25.00
SW/T.P.O./E, in double framed diamond, from 1873	25.00
South Western/T.P.O., single circle, from 1875	15.00
S.W. T.P.O./from the West, single circle, from 1876	7.50
S.W. T.P.O./from the East, single circle, from 1876	7.50
South Western T.P.O./Night Down, single circle, from 1897	7.50
South Western T.P.O./Night Up, single circle, from 1897	7.50
South Western T.P.O./Night Going West, single circle, 1909	8.00
South Western T.P.O./Night Down, double circle with BH and medium arcs, from 1910	10.00
South Western T.P.O./Night Up, double circle with BH and medium arcs, from 1910	10.00
South Western T.P.O./Night Down, single circle, from 1931	4.00
South Western T.P.O./Night Up, single circle, from 1931	4.00
South Western T.P.O. Nt Down/1 or 2, double circle thin arcs, from 1958	0.50
South Western T.P.O. Nt Up/1 or 2, double circle thin arcs, from 1958	0.50
South Western T.P.O./Nt Down, double circle short thin arcs, from 1970	5.00
South Western T.P.O. Up No 1 side, double circle thin arc, from 1972	1.00
South Western T.P.O. Up No 2 side, double circle thin arc, from 1972	1.00
South Western T.P.O. Going West/9.50 pm Mail, single circle, from 1910	10.00
South Western T.P.O./9.50 pm/Night Going West, single circle, from 1910	10.00
South Western T.P.O. Nt Down/3, double circle thin arc, with AM, from 1971	3.00

South Western T.P.O./Nt Down, as above but with 1 or 2 above
date, from 1971 . . . . 1.00
South Western T.P.O. Nt Down/AM, as above 1.00
South Western T.P.O./AM/Night Up, single circle 1.00
Posted without Late fee, boxed, from 1894 . . . . 3.00
1D/39–40/1/To pay/posted in/T.P.O./Late fee/Not Paid,
boxed, 1959 . . . . 1.00
As above but 2, 1959 . . . . 1.00
As above but without route numbers or stamp numbers, 1968 1.00

Stalybridge-Whitehaven T.P.O. see Whitehaven-Huddersfield T.P.O.
S.T. Hull see Hull Sorting Carriage.
St. Pancras-Derby S.T. see London-Derby S.C.
S. & T.R.P.O. see Shrewsbury-Tamworth T.P.O.
S.W.D.S.C., S.W.R.P.O., S.W.S.T. & S. West T.P.O. see South Western T.P.O.

Tamworth and Hereford Sorting Carriage (1902–14)
Tamworth & Hereford S.C. Up, single circle, from 1902 . . . . 12.00
Tamworth & Hereford S.C. Down, single circle, from 1902 . . . 15.00

Tamworth-Lincoln S.C. see Lincoln Sorting Carriage.
Tamworth-Shrewsbury R.S.C. see Shrewsbury-Tamworth T.P.O.
T.L.H. see London-Holyhead T.P.O.

Truro and Falmouth Sorting Tender (1895–1916)
Truro & Falmouth S.T., single circle, from 1895 . . . . 25.00

Up Special T.P.O. (from 1870)
North West T.P.O./Night Up, unframed dated circular, from
1870 . . . . 45.00
North West T.P.O./Night Up, single circle, from 1879 . . . . . 20.00
North Western T.P.O./Night Up, single circle, from 1897 . . . 8.00
Up Special Mail/T.P.O., single circle, from 1885 . . . . 6.00
Up Special/T.P.O., double circle with medium arcs, from 1921 . 5.00
Up Special/T.P.O., double circle with thicker, shorter arcs, from
1936 . . . . 5.00
Up Special/T.P.O., double circle with thin arcs, from 1950 . . . 2.00
As above but with star, from 1950 . . . . 2.00
As above but with index 1 or 2 above date, from 1952 . . . . 2.00
Up Special T.P.O./1, double circle with thin arcs, from 1957 . . 0.50
As above but 2, from 1957 . . . . 0.50
Up Special T.P.O./1, single circle, from 1957 . . . . 3.00
As above but 2, from 1957 . . . . 3.00
Up Special T.P.O./A and A1, double circle with thin arcs, from
1959 . . . . 1.00
Up Special T.P.O. (L)/1, double circle with thin arcs, from 1957 1.00
As above but 2, from 1957 . . . . 1.00

Up Special/T.P.O. No 1, rubber stamps 3.50
Posted without late fee, boxed, lower case letters 3.50
Posted without late fee/1d to pay, boxed 3.50
Late fee/Paid, boxed from 1939 . . . . 5.00
1d/41-1/to pay/posted in/T.P.O./Late Fee/Not Paid, boxed . 1.75
  As above but 17-1 . . . . 1.75
Up Special T.P.O./AM, Single circle 4.00
Up Special/AM/T.P.O., double circle with thin arcs 1.00

Up Special T.P.O. see also Glasgow-Carlisle S.C. and Edinburgh-Carlisle S.C.

West Cornwall Tender (1884–1892)

West Cornwall Tender, single circle 28.00

Whitehaven to Huddersfield T.P.O. (from 1875)

289 Whitehaven S.T., single circle, from 1875 . . . . 20.00
  As above but 'thimble', from 1882 . . . . 15.00
290 Carnforth & Whitehaven T.P.O., duplex, with numeral J54, from
  1891 . . . . 10.00
Whitehaven S.C., single circle, from 1904 . . . . 10.00
Whitehaven S.C., double circle, thick arcs and cross, 1920s . . . 6.00
Whitehaven S.C., double circle with thin arcs, from 1929 . . . 5.00
Whitehaven Preston T.P.O., double circle with thick arcs, from
  1930 . . . . 4.00
Preston Whitehaven T.P.O., double circle with thick arcs, from
  1930 . . . . 4.00
Whitehaven Preston T.P.O., double circle with thin arcs, from
  1957 . . . . 2.00
Preston Whitehaven T.P.O., double circle with thin arcs, from
  1957 . . . . 2.00
Whitehaven-Stalybridge T.P.O., double circle with thin arcs, from
  1965 . . . . 4.00
Stalybridge-Whitehaven T.P.O., double circle with thin arcs, from
  1965 . . . . 4.00
Whitehaven-Huddersfield T.P.O./2, double circle with thin arcs,
  from 1966 . . . . 0.50
Huddersfield-Whitehaven T.P.O./1, double circle with thin arcs,
  from 1966 . . . . 0.50

Huddersfield-Whitehaven T.P.O./AM/2 as above 1.00
More to Pay/Above . . . oz/077, boxed, 1930 . . . . 5.00
Liable to letter Rate/077, boxed, 1930 . . . . 5.00
Posted without late fee/077, boxed, 1930 . . . . 5.00
1d/To pay/077, unframed, 1930 . . . . 5.00
2d/To pay/077, unframed, 1930 . . . . 5.00
3d/to pay/077, unframed, 1930 . . . . 5.00
Posted without late fee/1d to pay, boxed, 1960 . . . . 3.00
1d/33–42/To pay/posted in/T.P.O./Late fee/Not Paid, boxed,
1965 . . . . 1.00

Whitehaven-Preston T.P.O. see Whitehaven-Huddersfield T.P.O.
Whitehaven-Stalybridge T.P.O. see Whitehaven-Huddersfield T.P.O.
York-Newcastle R.P.O. and T.P.O. see Edinburgh-York T.P.O.

York and Scarborough Sorting Carriage (1899–1928)
York & Scarboro' S.T., single circle, from 1899 . . . . 15.00

York-Shrewsbury Rly S.C. and T.P.O. see Shrewsbury-York T.P.O.

REMEMBER!
Prices in C.B.P. are minimum values
for a **clear strike on a clean card or cover.**
Have you read the notes
at the beginning?

PUZZLED?
From time to time all collectors find covers which have
curious or unexplained features. Send a photocopy (with SAE
or IRC) and I will send my comments or refer to a specialist in
a particular field. Some of the most interesting – or ones which
still cannot be explained – illustrated in the next
Collect British Postmarks.

14. MARITIME MARKINGS

Ship Letters

DOVER
SHIP LRE

291   A

DEAL
SHIP LRE

292   B

293   C

294   D

295   E

GUERNSEY
SHIP LETTER

296   F

SHIP LETTER
FALMOUTH

297   G

HULL
SHIP LETTER

298   H

SHIP LETTER
LIVERPOOL

299   J

SOUTHAMPTON
SHIP LETTER

300   K

301   L

302   M

BRISTOL
SHIP LETTER

303   N

SHIP LETTER
GREENOCK

304   P

149

SHIP LETTER.
AVONMOUTH.
BRISTOL.

305 Q   306   R

307 S

Ports using Ship Letter marks which appear on the market so seldom that no price guideline can be suggested are included with (?). All marks were struck in black unless otherwise stated.

London

Type A, with or without hyphen in 'Ship-Lre', in black.	25.00
As above but in red	100.00
Type E	30.00
Type M, unframed	45.00
Type M, framed	40.00
Type H	35.00
'Ship Letter' straight line types	10.00
Type L	7.50
As above with PAID	15.00
Post Paid Ship Letter marks	40.00
Paid Ship Letter marks	15.00
Post Paid withdrawn ship letters	150.00
Exempt ship letters	120.00

Aberdeen		Avonmouth		Beaumaris	
E	£120	S	£20	A	£200
F	£170	Ayr	(?)	H red	£150
H blue	£100	Ballycastle	(?)	Bideford	(?)
Shipletter, boxed	£25	Bangor (Wales)	(?)	Birmingham	(?)
Aldeborough	(?)	Bangor (Ireland)	(?)	Blyth	
Anstruther	(?)	Barnstaple		S	£30
Ardrossan	(?)	A	£175	Buckie	(?)
Arundel	(?)	D	£175	Buncrana	(?)
		H	£70	Burntisland	(?)
				Bridlington	(?)

Bridport

B	£150
B red	£200

Brighton

A	£200
B	£75
G	£50
H	£60
K	£50

Bristol

A	£40
E	£30
N red or black	£20
G red	£30
H	£30
H red	£30
K	£30
K blue	£30

Brixham

C	£200
E	£70
G red or black	£25
H	£20
H red	£50
K	£40

Caherciveen (?)

Campbeltown

A	£150
F	£200

Cardiff

H	£150
L	£45
Duplex	£50

Carrickfergus (?)

Chatham (?)

Chester (?)

Colchester

E red	£450
H red	£250

Coleraine (?)

Cork

N red or black	£75

Cove

A	£60
N	£40

Cowes

A	£50
G	£35
H red or black	£30
K red or black	£35
K blue	£75

Dartmouth

A	£60
D	£60
G	£50
H	£30
H red	£40
H green	£75
P red	£60

Devonport

A	£150
C	£150
D	£60
D red	£40
H red	£40
N red or black	£25
G red or black	£20

Dingle (?)

Douglas (I.O.M.)

A blue	£1000
G blue	£1300

Dover

A	£25
B	£25
E	£20
G	£20
G red	£35
G blue	£20
P	£20

Drogheda (?)

Dublin

N	£50
J red	£65
lower case 'Ship Letter' red or black	£50
Crowned dated type, red	£60

Dunbar (?)

Dundalk (?)

Dundee

E (with GR)	£150
H	£200

Eastbourne

D	£100
D blue	£200
D green	£250
H	£85

Edinburgh

A red	£200
D red (with ship)	£600
Octagon, Shipletter	£50
A	£300
E	£220
H	£100

Exmouth

H	£150

Falmouth

A	£35
C	£90
D	£50
E	£40
E red	£30
G	£40
G red	£20
H	£40
H red	£20
H blue	£35
P red	£40
L	£40

Faversham (?)

Fleetwood

P	£50

Folkestone

D	£150
H	£30
K	£25
K blue	£50

Fowey

H	£500

Fraserburgh (?)

Glasgow

E	£60
F	£20
F green	£50

Gosport (?)

Grangemouth (?)

Granton

Octagon, Ship Letter/ Granton	£75

Gravesend

A	£75
D	£60
E	£250
G	£35
G red	£40
G blue	£50
H	£30
K	£30
K green	£50
N	£45

Grays (?)

Goole (?)

Greenock

C	£120
D red or black	£40
E	£50
N	£35
H	£20
J red	£25

Grimsby

E	£300
Q	£30

Guernsey

E	£1300
F	£300
J red	£800
H	£1300

Harwich

G	£50
H	£70
F	£90
Q	£40

Hastings

A	£130
E	£180
G	£20
G red	£30
H	£20
H red	£30

Haverford West (?)

Helston (?)

Holyhead

A red	£250
H	£50
H red	£60
H blue	£100

Holywood (?)

Hull

C	£300
H	£25
G	£25
N	£20
R	£20
L	£15

Hythe

C	£350
H	£200

Ilfracombe (?)

Ipswich (?)

Irwine (?)

Isle of Wight

D	£500

Jersey

F	£250
J red	£2750
H red	£4000
K	£350
K blue	£4000
K yellow	£2750

Kilrush (?)

Kingsbridge

H	£25
H red	£40
G	£30
G green	£50

Kinsale

N	£70
N red	£90
N blue	£90
N yellow	£125

Kirkaldy (?)

Kirkwall

J	£200

Lancaster

A	£180
C	£350
D	£135
D red	£175
H	£100
H red	£150

Leith

E	£100
E red	£115
E (with GR)	£350
E (dated)	£200
H	£70
Oval Shipletter/Leith	£50
Leith Shipletter, thimble	£25
L	£50

Lerwick

H	£150
H green	£200

Lewes

H	£75

Limerick

F	£50
Scroll, red	£180

Liverpool

A	£12
D	£15
E red or black	£12
E dated, red or black	£50
H	£15
G	£10
J	£10
J red	£30
F	£10
N red or black	£10
Circular unframed, red or black	£10
As above, green	£25
Q	£10
Q red	£50
R	£10
R red	£40
L ('ship')	£8

Londonderry

E	£220
E red	£200

Looe (?)

Lowestoft (?)

Lynn (?)

Lyme

A	£200
G red	£160
H	£150

Lymington

A	£80
A red	£90
A blue	£125
D blue	£250

Maldon (?)

Marazion

(289 mileage)	£250
H	£200

Margate

A	£35
A blue	£60
G red or black	£25
H	£40

Mevagissey

H	£250

Milford

A	£250
E blue	£250
H	£60
H red	£100
H blue	£90

Middlesbrough

L	£60

Montrose (?)

Newburgh (?)

Newcastle-on-Tyne

P red	£100
F	£100
N	£100

Newry

A	£400
N	£100
Oval type	£500

Newton Abbot

H	£275

North Shields

E	£350
H	£200
F green	£200

Padstow (?)

Passage (?)

Pembroke

G	£200

Penzance

D	£100
H	£30
H red	£40
H blue	£50
P	£45

Peterhead

Q	£50

Plymouth

A	£50
D	£40
E	£35
G	£40
G red	£40
L ('letters')	£10
L ('letter')	£6
L unframed	£20

Polperro . . . . . . (?)

Poole

A	£150
E	£150
G red	£150
H	£100

Port Askaig . . . . (?)

Port Glasgow

A	£100
D	£70
N	£40
E dated	£250
H	£20
Oval	£15

Pwllheli . . . . . (?)

Queenborough

A	£120
B	£200
G red	£60

Queenstown

L	£50

Ramsgate

A	£100
G	£150
H	£60
E	£125

Rochford . . . . . (?)

Rochester

E	£200
F	£150
G	£150

(New) Romney

D	£175
F	£30
F green	£50
H	£50

Rostrevor . . . . (?)

Rothesay . . . . . (?)

Ryde

E	£350
H	£70
H red or blue	£95
P	£40
K	£35
K red	£45
K blue	£60

Rye . . . . (?)

St. Ives

H	£200

St. Mawes

G	£150
G blue	£350

Sheerness

D red	£200
H red	£150

Shoreham

H	£200

Sidmouth . . . . (?)

Sittingbourne . . . . (?)

Skibbereen

A	£90
A red	£100
Lower case 'ship letter'	£150
As above, blue	£250

Southampton

A	£50
D	£50
E	£50
E red	£60
F	£30
F blue	£50
N	£25
N red	£35
P	£18
K red or black	£17
L	£8

South Shields

P	£50

Southwold

E	£350

Sutherland . . . . (?)

Stornoway

Boxed, Shipletter	£50

Stranraer

A	£100
A blue	£150

Swanage

E	£200
F	£75
F red	£50
N	£75
G	£45
H	£40
P framed red or black	£40

Swansea

A	£350
N	£60
N red	£80
H	£60
L	£25

Teignmouth

G	£250
H magenta	£300

Tobermory . . . . (?)

Torquay

K	£90
K blue	£100

Troon

E (with GR)	£400
J	£300

Warren Point . . . . (?)

Waterford

N	£75
N red	£100
N blue	£150
N green	£150

Weymouth

A	£80
D	£70
E	£250
G red or black	£40
H	£30

Wexford . . . . . (?)

Whitby . . . . . (?)

Whitehaven

B	£250
H red or black	£200

Wicklow . . . . . (?)

Worthing

H	£250
H blue	£300

Yarmouth (IOW)

E	£250
G	£125

Yarmouth (Norfolk)

A	£250
D	£150
G	£120
H	£50

Youghal

N	£220

India Letters (Struck in black unless stated otherwise).

308

INDIA LETTER
WEYMOUTH

309

310

London:

Framed	15.00	Circular Types with crown	. 45.00
As above but in red . . .	25.00	Circular Types without	
Step Type (red)	40.00	crown	100.00
		Ship Letter/from/India	. . 500.00

	308	309	310
Brighton, black or red	45.00		
Bristol	45.00		
Brixham, black or red	50.00		
Cork, black or red	50.00		
Cove	60.00		
Cowes, black or red	40.00		
Dartmouth, red		25.00	
Deal	20.00		
Deal, blue	50.00		
Deal, red			15.00
Devonport, black or red	40.00	25.00	
Dover, black or red	15.00	18.00	15.00
Eastbourne	40.00		
Eastbourne, green	70.00		
Exeter, black or red	80.00		
Exmouth	200.00		
Falmouth, black or red	15.00	10.00	
Folkestone, black or red	60.00		
Gravesend, black or red	20.00	30.00	25.00
Greenock, black or red	20.00		25.00
Guernsey	4000.00		
Harwich	180.00		
Hastings	25.00		
Holyhead	60.00		
Holyhead, red	40.00		
Hull, red	50.00		

	Framed	Unframed	Step
Isle of Wight	90.00		
Kingsbridge, black or red	25.00		
Leith, blue	150.00		
Lewes, black	30.00		
Lewes, red	60.00		
Lyme	150.00		
Lymington	75.00		
Lymington, red	90.00		
Margate, black or red	30.00		
Milford	100.00		
Penzance	20.00		
Penzance, red	25.00	40.00	
Plymouth	16.00	15.00	
Plymouth, red	20.00		15.00
Poole	85.00		
Port Glasgow	40.00		
Portsmouth, black or red	12.50		
Queenborough	200.00		
Ramsgate, black or red	40.00		
(New) Romney, black or red	50.00		50.00
Ryde		50.00	40.00
St. Ives	200.00		
Sheerness, red	200.00		
Southampton	25.00		
Swanage	60.00		
Swanage, red	55.00		40.00
Weymouth, black or red	40.00	50.00	

Paquebot

Applied at British Ports, either to cancel stamps or as cachet, to mail posted on board ship.

PAQUEBOT

311
Straight Line
(size and spacing of
letters vary)

PAQUEBOT.

312
Boxed
(size of letters and
box vary)

313
Posted at Sea

PAQUEBOT ≡
POSTED AT SEA ≡

314

Universal machine with framed
two line Paquebot slogan

315
Double circle
with thin arcs

Port	From	Type	
Aberdeen	1937	Aberdeen/Paquebot, single circle	25.00
Ardrossan	1956	Straight line	10.00
Belfast	1928	Posted at sea	5.00
	1925	Hey Dolphin machine, two line slogan	10.00
	1935	Universal machine, two line slogan	20.00
	1968	Boxed	5.00
Birmingham	1910	Birmingham/Ship, double circle medium arcs	50.00
Blackpool	1975	Straight line	10.00
Bournemouth	1974	Boxed	10.00
Bristol	1910	Straight line	45.00
	1913	Krag machine with five wavy bars	30.00
	1923	Straight line	4.00
	1929	Hey Dolphin machine, boxed Paquebot	5.00
	1934	Universal machine, two line slogan	10.00
Brixham	1950	Straight line	10.00
	1959	Double circle, thin arcs	8.00
	1959	Universal machine, two line slogan framed	3.00
Buckie	1966	Straight line	10.00
Burnham on Crouch	1970	Straight line	15.00
Cardiff	1910	Posted at sea	10.00
	1911	Krag machine, straight or wavy bars	10.00
Cowes	1974	Straight line	8.00
Douglas I.O.M.	1973	Double circle, thin arcs	90.00
Dover	1905	Straight line	45.00
	1911	Posted at sea	3.00
Dundee	1967	Boxed	3.00
Edinburgh	1912	Straight line	10.00
	1937	Universal machine with wavy lines	3.00
		As above but with slogans	4.00
	1938	Edinburgh/Paquebot, double circle thick arcs	3.00
Falmouth	1976	Straight line	6.00
Felixstowe	1970	Boxed	4.00

Folkestone	1905	Straight line	3.00
	1968	Boxed	2.00
	1968	Straight line, mis-spelt 'Pacquebot'	30.00
	1972	Posted at sea, illustrated	5.00
Glasgow	1894	Oval, Packet letter/Glasgow	7.50
	1902	Straight line	10.00
	1933	Boxed	5.00
	1929	Universal machine, two line slogan	3.00
	1940	Dated box	10.00
Goole	1970	Boxed	7.50
Grangemouth	1910	Straight line	50.00
	1904	Boxed	10.00
Grays	1951	Boxed	10.00
	1968	Universal machine, two line, framed	3.00
Gt. Yarmouth	1971	Straight line	4.00
Greenock	1901	Straight line	10.00
	1959	Universal machine, two line, framed	2.00
Grimsby	1895	Straight line	3.00
Guernsey	1903	Straight line	3.00
Harwich	1951	Boxed	2.00
Holyhead	1922	Posted at sea	5.00
Hull	1896	Straight line	3.00
	1906	Paquebot/Hull, double circle medium arcs	10.00
	1938	Universal machine, two line	18.00
Ilford	1970	Straight line	5.00
	1972	Dated packet type, with central lines	5.00
Invergordon	1967	Boxed	5.00
Ipswich	1971	Straight line	5.00
Jersey	1903	Straight line	10.00
Kings Lynn	1973	Straight line	5.00
Kirkwall	1969	Boxed	5.00
	1973	Straight line	3.00
Lancaster	1970	Paquebot;/Posted at sea/Received	2.50
Leith	1899	Straight line	25.00
Lerwick	1933	Straight line	50.00
	1967	Lerwick, Shetland/Paquebot, single circle	4.00
Liverpool	1894	Straight line	10.00
	1895	Paquebot;/Liverpool, double circle medium arcs	2.00
	1906	As above but Liverpool 1	3.00
	1910	Posted at sea	3.00
	1912	Colombia machines, straight or wavy bars	8.00
	1924	Hey Dolphin with Paquebot in wavy bars	2.00
	1934	Universal machine, two line	8.00
	1955	Paquebot/Liverpool 1, single circle	2.50
London	1895	Straight line	3.00
	1911	Krag machine with straight or wavy bars	2.00
	1921	Machine: London FS datestamp, Paquebot in wavy bars	2.00
	1924	London/F.S/Paquebot, single circle	2.00
	1934	Universal, London FS, two line	2.00
	1935	As above but boxed slogan	2.50
	1936	London F.S/Paquebot, double circle, thick arcs	2.00
	1950	London/Paquebot, packet type, date between bars	2.00
	1971	As above but no bars	3.00
	1971	London/F.S./Paquebot, double circle, thin arcs	2.00

Londonderry	1955	Straight line	7.00
	1966	Boxed	5.00
Lowestoft	1972	Straight line	3.50
Maldon	1955	Straight line	15.00
Manchester	1912	Straight line	8.00
Methil	1907	Straight line	50.00
Middlesbrough	1953	Straight line	3.50
Milford Haven	1970	Posted at Sea	6.00
Newcastle-on-Tyne	1903	Straight line	8.00
	1971	Boxed	4.00
Newhaven	1966	Straight line	4.00
	1966	Universal machi=0	
	1966	Newhaven. Sussex/Paquebot, double circle, thin arcs	3.50
	1975	As above but Newhaven East Sussex	3.00
Newport	1959	Straight line	5.00
	1969	Posted at Sea, Newport Mon.	5.00
	1975	As above but Newport Gwent	4.00
North Shields	1929	Straight line	4.00
Oban	1961	Straight line	4.00
Plymouth	1897	Straight line	10.00
	1904	Paquebot/Plymouth, double circle, medium arcs	2.00
	1907	Paquebot. Plymouth/2, as above	2.00
	1910	Colombia machine, six straight bars	2.00
	1913	Krag machine, five wavy bars, continuous	3.00
	1923	Hey Dolphin machine, boxed Paquebot	4.00
	1922	Machine (no year) five wavy bars	20.00
	1935	Universal machine, two line	2.00
	1933	Paquebot Plymouth/Devon 1, double circle	3.00
	1936	Krag, five wavy, Plymouth/Posted at Sea	40.00
Portsmouth	1953	Portsmouth and Southsea/Paquebot, double circle	10.00
	1971	Boxed	5.00
	1972	Straight line	3.00
Port Talbot	1974	Port Talbot. Glam/Paquebot, single circle	3.00
Preston	1954	Boxed	4.00
Queenstown	1894	Straight line	25.00
	1922	Paquebot Queenstown, double circle	4.00
Ryde	1973	Straight line	5.00
Saltcoats	1974	Straight line	5.00
Scarborough	1971	Straight line	5.00
Southampton	1899	Straight line	5.00
	1908	Paquebot/Southampton, double circle	5.00
	1911	Colombia machine, five or six straight bars	4.00
	1910	Posted at sea	2.00
	1924	Universal machine with wavy lines	1.50
		As above but with slogan, 1930s	3.00
		As above but 1940s	2.00
		As above but 1950s	1.50
	1931	Universal machine, two line	1.50
	1957	As above but framed two line	1.50
South Devon	1969	Paquebot/South Devon, Double circle thin arcs	3.00
(Torquay)	1973	Universal machine, two line, transposed	4.00
South Shields	1897	Straight line	5.00
Stornoway	1966	Straight line	15.00
	1967	Stornoway. Isle of Lewis/Paquebot	4.00

Stromness	1970	Boxed	5.00
Sunderland	1968	Straight line	4.00
	1975	Boxed	3.00
Swansea	1935	Swansea Glam/Paquebot, double circle thick arcs	5.00
	1976	West Glamorgan/Paquebot, double circle thin arcs	3.00
Thurso	1976	Boxed	4.00
Weymouth	1973	Paquebot/Weymouth, skeleton	15.00
	1975	Universal machine, two line, transposed	4.00
	1976	Posted at sea	3.00

Some of the foreign Paquebot marks to be found on mail franked with British Stamps:

Aden:	Boxed Paquebot, from 1894	1.50
	Circular with shaded bottom half, from 1908	1.50
	Paquebot/Aden, shaded background, from 1933	2.00
	Paquebot/Aden G.P.O., single circle, from 1953	2.00
	Paquebot machine marks	2.00
Alexandria:	Boxed Paquebot, from 1902	3.50
	Circular Paquebot/Alexandrie, with Arabic, from 1924	2.00
	Straight line types	8.00
Balboa:	Duplex types, from 1917	1.50
	Straight line types, from 1920	8.00
	Machine types, from 1931	1.50
Bergen:	Straight line types, from 1925	2.00
	Boxed types, from 1905	3.50
	Machine types, from 1938	2.00
Bombay:	Boxed Paquebot, from 1904	2.00
	Straight line types, from 1900	8.00
	Circular Bombay Foreign types, from 1913	1.50
Capetown:	Circular types, from 1914	1.50
	Machine types, from 1914	2.00
Cherbourg:	Straight line types, from 1920	1.50
	Continuous impression machine, Paquebot between bars, from 1926	1.50
	Machine with tourist slogan, from 1955	3.50
	Machine with boxed Paquebot between wavy bars, from 1965	1.50
Colombo:	Straight line types, from 1894	2.00
	Circular types, from 1912	2.00
	Machine types, slogans or bars, from 1927	2.00
Dublin:	Circular Baile Atha Cliath types, from 1935	2.00
Dun Laoghaire:	Posted at Sea type, from 1923	1.50
Durban:	Double circle types, from 1937	1.50
	Machine types, from 1941	2.00
Funchal:	Straight line types, from 1904	3.50
	Paquebot in oval frame, from 1910	8.00
	Boxed Paquebot, from 1913	1.50
	Circular dated type, from 1968	5.00
Gibraltar:	Straight line types, from 1894	2.00
	Gibraltar/Paquebot single circle, from 1910	2.00
	Pictorial mark with ship, from 1967	2.00
Hamilton,	Straight line types, from 1907	2.00
Bermuda	Paquebot/Bermuda, single circles, from 1947	1.50
	Machine with Paquebot boxed, from 1951	20.00

Lisbon:	Paquete, straight line types, from 1895	2.00
	Paquebot, straight line type, from 1897	1.50
	Double circle types with Paquete at base, from 1906	2.00
	Double circle types with Lisboa at base, from 1949	1.50
Malta:	All types	2.00
New York:	Straight line types with (N.Y. 2D DIV) from 1894	2.00
	As above but (N.Y.P.O. For. Sec.), from 1913	20.00
	Single circle types, from 1905	3.50
	Duplex types, from 1915	1.50
	Machine types, from 1924	1.50
Oslo:	Boxed Paquebot, from 1931	2.00
	Machine type, from 1937	8.00
	Paquebot straight line type, from 1972	5.00
Port Said:	Straight line type, from 1905	3.50
	Pleine Mer, unframed, from 1896	8.00
	Boxed Paquebot, from 1899	1.50
	Circular type, from 1912	1.00
Port Sudan:	Boxed Paquebot, from 1927	2.00
Port Taufiq:	Boxed Paquebot, from 1901	1.50
	Circular type with wording inside arcs, from 1939	2.00
	Circular type with wording across, from 1957	1.50
Quebec:	Straight line types, from 1914	8.00
	Two line, Exempt from War tax, from 1915	30.00
	Boxed, Exempt from War tax, from 1919	8.00
	Mailed on the High Seas, unframed, from 1920	3.50
	Mailed on High Seas, unframed, from 1923	3.50
	Depose en mer/mailed on high sea, unframed, from 1937	1.50
	Machine with Paquebot/Posted/At Sea, from 1926	1.50
Suez:	Boxed or unboxed Paquebot, from 1902	2.00

(Full details of all Paquebot marks are given by Roger Hosking including many not included in the above lists.)

Posted on the High Seas

316

Oval cachets, Posted on the/High Seas, without ship's name	. .	6.00
As above but with name of ship or company:		
316 Royal Mail Steam Packet company	. . . .	6.50
R.M.S.P. Coy, dated cachets with ship's name.	. . . . . .	7.00
Donaldson Line, e.g. S.S. Saturnia.	. . . .	8.50
Canadian Pacific e.g. R.M.S. Metagama	. . . .	12.50
Other cachets with ships' names, e.g. Drina.	. . . . . .	7.50
Posted on Board ship/I.S., boxed T shaped.	. . . .	15.00

Packet Stamps: Overseas Mail

317

318

319

320

317 Circular, Falmouth Packet Lre, unframed green or black, from
1807 . . . . 60.00
Falmouth/Packet Letter, unframed green or black, from 1809 . 110.00
318 Unframed skeleton type marks with F (Falmouth) and Lisbon,
Malta, Brasil etc. 75.00
319 Oval marks with L (Liverpool) in centre and America above,
from 1840 . . . . 20.00
Circular Liverpool marks with America above, black or green,
from 1845 . . . . 10.00
Circular, Paid/Liverpool/US Packet/date, red or black from
1850s 12.00
320 Single circle types, eg. Southampton/Packet-Letter, from 1870s 8.00

Packet Stamps: Home Mail

*City of Dublin Steam Packet Company, Holyhead and Kingston
Service, 1860–1925*

321   **322**   **323**   **324**

321 H & K Pact, dated, with side arcs (backstamp) 15.00
    As above but surmounted by 'Night Mail' 65.00
    As above but duplex: with diamond numeral 186 . . . . . . 50.00
322 H & K Packet, double circle types, from 1880s 40.00
    H & K Packet, single circle type, from 1884 . . . . 30.00
323 As above but larger, C 1–4 (Connaught), L 1–4 (Leinster), M 1–
    4 (Munster), U 1–4 (Ulster), from 1901 . . . . 20.00
    As above but C5, L5, M5, or U5, rubber, in purple, H & K
    Packet P.O. 35.00
324 H & K Packet, double circle thick arcs broken by cross, from 1919 25.00

Belfast Packet Services

325

325 Prince of/Wales, circular, from 1843 . . . . 200.00
    Fleetwood & Belfast, circular, from 1843 . . . . 200.00

North Wales Coastal Services

POSTED ON

"LA MARGUERITE"

326

326 Posted on/"La Marguerite", unframed cachet in blue, from 1907 35.00
    Posted on La Marguerite, double circle in violet, from 1911 . . 85.00
    As above but sans-serif letters and crosses, from 1914 . . . . 100.00
    Posted on St. Tudno, oval purple cachet, from 1912 . . . . . . 175.00
    Posted on St. Elvies, circular purple cachet, from 1912 . . . . 175.00
    Per. Passgr. S. 'Trefiw-Belle', small violet cachet, from 1904 . . 175.00
    Posted on Snowdon 175.00

Isle of Man

MONA'S ISLE
327

327 Straight line Isle of Man Steam Packet Company cachets eg. Ben-
    My-Chree, Manx Maid, Mona's Isle, black, purple or red . 1.00
    Boxed cachets with vessel details, black, purple or red 1.50

CAMPBELTON
STEAM BOAT
328

328 Campbelton/Steam Boat, unframed, from 1830 . . . . 100.00

Skye Packet Services
Uist to/Dunvegan, unframed, from 1836 . . . . 200.00

Glasgow and Inveraray Steamboat Company

329

331

330

329 Posted on board/Lord of the Isles/Steamer, unframed, oval in
magenta 80.00
330 Posted on board S.S. 'Fairy Queen'/Loch Eck/Argyllshire,
double circle 80.00
331 R.M.S. 'Lord of the Isles', double oval with date, violet 50.00

D. Hutcheson & Co.

332

332 Posted on Board/'Columba'/date/D. Hutcheson & Co., double
oval 150.00

Lochgoil and Lochlong Steamboat Company

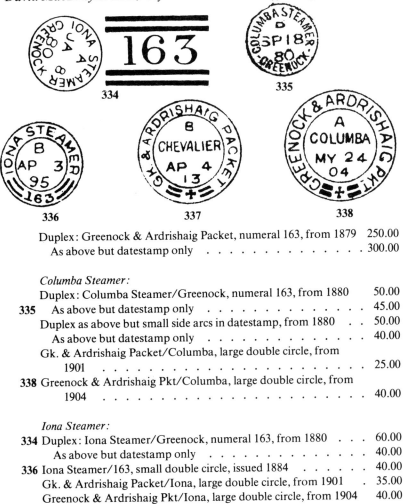

333

333 Posted on Board/'Edinburgh Castle'/Steamer, unframed oval   160.00

David MacBrayne Ltd., Clyde Steamer Post Offices, from 1879

Duplex: Greenock & Ardrishaig Packet, numeral 163, from 1879   250.00
As above but datestamp only 300.00

Columba Steamer:
Duplex: Columba Steamer/Greenock, numeral 163, from 1880   50.00
335 As above but datestamp only 45.00
Duplex as above but small side arcs in datestamp, from 1880 . . 50.00
As above but datestamp only 40.00
Gk. & Ardrishaig Packet/Columba, large double circle, from
1901 . . . . 25.00
338 Greenock & Ardrishaig Pkt/Columba, large double circle, from
1904 . . . . 40.00

Iona Steamer:
334 Duplex: Iona Steamer/Greenock, numeral 163, from 1880 . . . 60.00
As above but datestamp only 40.00
336 Iona Steamer/163, small double circle, issued 1884 . . . . . 40.00
Gk. & Ardrishaig Packet/Iona, large double circle, from 1901 . 35.00
Greenock & Ardrishaig Pkt/Iona, large double circle, from 1904 40.00

Grenadier Steamer:
Grenadier Steamer/666, double circle, from 1895 . . . . . . 200.00
Gk. & Ardrishaig Packet/Grenadier, large double circle, from
1901 . . . . 150.00
Greenock & Ardrishaig Pkt/Grenadier, large double circle, from
1903 . . . . 175.00

Chevalier Steamer:
337 Gk. & Ardrishaig Packet/Chevalier, large double circle, from
1902 . . . . 250.00

Gk. & Ardrishaig Packet, large double circle with ship name
removed, from 1916 . . . . 300.00

Cachets used on other coastal services
Ivanhoe, straight line, violet, 1904 . . . . 100.00
At sea/M.V. Royal Daffodil, red, 1951 . . . . 7.50

Postal Markings of the Royal Navy

| 339 | 340 | 341 |

Navy Post Office, straight line, unframed, 1840s 250.00
339 Navy Post Office, circular double arc type, in blue, 1850s . . . 150.00
Duplex: Plymouth/H.M.S. with numeral 620, from 1852 . . . 50.00
Duplex: Devonport/H.M.S., with numeral 250, 1860s 50.00
340 Fleet Post Office, single circle, from 1914 . . . . 7.50
Fleet P.O., single circle, from 1915 . . . . 7.50
Krag machines, fitted with F.P.O., dies for anonymity 2.50
Krag machines with dies of bars, crosses or plus signs 2.00
Locally made crosses, circles etc., probably rubber or cork . . . 4.00
341 Dumb cancel of seven or eight vertical bars across circle 1.00
Received from H.M. Ship/No charge to be Raised, boxed or
unboxed 1.25
First War Ship Censor Markings, with name of ship 7.50

RECEIVED FROM

H.M. SHIPS
342

RECEIVED FROM

H.M.S ....

ABROAD.
343

Machine, Received from H.M. Ships/No Charge to be raised, boxed	0.75
Machine, Received from H.M. Ships, boxed	0.75
342 As above but unboxed	0.65
343 Received from/H.M.S. . . . ./ Abroad, unframed	2.00

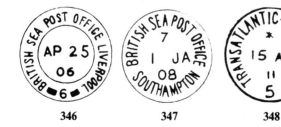

344   345

Received from/H.M. Ships, undated large circles, 1939	3.50
Received from/H.M. Ships, single circle, dated, 1939	3.00
344 Received from/H.M. Ships, double circle short thick arcs, 1939 .	3.00
London/H.M. Ships, double circle short thick arcs, 1939 . . .	4.00
Edinburgh/H.M. Ships, double circle short thick arcs, 1939 . .	4.00
Machine cancellations with census diamond instead of datestamp, 1939	2.00
Post Office/Maritime Mail, double circle short thick arcs, from 1942	2.00
Machine with 'Post Office' in circle for datestamp, Maritime Mail Slogan, black or red, from 1942	0.50
345 Post Office/Maritime Mail, rubber stamps, several designs . . .	1.75

Sea Post Offices

346   347   348   349

166

Transatlantic:

346 British Sea Post Office Liverpool/number 1–7, double circle from
1905 . . . . 50.00
347 British Sea Post Office/Southampton, numbered 1–10, single
circle, from 1907 . . . . 80.00
348 Transatlantic Post Office/number 1–11, single circle, 1908–14 . 18.00
349 Transatlantic Post Office Plymouth/number 1–4, double circle,
from 1905–7 . . . . 100.00

350

351

India/Aden route:
350 Sea Post Office, single circle 0.75

UK/South Africa route:
351 United Kingdom & S. Africa Sea P.O./number, double circle . . 30.00

Moveable Box Marks

352

353

Boxed M.B., Southampton service, in blue, from 1844 . . . . . 50.00
Milestone Southampton M.B. type with year in full, from 1857 . 25.00
352 As above but year with two figures only, from 1884 . . . . . 15.00
353 Circular Southampton M.B. types, 1893–1939 . . . . 8.50
Jersey Octagonal M.B. types, 1857–1914 . . . . 95.00
Jersey milestone type, 1914–39 . . . . 85.00
London circular M.B. type 9.50

15. MILITARY AND CAMP POSTMARKS

Wars and Campaigns

354

355

356

War of the Austrian Succession, 1740–48
354 Circled ('Armée Britannique') 400.00

French Revolutionary War, 1799
355 Army Bag, circular, in black 750.00
Army Bag, double oval, in red 1400.00

Napoleonic and Peninsular Wars, 1803–15
Lisbon town markings on campaign letters 50.00
356 Transport office double circle on Prisoner of War mail 150.00

Crimean War, 1854–56

357

358

357 Barred type with crown and stars, 1854–55 . . . . 250.00
358 Barred type with star and cyphers, 1855–56 . . . . 150.00
Post Office/British Army, unframed circular types, black, blue,
red or green from 1854 . . . . 50.00

(On pieces these postmarks are worth about a half of the prices quoted, on
loose stamps about a third.)

British Expeditions to Egypt (1882) and Sudan (1885)

359

359 British Army Post Office/Egypt, single circle 250.00
Barred type with B.A./E. . . . . ?

(On pieces these postmarks are worth about a third of the prices quoted, on loose stamps about a quarter.)

South African War (1899–1902)

360   **361**   **362**

360 Field Post Office B.O./British Army S. Africa, double circle . . 17.50
361   As above but without B.O. 20.00
     Field P.O./British Army S. Africa, single circle 7.00
     Army Post Office/South Africa, large circle with double rim and
     town or code 40.00
     Army Post Office/town, double circle types 7.00
     Army Post Office/T.P.O. double circles 25.00
362 Octagonal Natal Field Force marks 50.00
     Parcel marks with NFF, FPO, PAO, etc 50.00
     Instructional marks, 'Not to be found' etc 25.00

REMEMBER!
Prices in C.B.P. are minimum values
for a **clear strike on a clean card or cover.**
Have you read the notes
at the beginning?

First World War, 1914–19

(Note: Prices are for the cheapest period of use. Values vary according to location of unit and date. APO single circles used pre–1914 are worth considerably more. Full details are in Kennedy/Crabb and Proud.)

| 363 | 364 | 365 |

Advance Base Post Office, double circle	. . . .	7.50
Army Base Post Office, single circles	. . . .	0.45
363 As above but indexes 17–20 at foot	. . . .	17.50
364 Army Base Post Office, double circles	. . . .	0.45
365 Army Courier Office. (British Army of the Rhine, 1919–29)	. .	3.00
Army Letter Office/London, double circles	. . . .	6.00

| 366 | 367 |

366 Army Post Office, single circles with number of infantry brigade at foot:

1	0.50	5	0.50	9	2.50	13	1.00	17	1.00
2	1.00	6	2.50	10	2.50	14	1.00	18	1.00
3	1.00	7	2.50	11	2.50	15	1.00		
4	0.50	8	2.50	12	2.50	16	1.00		

367 Army Post Office, double circle with index at foot:

1	Army Base P.O.	. . 0.20	27	3 Inf. Div.	. . . 1.50	39	1st Army Troops	. 1.50
2	Postal Transfer Dt	. 0.20	28	4 Inf. Div.	. . . 1.00	40	I Corps	. . . . . 1.50
3	Postal Reg. DT	. . 0.20	29	5 Inf. Div.	. . . 1.00	41	II Corps	. . . . 1.50
4	(APO S14)	. . . . 0.30	30	6 Inf. Div.	. . . 1.00	42	Marseilles	. . . . 1.50
19	1 Inf. Div.	. . . . 2.00	31	1 Cav Bde.	. . . . 2.00	43	III Corp	. . . . 1.00
20	2 Inf. Div.	. . . . 3.00	32	2 Cav Bde.	. . . . 1.00	44	19 Inf. Bde.	. . . 1.50
21	3 Inf. Div.	. . . . 5.00	33	3 Cav Bde.	. . . . 5.00	45	2 Cav Div.	. . . 2.00
22	4 Inf. Div.	. . . . 1.00	34	4 Cav Bde.	. . . . 1.00	46	W. Front	. . . . 1.50
23	5 Inf. Div.	. . . . 1.00	35	5 Cav Bde.	. . . . 1.00	47	Postal Transfer	
24	6 Inf. Div.	. . . . 1.00	36	1 Cav Div.	. . . . 1.00		Depot	. . . . 0.50
25	1 Inf. Div.	. . . . 1.00	37	Sta. off. Boulogne	. 0.50	48	Sta. off. Orleans	. . 1.50
26	2 Inf. Div.	. . . . 1.00	38	Sta. off. St. Nazaire	1.00	49	Sta. off. Nantes	. . 1.00

50 Sta. off. Le Mans . 2.00	L15 Austria . . . . . ?	R50 50 Div. Rail . . . 1.00
51 I Corp Railhead . . 0.50	L16 Yugoslavia . . . 30.00	RN 50 Div. Rail . . . 1.00
52 II Corp Railhead . 1.00	PB1 Russia 15.00	R51 51 Div. Rail . . . 0.50
53 III Corp Railhead . 1.50	PB2 Russia 15.00	RHD 51 Div. Rail . . . 2.50
54 W. Front 2.00	PP1 Italy 2.00	R52 52 Div. Rail . . . 5.00
55 Lahore Div. Train . 3.00	R1 I Corps Rail . . . 0.50	R53 53 Div. Rail . . . ?
56 W. Front 2.00	R2 II Corps Rail . . 0.50	R54 54 Div. Rail . . . ?
57 W. Front 2.00	R2A 27 Div. Rail . . . 5.00	R55 55 Div. Rail . . . 0.50
58 W. Front 1.50	R3 III Corps Rail . . . 0.40	R56 56 Div. Rail . . . 1.00
59 W. Front 2.00	R4 IV Corps Rail . . . 0.40	R57 57 Div. Rail . . . 2.00
60 7 Cav Bde. 1.50	R5 V Corps Rail . . . 0.40	R58 58 Div. Rail . . . 1.00
61 W. Front 2.00	R5A Branch off V Corps 5.00	R59 59 Div. Rail . . . 1.00
62 7 Div. H.Q. 2.00	R6 6 Div. Rail 0.40	R60 60 Div. Rail . . . 3.00
63 7 Div. Train . . . 2.00	R7 7 Div. Rail . . . 1.00	R61 61 Div. Rail . . . 1.00
64 20 Bde. 2.00	R8 8 Div. Rail 0.50	R62 62 Div. Rail . . . 1.00
65 21 Bde. 2.00	R9 9 Div. Rail 0.50	R63 63 Div. Rail . . . 1.00
66 22 Bde. 2.00	R10 10 Div. Rail . . 15.00	R64–5 not used
67 IV Corp H.Q. . . . 3.00	R11 11 Div. Rail . . . 1.00	R66 66 Div. 1.00
68 8 Div. H.Q. 2.00	R12 12 Div. Rail . . . 0.50	R67–73 not used
69 8 Div. Train . . . 2.00	R13 13 Div. Rail . . . 0.50	R74 74 Div. 2.00
70 23 Bde. 2.00	R14 14 Div. Rail . . . 0.50	R75 75 Div. Rail not used
71 24 Bde. 3.00	R15 15 Div. Rail . . . 0.50	RA1 1 Rail 0.50
72 25 Bde. 3.00	R16 16 Div. Rail . . . 0.40	RA2 2 Rail 1.00
73 W. Front 4.00	R17 17 Div. Rail . . . 0.40	RB Guards Div. Rail . 0.50
74 W. Front 4.00	R18 18 Div. Rail . . . 0.50	RC1 1 Cav Div. Rail . 0.30
75 Sta. off. Paris . . . 3.00	R19 19 Div. Rail . . . 0.40	RC2 2 Cav Div. Rail . 0.30
76 W. Front 4.00	R20 20 Div. Rail . . . 0.40	RC3 3 Cav Div. Rail . 0.50
77 W. Front 3.00	R21 21 Div. Rail . . . 0.80	RC4 Cav Div. Rail . . . 4.00
78 Sta. off. Dunkirk . 3.00	R22 22 Div. Rail . . . 2.00	RG G.H.Q. Rail . . . 4.00
79 W. Front 1.50	R23 23 Div. Rail . . . 1.00	RX16 XVI Corps Rail . 20.00
80 W. Front 1.50	R24 24 Div. Rail . . . 0.50	RY used by 59–63 Div. 1.00
81 ? W. Front	R25 25 Div. Rail . . . 1.00	S1 Abbeville 0.20
82 Sta. off. Etretat? . 3.00	R26 26 Div. Rail . . . 2.00	S2 France 0.50
83–4 ?	R27 27 Div. Rail . . . 3.00	S3 France 1.00
85 W. Front 5.00	R28 28 Div. Rail . . . 2.00	S4 Belgium 1.00
86 27th Div. Train . 10.00	R29 29 Div. Rail . . . 1.00	S5 France 0.50
87 W. Front 5.00	R30 30 Div. Rail . . . 1.00	S6 France 0.50
88 W. Front . . . 10.00	R31 31 Div. Rail . . . 2.00	S7 France 0.50
89 W. Front 5.00	R32 32 Div. Rail . . . 2.00	S8 France 0.50
91–3 ?	R33 33 Div. Rail . . . 1.00	S9 France 3.00
94 W. Front . . . 10.00	R34 34 Div. Rail . . . 1.00	S10 France 0.20
100 Etaples? 5.00	R35 35 Div. Rail . . . 0.50	S11 Etaples 0.40
GR German Railhead . 5.00	R36 36 Div. Rail . . . 0.50	S12 Harfleur 0.20
L1 Italy, Base 2.00	R37 37 Div. Rail . . . 1.00	S13 Le Treport 0.20
L2 Italy 3.00	R38 38 Div. Rail . . . 1.00	S14 France 0.30
L3 Italy 4.00	R39 39 Div. Rail . . . 0.50	S15 Rouen 0.20
L4 Italy 6.00	R40 40 Div. Rail . . . 1.00	S16 Serqueux 0.20
L5 Italy 6.00	R41 41 Div. Rail . . . 1.00	S17 Etaples 0.20
L6 Italy 6.00	R42 42 Div. Rail . . . 1.00	S18 Camiers 0.30
L7 Italy 5.00	R43–45 not used	S19 France 0.40
L8 Italy 4.00	R46 46 Div. Rail . . . 0.50	S20 France 0.40
L9 Italy 5.00	R47 47 Div. Rail . . . 1.00	S21 France 0.40
L11 Italy 5.00	RL 47 Div. Rail . . 10.00	S22 Etaples 1.00
L12 Italy 7.50	R48 48 Div. Rail . . . 0.50	S23 France 0.50
L13 France 7.50	R49 49 Div. Rail . . . 1.00	S24 Calais 0.40
L14 Italy 30.00	RWR 49 Div. Rail . . . 5.00	S25 France 0.40

S26	France	0.50	S65	Belgium	0.50	S104	Nancy	12.00
S27	Caudebec	1.50	S66	France	0.50	S105	France	4.00
S28	St. Saens	1.00	S67	Cassel	3.00	S106	Belgium	12.00
S29	France	1.50	S68	France	1.00	S107	Belgium	4.00
S30	France	0.40	S69	Lens	10.00	S108	France	12.00
S31	France	0.40	S70	Italy	3.00	S109	Motteville	7.50
S32	France	0.40	S71	France	1.00	S110	Antwerp	12.00
S33	France	0.50	S72	France	2.00	S111	Dieppe	5.00
S34	France	1.00	S73	Vendroux	0.50	S112	W. Front	?
S35	France	1.00	S74	France	1.00	S113	France	?
S36	Zeneghem	2.00	S75	France	0.50	S114	Spa	5.00
S37	France	0.40	S76	France	0.50	S115	Charleroi	5.00
S38	Wimereaux	0.50	S77	France	0.50	S116	Amiens	4.00
S39	Dannes	0.50	S78	France	0.50	S117	W. Front	2.00
S40	France	1.00	S79	Le Touquet	0.50	S118	Lille	12.00
S41	France	0.50	S80	France	0.50	S119	Cambrai	4.00
S42	France	0.50	S81	France	0.50	S120	Germany	5.00
S43	France	0.50	S82	Rue	5.00	S121	W. Front	?
S44	Buchy	1.00	S83	Trouville	0.50	SX1	Greece	1.00
S45	France	1.00	S84	Lilliers	2.00	SX2	Salonika	2.00
S46	France	0.50	S85	France	3.00	SX3	Greece	4.00
S47	France	0.50	S86	France	2.00	SX4	Salonika	3.00
S48	France	1.00	S87	France	2.00	SX5	Greece	2.00
S49	France	1.50	S88	Boulogne	3.00	SX6	Vertekop	7.50
S50	Cherbourg	0.50	S89	France	5.00	SX7	Stavros	7.50
S51	France	0.50	S90	France	2.00	SX8	Greece	3.00
S52	France	0.50	S91	France	4.00	SX9	Greece	7.50
S53	France	0.50	S92	Bethune	2.00	SX10	Greece	7.50
S54	France	0.50	S93	Courban	5.00	SX11	Greece	4.00
S55	Marseilles	2.00	S94	Hesdin	1.00	SX12	Greece	7.50
S56	France	0.50	S95	St. Pol	3.00	SX13	Eurendzik	5.00
S57	France	3.00	S96	France	?	SX14	Greece	20.00
S58	France	1.00	S97	Nancy	7.50	SZ1	Turkey	3.00
S59	France	0.50	S98	France	?	SZ2	Greece	3.00
S60	France	0.50	S99	France	2.00	SZ3	Turkey	5.00
S61	France	1.00	S100	Taranto	3.00	T42	42 Div. Train	0.80
S62	Cassel	0.50	S101	Arquata	4.50	T62	62 Div. Train	1.00
S63	W. Front	0.50	S102	France	3.00	Y1	Turkey	1.00
S64	France	1.00	S103	Aulnois	7.50			

368

368 Army Post Office, skeletons, various sizes, usually with index at base:

	No Index	. . . 6.00	SX9	Greece	. . . . 10.00	SZ22	Port Said	. . . . 2.00
1	Base Army P.O.	. . . 0.20	SX11	Greece	. . . . 12.00	SZ23	Egypt	. . . . . 15.00
A	Postal Transfer Dt	. 0.50	SX12	Greece	. . . . 10.00	SZ24	Alexandria	. . . . 4.00
B	?		SX13	Eurendzik	. . . . 5.00	SZ24X	Egypt	. . . . 4.00
C	GHQ?	. 4.00	SX14	Greece	. . . . 20.00	SZ25	Egypt	. . . . . . 7.50
E	W. Front	. . . 5.00	SX15	Greece	. . . . 10.00	SZ26	Egypt	. . . . 10.00
F2	Abbasia	. . . . 4.00	SX16	Greece	. . . . 20.00	SZ26T	Egypt	. . . 15.00
R5	V Corps Rail	. . . 5.00	SX17	Sarigol	. . . . 15.00	SZ27	Egypt	. . . . . . 7.50
R22	22 Div. Rail	. . 10.00	SX18	Burgas	. . . . . . ?	SZ28	Egypt	. . . . . . 7.50
R26	26 Div. Rail	. . 10.00	SX19	Rupel	. . . . 20.00	SZ32	Palestine	. . . . 25.00
R27	27 Div. Rail	. . . 3.00	SX20	Hirsova	. . . . 20.00	SZ33	Egypt	. . . . 10.00
R28	28 Div. Rail	. . 10.00	SX21	Bulgaria	. . . . 30.00	SZ34	Palestine	. . . . 15.00
RW	W.F. Rail	. . . 25.00	SX22	Batum	. . . . . 50.00	SZ35	Palestine	. . . . 17.50
RX16	16 Cps Rail	. . . 20.00	SX23	Greece	. . . . . . ?	SZ36	Egypt	. . . . 10.00
RZ	N.Z. Div. Rail	. . . ?	SX24	Greece	. . . . . . ?	SZ37	Lebanon	. . . . 12.50
S15	Rouen	. 2.00	SY1	Chanak	. . . . 10.00	SZ38	Palestine	. . . . 25.00
S17	France	. . . . 20.00	SY2	Turkey	. . . . 15.00	SZ39	Palestine	. . . . 25.00
S28	France	. . . . 3.00	SY3	Bostanji	. . . . 15.00	SZ40	Jaffa	. . . . . 20.00
S35	France	. . . . 6.00	SY4	Turkey	. . . . 15.00	SZ41	Egypt	. . . . 10.00
S46	France	. . . . 4.00	SY5	Turkey	. . . . 30.00	SZ42	Egypt	. . . . 12.50
S47	France	. . . . 4.00	SZ1	Turkey	. . . . . 3.00	SZ43	El Arish	. . . . 15.00
S50	France	. . . . 3.00	SZ2	Greece	. . . . . 4.00	SZ44	Jerusalem	. . . 10.00
S56	France	. . . . 5.00	SZ3	Egypt	. . . . . 3.00	SZ45	Jaffa	. . . . 20.00
S59	France	. . . . 2.50	DLO	SZ3 Egypt	. . 30.00	SZ46	Palestine	. . . 25.00
S72	France	. . . . 9.00	SZ4	Egypt	. . . . . 2.00	SZ47	Palestine	. . . 25.00
S76	France	. . . . 5.00	SZ5	Turkey	. . . . . 4.00	SZ48	Palestine	. . . 25.00
S77	France	. . . . 5.00	SZ6	Greece	. . . . . 6.00	SZ49	Mulebbis	. . . 20.00
S81	France	. . . . 2.50	SZ7	Malta	. . . . . 5.00	SZ50	Turkey	. . . . 30.00
S83	France	. . . . 0.50	SZ8	Greece	. . . . . 7.50	SZ51	Egypt	. . . . 10.00
S86	France	. . . . 6.00	SZ9	Egypt	. . . . . 5.00	SZ52	Palestine	. . . 30.00
S91	France	. . . 12.00	SZ10	Cairo	. . . . . 1.00	SZ53	Palestine	. . . 25.00
S94	France	. . . . 5.00	SZ10T	Cairo	. . . . . 1.00	SZ54	Egypt	. . . . 15.00
S95	France	. . . . 6.00	SZ11	Cairo	. . . . . 4.00	SZ56	Syria	. . . . . . ?
S97	France	. . . . 15.00	SZ12	Egypt	. . . . . 3.00	SZ58	Egypt	. . . . . . 7.50
S101	Italy	. . . . 13.50	SZ13	Egypt	. . . . . 5.00	SZ61	Safed	. . . . 30.00
S111	France	. . . . 5.00	SZ14	Egypt	. . . . . 5.00	SZ62	Damacus	. . . 15.00
SX1	Greece	. . . . 4.00	SZ15	Egypt	. . . . . 5.00	X	Greece	. . . . 1.00
SX2	Greece	. . . . 6.00	SZ16	Egypt	. . . . 10.00	Y1	Chanak	. . . . 10.00
SX3	Greece	. . . . 4.00	SZ17	Egypt	. . . . . 5.00	Y2	Turkey	. . . 15.00
SX4	Greece	. . . . 6.00	SZ18	Egypt	. . . . . 7.50	Y3	Bostanji	. . . 15.00
SX5	Greece	. . . . 6.00	SZ19	Egypt	. . . . . 7.50	Base X	Greece	. . . . 1.00
SX7	Stavros	. . . . 15.00	SZ20	Egypt	. . . . . 7.50		Kantara	. . . . . 1.50
SX8	Greece	. . . . 3.00	SZ21	Egypt	. . . . . 6.00			

ARMY POST OFFICE 3

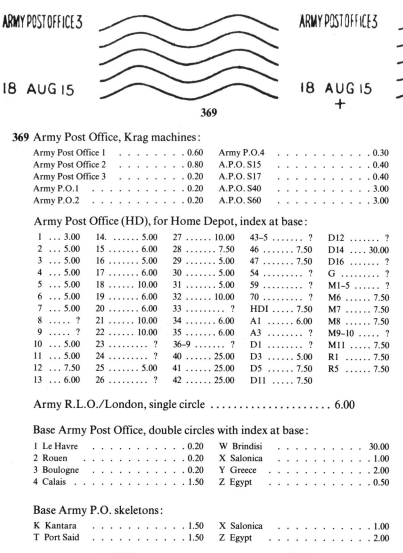

18 AUG 15

369

ARMY POST OFFICE 3

18 AUG 15
+

369 Army Post Office, Krag machines:

Army Post Office 1	. . . . 0.60	Army P.O.4	. . . . 0.30
Army Post Office 2	. . . . 0.80	A.P.O. S15	. . . . 0.40
Army Post Office 3	. . . . 0.20	A.P.O. S17	. . . . 0.40
Army P.O.1	. . . . 0.20	A.P.O. S40	. . . . 3.00
Army P.O.2	. . . . 0.20	A.P.O. S60	. . . . 3.00

Army Post Office (HD), for Home Depot, index at base:

1 ... 3.00	14. ...... 5.00	27 ...... 10.00	43–5 .... ?	D12 .... ?
2 ... 5.00	15 .... 6.00	28 .... 7.50	46 .... 7.50	D14 .... 30.00
3 ... 5.00	16 .... 5.00	29 .... 5.00	47 .... 7.50	D16 .... ?
4 ... 5.00	17 .... 6.00	30 .... 5.00	54 .... ?	G .... ?
5 ... 5.00	18 ...... 10.00	31 .... 5.00	59 .... ?	M1–5 ...... ?
6 ... 5.00	19 .... 6.00	32 ...... 10.00	70 .... ?	M6 ...... 7.50
7 ... 5.00	20 .... 6.00	33 .... ?	HDI 7.50	M7 ...... 7.50
8 ..... ?	21 ...... 10.00	34 .... 6.00	A1 ...... 6.00	M8 ...... 7.50
9 ..... ?	22 ...... 10.00	35 .... 6.00	A3 .... ?	M9–10 ..... ?
10 ... 5.00	23 .... ?	36–9 .... ?	D1 .... ?	M11 ..... 7.50
11 ... 5.00	24 .... ?	40 ...... 25.00	D3 ...... 5.00	R1 ...... 7.50
12 ... 7.50	25 .... 5.00	41 ...... 25.00	D5 ...... 7.50	R5 ...... 7.50
13 ... 6.00	26 .... ?	42 ...... 25.00	D11 ..... 7.50	

Army R.L.O./London, single circle 6.00

Base Army Post Office, double circles with index at base:

1 Le Havre	. . . . 0.20	W Brindisi	. . . . 30.00
2 Rouen	. . . . 0.20	X Salonica	. . . . 1.00
3 Boulogne	. . . . 0.20	Y Greece	. . . . 2.00
4 Calais	. . . . 1.50	Z Egypt	. . . . 0.50

Base Army P.O. skeletons:

K Kantara	. . . . 1.50	X Salonica	. . . . 1.00
T Port Said	. . . . 1.50	Z Egypt	. . . . 2.00

370

371

Dublin marks used after Easter rising, 1916

Parcle Post types **370** 5.00
Single rim skeletons 7.50
Double rim skeletons 8.50

Field Post Office, double circles (371) or skeletons with index at base:

Index	Used by	d/c	sk	Index	Used by	d/c	sk
1	1 Inf. Bde. 1 Div.	0.30	0.30	43	43 Bde. 14 Div.	0.30	
2	2 Inf. Bde. 1 Div.	0.30		44	44 Bde. 15 Div.	0.30	
3	3 Inf. Bde. 1 Div.	0.50		45	45 Bde. 15 Div.	0.30	
4	4 Inf. Bde. 2 Div.	0.80		46	46 Bde. 15 Div.	0.30	
5	5 Inf. Bde. 2 Div.	0.30		47	47 Bde. 16 Div.	0.30	
6	6 Bde. 2 Div.	0.30		48	48 Bde. 16 Div.	0.30	
7	7 Bde. 3 Div.	0.30		49	49 Bde. 16 Div.	0.50	
8	8 Bde. 3 Div.	0.30		50	50 Bde. 17 Div.	0.30	
9	9 Bde. 3 Div.	0.30		51	51 Bde. 17 Div.	0.30	
10	10 Bde. 4 Div.	0.40		52	52 Bde. 17 Div.	0.30	
11	11 Bde. 4 Div.	0.30		53	53 Bde. 18 Div.	0.30	
12	12 Bde. 4 Div.	0.30		54	54 Bde. 18 Div.	0.40	
13	13 Bde. 5 Div.	0.40		55	55 Bde. 18 Div.	0.30	
14	14 Bde. 5 Div.	0.30		56	56 Bde. 19 Div.	0.30	
15	15 Bde. 5 Div.	0.30		57	57 Bde. 19 Div.	0.50	
16	16 Bde. 6 Div.	0.30		58	58 Bde. 19 Div.	0.30	
17	17 Bde. 6 Div.	0.30		59	59 Bde. 20 Div.	0.30	
18	18 Bde. 6 Div.	6.00		60	60 Bde. 20 Div.	0.30	
19	19 Bde. 33 Div.	0.30		61	61 Bde. 20 Div.	0.30	
20	20 Bde. 7 Div.	0.30		62	62 Bde. 21 Div.	0.30	
21	21 Bde. 7 Div.	0.30		63	63 Bde. 21 Div.	0.30	
22	22 Bde. 7 Div.	0.30		64	64 Bde. 21 Div.	0.30	
23	23 Bde. 8 Div.	0.50		65	65 Bde. 22 Div.	2.00	
24	24 Bde. 8 Div.	0.40		66	66 Bde. 22 Div.	2.00	
25	25 Bde. 8 Div.	0.30		67	67 Bde. 22 Div.	2.00	
26	26 Bde. 9 Div.	0.30		68	68 Bde. 23 Div.	0.30	
27	27 Bde. 9 Div.	0.30		69	69 Bde. 23 Div.	0.50	
28	28 Bde. 9 Div.	0.50		70	70 Bde. 23 Div.	0.40	
29	29 Bde. 10 Div.	6.00		71	71 Bde. 24 Div.	0.40	
30	30 Bde. 10 Div.	5.00		72	72 Bde. 24 Div.	0.40	
31	31 Bde. 10 Div.	5.00	10.00	73	73 Bde. 24 Div.	0.40	
32	32 Bde. 11 Div.	5.00		74	74 Bde. 25 Div.	0.40	
33	33 Bde. 11 Div.	0.50		75	75 Bde. 25 Div.	0.40	
34	34 Bde. 11 Div.	0.30		76	76 Bde. 25 Div.	0.50	
35	35 Bde. 12 Div.	0.30		77	77 Bde. 26 Div.	2.00	
36	36 Bde. 12 Div.	0.30		78	78 Bde. 26 Div.	2.00	
37	37 Bde. 12 Div.	0.30		79	79 Bde. 26 Div.	3.00	
38	38 Bde. 13 Div.	10.00		80	80 Bde. 27 Div.	1.00	
39	39 Bde. 13 Div.	10.00		81	81 Bde. 27 Div.	0.50	
40	40 Bde. 13 Div.	10.00		82	82 Bde. 27 Div.	0.50	
41	41 Bde. 14 Div.	0.30		83	83 Bde. 28 Div.	0.50	
42	42 Bde. 14 Div.	0.30		84	84 Bde. 28 Div.	0.50	

Index	Used by	d/c	sk	Index	Used by	d/c	sk
85	85 Bde. 28 Div.	0.50		6L	142 Bde. 47 Div.	0.90	
86	86 Bde. 29 Div.	0.50		143	143 Bde. 48 Div.	0.30	
87	87 Bde. 29 Div.	0.50		1SM	143 Bde. 48 Div.	0.60	
88	88 Bde. 29 Div.	0.40		144	144 Bde. 48 Div.	0.30	
89	89 Bde. 30 Div.	0.30		2SM	144 Bde. 48 Div.	0.60	
90	90 Bde. 30 Div.	0.30		145	145 Bde. 48 Div.	0.30	
91	91 Bde. 30 Div.	0.40		3SM	145 Bde. 48 Div.	0.60	
92	92 Bde. 31 Div.	0.30		146	146 Bde. 49 Div.	0.30	
93	93 Bde. 31 Div.	0.30		1WR	146 Bde. 49 Div.	1.50	
94	94 Bde. 31 Div.	0.30		147	147 Bde. 49 Div.	0.30	
95	95 Bde. 32 Div.	0.30		2WR	147 Bde. 49 Div.	1.50	
96	96 Bde. 32 Div.	0.30		148	148 Bde. 49 Div.	0.30	
97	97 Bde. 32 Div.	0.50		3WR	148 Bde. 49 Div.	0.30	
98	98 Bde. 33 Div.	0.30		149	149 Bde. 50 Div.	0.30	
99	99 Bde. 33 Div.	0.30		1N	149 Bde. 50 Div.	3.00	
100	100 Bde. 33 Div.	0.30		150	150 Bde. 50 Div.	0.30	
101	101 Bde. 34 Div.	0.40		2N	150 Bde. 50 Div.	3.00	
102	102 Bde. 34 Div.	0.40		151	151 Bde. 50 Div.	0.30	
103	103 Bde. 34 Div.	0.30		3N	151 Bde. 50 Div.	3.00	
104	104 Bde. 35 Div.	0.40		152	152 Bde. 51 Div.	0.30	
105	105 Bde. 35 Div.	0.40		1HD	152 Bde. 51 Div.	3.00	
106	106 Bde. 35 Div.	0.50		153	153 Bde. 51 Div.	0.40	
107	107 Bde. 36 Div.	0.50		2HD	153 Bde. 51 Div.	4.00	
108	108 Bde. 36 Div.	0.40		154	154 Bde. 51 Div.	0.40	
109	109 Bde. 36 Div.	0.40		3HD	154 Bde. 51 Div.	0.40	
110	110 Bde. 37 Div.	0.30		155	155 Bde. 52 Div.	1.00	1.00
111	111 Bde. 37 Div.	0.30		1LL	155 Bde. 52 Div.	1.00	
112	112 Bde. 37 Div.	0.30		156	156 Bde. 52 Div.	1.00	
113	113 Bde. 38 Div.	0.30		2LL	156 Bde. 52 Div.	2.00	
114	114 Bde. 38 Div.	0.30		157	157 Bde. 52 Div.	1.00	
115	115 Bde. 38 Div.	0.40		3LL	157 Bde. 52 Div.	1.00	
116	116 Bde. 39 Div.	0.30		158	158 Bde. 53 Div.	10.00	
117	117 Bde. 39 Div.	0.30		159	159 Bde. 53 Div.	7.50	
118	118 Bde. 39 Div.	0.30		160	160 Bde. 53 Div.	10.00	
119	119 Bde. 40 Div.	0.80		161	161 Bde. 54 Div.	7.50	
120	120 Bde. 40 Div.	0.80		161T	161 Bde. 54 Div.		15.00
121	121 Bde. 40 Div.	0.40		162	162 Bde. 54 Div.	6.00	
122	122 Bde. 41 Div.	0.40		163	163 Bde. 54 Div.	6.00	
123	123 Bde. 41 Div.	0.40		164	164 Bde. 55 Div.	0.30	
124	124 Bde. 41 Div.	0.50		165	165 Bde. 55 Div.	0.30	
125	125 Bde. 42 Div.	0.40		166	166 Bde. 55 Div.	0.30	
126	126 Bde. 42 Div.	0.50		167	167 Bde. 56 Div.	0.50	
127	127 Bde. 42 Div.	0.50		168	168 Bde. 56 Div.	1.00	
128–36	Not used			169	169 Bde. 56 Div.	0.40	
137	137 Bde. 46 Div.	0.40		170	170 Bde. 57 Div.	1.00	
1M	137 Bde. 46 Div.	0.80		171	171 Bde. 57 Div.	0.80	
138	138 Bde. 46 Div.	0.40		172	172 Bde. 57 Div.	1.00	
2M	138 Bde. 46 Div.	0.80		173	173 Bde. 58 Div.	0.40	
139	139 Bde. 46 Div.	0.40		174	174 Bde. 58 Div.	1.00	
3M	139 Bde. 46 Div.	0.80		175	175 Bde. 58 Div.	0.50	
140	140 Bde. 47 Div.	0.30		176	176 Bde. 59 Div.	1.00	
4L	140 Bde. 47 Div.	0.90		177	177 Bde. 59 Div.	2.00	
141	141 Bde. 47 Div.	0.30		178	178 Bde. 59 Div.	1.00	
5L	141 Bde. 47 Div.	0.90		179	179 Bde. 60 Div.	1.00	1.00
142	142 Bde. 47 Div.	0.30		X179	179 Bde. 60 Div.		2.00

Index	Used by	d/c	sk
180	180 Bde. 60 Div.	1.00	
X180	180 Bde. 60 Div.		1.00
181	181 Bde. 60 Div.	1.00	1.00
X181	181 Bde. 60 Div.		1.00
182	182 Bde. 61 Div.	0.60	
183	183 Bde. 61 Div.	0.60	
184	184 Bde. 61 Div.	0.80	
185	185 Bde. 62 Div.	1.00	
186	186 Bde. 62 Div.	1.00	
187	187 Bde. 62 Div.	1.00	
188	188 Bde. 63 Div.	1.00	
NL1	188 Bde. 63 Div.	1.00	
189	189 Bde. 63 Div.	1.00	
NL2	189 Bde. 63 Div.	1.00	
190	190 Bde. 63 Div.	0.40	
NL3	190 Bde. 63 Div.	0.40	
191–96	Not used		
197	197 Bde. 66 Div.	1.00	
198	198 Bde. 66 Div.	1.00	
199	199 Bde. 66 Div.	1.00	
200	N. Russia	30.00	
201	Russia	25.00	
202	N. Ireland	25.00	
203–27	Not used		
228	Salonika	10.00	10.00
229	229 Bde.	1.00	
2DY	229 Bde.		10.00
HY	229 Bde.		10.00
SWY2	229 Bde.	1.00	
230	230 Bde. 74 Div.	1.00	1.00
3DY	230 Bde. 74 Div.		15.00
EY	230 Bde. 74 Div.	15.00	
231	231 Bde.	1.50	
4DY	231 Bde.		20.00
WBY	231 Bde.	7.50	
232	232 Bde. 75 Div.	7.50	7.50
233	233 Bde. 75 Div.	7.50	20.00
234	234 Bde. 75 Div.	7.50	7.50
A1	1 Army H.Q.	0.30	
AT1	1 Army H.Q.	0.30	
A2	2 Army H.Q.	0.40	2.00
A2A	Adv. Army H.Q.		0.40
A3	3 Army H.Q.	0.40	
A4	4 Army H.Q.	0.40	
A4X	Adv. Army H.Q.	1.20	
A5	5 Army H.Q.	0.50	
AR	5 Army H.Q.	0.50	
A5X	Adv. Army H.Q.	0.50	
AD1	1 A.D.O.	0.40	0.40
AD2	2 A.D.O.	0.40	
AD3	3 A.D.O.	0.50	
AD4	4 A.D.O.	1.00	
AD5	5 A.D.O.	1.00	
AGX	Adv. G.H.Q.	?	
AN8–14	Australian Bdes.?		

Index	Used by	d/c	sk
AQ3	3 Tank Group H.Q.	1.00	
1B	1 Guards Bde.	0.30	
2B	2 Guards Bde.	0.30	
3B	3 Guards Bde.	0.40	
4B	4 Guards Bde	0.50	
C1	1 Cavalry Bde.	0.30	
C2	2 Cavalry Bde.	0.30	
C3	3 Cavalry Bde.	0.30	
C4	4 Cavalry Bde.	0.30	
C5	5 Cavalry Bde.	0.30	
C6	6 Cavalry Bde.	0.30	
C7	7 Cavalry Bde.	0.30	
C8	8 Cavalry Bde.	0.40	
C9	9 Cavalry Bde.	0.30	
C10	10 Cavalry Bde.	20.00	20.00
2Y	10 Cavalry Bde.	25.00	
6Y	10 Cavalry Bde.	20.00	
C11	11 Cavalry Bde.	15.00	
4Y	11 Cavalry Bde.	15.00	
8Y	11 Cavalry Bde.	15.00	
C12	12 Cavalry Bde.	20.00	
22Y	12 Cavalry Bde.	25.00	15.00
NMY	12 Cavalry Bde.	15.00	
C13	13 Cavalry Bde.	20.00	20.00
5Y	13 Cavalry Bde.	10.00	
C14	14 Cavalry Bde.		25.00
3Y	14 Cavalry Bde.		6.00
7Y	14 Cavalry Bde.	6.00	6.00
C15	15 Cavalry Bde.	?	?
CD3	Kantara	15.00	
C18	Camel Corps		25.00
M1	Camel Corps	20.00	20.00
CZ	Camel Corps	20.00	20.00
D1	1 Div. H.Q.	0.50	
D2	2 Div. H.Q.	0.50	
D3	3 Div. H.Q.	0.40	
D4	4 Div. H.Q.	0.50	
D5	5 Div. H.Q.	0.40	
D6	6 Div. H.Q.	0.40	
D7	7 Div. H.Q.	1.00	
D8	8 Div. H.Q.	0.50	
D9	9 Div. H.Q.	0.50	
D10	10 Div. H.Q.	5.00	
D11	11 Div. H.Q.	0.50	
D12	12 Div. H.Q.	0.50	
D13	13 Div. H.Q.	15.00	
D14	14 Div. H.Q.	0.50	
D15	15 Div. H.Q.	0.40	
D16	16 Div. H.Q.	0.40	
D17	17 Div. H.Q.	0.40	
D18	18 Div. H.Q.	0.50	
D19	19 Div. H.Q.	0.40	
D20	20 Div. H.Q.	0.40	
D21	21 Div. H.Q.	0.40	
D22	22 Div. H.Q.	2.00	

Index	Used by	d/c	sk		Index	Used by	d/c	sk
D23	23 Div. H.Q.	0.60			DB	Guards Div.	0.50	
D24	24 Div. H.Q.	0.50			DC1	1 Cavalry Div.	0.30	
D25	25 Div. H.Q.	0.80			DC2	2 Cavalry Div.	0.40	
D26	26 Div. H.Q.	2.00			DC3	3 Cavalry Div.	0.40	
D27	27 Div. H.Q.	0.50			DC4	4 Cavalry Div. H.Q.	3.00	
D28	28 Div. H.Q.	2.00			DM3	4 Cavalry Div. H.Q.	20.00	
D29	29 Div. H.Q.	0.40			DC5	5 Cavalry Div. H.Q.	20.00	
D30	30 Div. H.Q.	0.40			DM4	5 Cavalry Div. H.Q.	15.00	
D31	31 Div. H.Q.	0.40			DK	W. Front	0.50	
D32	32 Div. H.Q.	0.80			DM2	Australian mtd Div.	?	
D33	33 Div. H.Q.	0.50			DM1	A and NZ mtd Div.	?	
D34	34 Div. H.Q.	0.40			DN	W. Front	0.40	
D35	35 Div. H.Q.	0.30			DP1–DP4 Canadian Div. H.Q.		1.00	
D36	36 Div. H.Q.	0.30			DQ	Tank corps H.Q.	1.00	
D37	37 Div. H.Q.	0.40			DW	Egypt		25.00
D38	38 Div. H.Q.	0.60			DW1–DW5 Australian Div. H.Q.		?	
D39	39 Div. H.Q.	0.40			DX1–DX4 Canadian Div. H.Q.		0.40	
D40	40 Div. H.Q.	0.80			DY	2 mtd Div. H.Q.	15.00	
D41	41 Div. H.Q.	0.50			DZ	N.Z. Div. H.Q.	0.80	
D42	42 Div. H.Q.	0.40			EY	1 mtd Bde.	20.00	
D43–45	Not used				F1	E.F.F. H.Q.		10.00
D46	46 Div. H.Q.	0.60			F2	Abbasia		4.00
DM	46 Div. H.Q.	2.40			FD1	Field Depot Italy	3.00	
D47	47 Div. H.Q.	0.60			FD2	Field Depot Italy	7.00	
DL2	47 Div. H.Q.	2.40			FD3	Field Depot Italy	7.50	
D48	48 Div. H.Q.	0.40			FD4	Field Depot Italy	7.50	
DSM	48 Div. H.Q.	1.20			FD5	Field Depot Italy	6.00	
D49	49 Div. H.Q.	0.60			FD6–FD7 Not used			
DWR	49 Div. H.Q.	3.00			FD8	Field Depot Italy	5.00	
D50	50 Div.	0.40			FD9	Field Depot Italy	5.00	
DN	50 Div.	2.00			G	G.H.Q. B.E.F.	0.30	
D51	51 Div. H.Q.	0.50			LSK	G.H.Q. B.E.F.		0.30
DHD	51 Div. H.Q.	0.50			GM	G.H.Q. E.E.F.		5.00
D52	52 Div. H.Q.	2.00			GM1	G.H.Q. E.E.F.		10.00
DLL	52 Div. H.Q.	20.00			GM2	G.H.Q. E.E.F.		5.00
D53	53 Div. H.Q.	10.00			GQ	Italy G.H.Q.	4.00	
D54	54 Div. H.Q.	10.00			GQ2	Italy G.H.Q.	4.00	
D55	55 Div. H.Q.	0.50			GX	British Salonika Army	2.50	
D56	56 Div. H.Q.	1.00			GZ	G.H.Q. M.E.F.	7.50	
D57	57 Div. H.Q.	1.00			H1	I Corps H.Q.	0.30	
D58	58 Div. H.Q.	1.00			H2	II Corps H.Q.	0.30	
D59	59 Div. H.Q.	1.00			H3	III Corps H.Q.	0.30	
D60	60 Div. H.Q.	20.00	1.00		H4	IV Corps H.Q.	0.30	
D61	61 Div. H.Q.	1.00			H5	V Corps H.Q.	0.30	
D62	62 Div. H.Q.	1.00			H6	VI Corps H.Q.	0.30	
D63	63 Div. H.Q.	0.80			H7	VII Corps H.Q.	0.30	
DNL	63 Div. H.Q.	15.00			H8	VIII Corps H.Q.	0.40	
D64–5	Not used				MH2	VIII Corps H.Q.	15.00	
D66	66 Div. H.Q.	1.00			H9	IX Corps	0.40	
66D	66 Div. H.Q.		5.00		MH3	IX Corps	15.00	
D67–73	Not used				H10	X Corps H.Q.	0.40	
D74	74 Div. H.Q.	2.00	4.00		H11	XI Corps H.Q.	0.40	
D75	75 Div. H.Q.	10.00			H12	XII Corps H.Q.	2.00	
DAN 4	4 Australian Div.	?			H13	XIII Corps	0.30	
DAN 5	5 Australian Div.	?			H14	XIV Corps	0.30	

Index	Used by	d/c	sk	Index	Used by	d/c	sk
H15	XV Corps	0.50	20.00	S74	France	3.00	
H16	XVI Corps H.Q.		6.00	S77	France	0.50	
AH16	XVI Corps Adv. H.Q.		6.00	SA1	S.A. Inf. Bde.	?	
H17	XVII Corps H.Q.	0.30		SEY	S.E. mtd Bde.	15.00	
H18	XVIII Corps	0.30	2.00	SWY2	2nd S.W. mtd Bde.	15.00	
H19	XIX Corps	0.40		SX2	Greece		6.00
H20	XX Corps		15.00	SX3	Salonika		10.00
H20T	XX Corps		20.00	SZ1	Turkey		3.00
H21	XXI Corps H.Q.		20.00	SZ1T	Egypt		3.00
H22	XXII Corps H.Q.	0.60		SZ3	Turkey		5.00
HC1	Cavalry H.Q.	0.50		SZ5	Syria		20.00
HC2	W. Front	0.40		SZ8	Lebanon		15.00
HC3	W. Front	0.40		SZ9	Lebanon		20.00
HK	II American Corps	?		SZ11	Egypt		4.00
HM	H.Q. Desert Column	15.00	20.00	SZ15	Egypt		5.00
HP	Canadian Corps	?		SZ16	Haifa		25.00
HR	Reserve Corps H.Q.	?		SZ18	Egypt		15.00
HW	1 Anzac Corps H.Q.	?		SZ19	Lebanon		15.00
HW2	2 Anzac Corps H.Q.	?		SZ19T	Egypt		7.50
HX	Canadian Corps H.Q.	?		SZ20	Ludd		7.50
HY	Highland mtd Bde. H.Q.	15.00		SZ21	Egypt		6.00
IK–3K	Security purposes	?		SZ23	Egypt		15.00
LY	Lowland mtd Bde.	20.00		SZ34	Jaffa		10.00
MD1	Anzac mtd Div.	?		SZ36	Egypt		10.00
MD2	Australian mtd Div.	?		SZ48	Palestine		20.00
MDT1	Anzac mtd Div. Train	?		SZ49	Mulebbis		20.00
MX1	mtd Bde.	?		SZ53	Palestine		20.00
1P–12P	Canadian Bde. H.Q.	?		SZ55	Egypt		15.00
PB1	Egypt		20.00	SZ57	Haifa		20.00
PB11	Russia	50.00		SZ58	Jericho		15.00
PB12	Russia	40.00		SZ59	Tul Karem		25.00
PB13	Russia	40.00		SZ60	Tiberias		25.00
PB14	Russia	40.00		SZ61	Palestine		25.00
PB15	Russia	40.00		SZ62	Damascus		15.00
PB22	Russia	40.00		T1	1 Div. Train	0.50	
PB33	Russia	40.00		T2	2 Div. Train	0.50	
PB44	Russia	40.00		T3	3 Div. Train	0.40	
PB55	Russia	40.00		T4	4 Div. Train	0.50	
PB66	Russia	40.00		T5	5 Div. Train	0.40	
PB77	Russia	45.00		T6	6 Div. Train	0.40	
PB88	Russia	45.00		T7	7 Div. Train	1.00	
PB99	Russia	50.00		T8	8 Div. Train	0.30	
Q1	1 Bde. Tank Corps	1.00		T9	9 Div. Train	0.50	
Q2	2 Bde. Tank Corps	1.00		T10	10 Div. Train	5.00	
Q3	3 Bde. Tank Corps	1.00		T11	11 Div. Train	1.00	
Q4	4 Bde. Tank Corps	2.00		T12	12 Div. Train	0.50	
Q5	5 Bde. Tank Corps	2.00		T13	Not used		
R10	10 Div. Rail		15.00.	T14	14 Div. Train	0.50	
S26	France	2.00		T15	15 Div. Train	0.40	
S29	France	20.00		T16	16 Div. Train	0.50	
S58	France	4.00		T17	17 Div. Train	0.40	
S62	France	1.50		T18	18 Div. Train	0.30	
S63	W. Front	4.00		T19	19 Div. Train	0.30	
S64	France	4.00		T20	20 Div. Train	0.30	
S66	France		4.00	T21	21 Div. Train	0.30	

Index	Used by	d/c	sk	Index	Used by	d/c	sk
T22	22 Div. Train	2.00		T57	57 Div. Train	2.00	
T23	23 Div. Train	0.50		T58	58 Div. Train	2.00	
T24	24 Div. Train	0.30		T59	59 Div. Train	1.00	
T25	25 Div. Train	0.30		T60	60 Div. Train	15.00	
T26	26 Div. Train	2.00		T61	61 Div. Train	1.00	
T27	27 Div. Train	0.50		T62	62 Div. Train	1.00	
T28	28 Div. Train	2.00		T63	63 Div. Train	0.50	
T29	29 Div. Train	0.30		TNL	63 Div. Train	25.00	
T30	30 Div. Train	0.30		T64–T65	Not used		
T31	31 Div. Train	0.50		T66	66 Div. Train	2.00	
T32	32 Div. Train	0.50		T67–T73	Not used		
T33	33 Div. Train	0.50		T74	74 Div. Train	?	
T34	34 Div. Train	0.40		TAN 4	4 Aust. Div. Train	?	
T35	35 Div. Train	0.50		TAN 5	5 Aust. Div. Train	?	
T36	36 Div. Train	0.50		TB	Guards Div. Train	0.40	
T37	37 Div. Train	0.40		TC 4	Cal Div. Train	2.00	
T38	38 Div. Train	0.40		TC	Cal Div. Train		2.00
T39	39 Div. Train	0.40		TG	G.H.Q. Train	0.30	
T40	40 Div. Train	0.40		TK	Spare D/S	?	
T41	41 Div. Train	0.40		TW	W.F.F. Train	20.00	
T46	46 Div. Train	0.40		TW1	5 Aust. Div. Train	?	
TM	46 Div. Train	2.00		TX–TX4	Canadian Trains	?	
T47	47 Div. Train	0.40		TY	Spare D/S	?	
TL2	47 Div. Train	2.00		TZ	N.Z. Div. Train	0.40	
T48	48 Div. Train	0.50		W1	W.W.F. Egypt		15.00
TSM	48 Div. Train	2.50		W1	B.M.M. Italy	20.00	
T49	49 Div. Train	0.40		W2	W.W.F. Egypt		17.50
TWR	49 Div. Train	3.20		W2	B.M.M. Greece		15.00
T50	50 Div. Train	0.40		W2	B.M.M. Greece	15.00	
TN	50 Div. Train	3.20		W3	B.M.M.	20.00	
T51	51 Div. Train	0.40		W4	Greece	20.00	
THD	51 Div. Train	6.00		WSY	Mtd Bde.	?	
T52	52 Div. Train	5.00		1W–8W	Aust. Bdes.	0.50	
TLL	52 Div. Train	72.00		W10–W11	Aust. Bdes.	0.50	
T53	53 Div. Train	20.00		12W–15W	Aust. Bdes.	0.50	
T54	Not used			1X–12X	Canadian Bdes.	0.50	
T55	55 Div. Train	0.40		1Y	1 mtd Bde.	10.00	
T56	56 Div. Train	0.40		1Z–4Z	N.Z. Bdes.	0.50	

Instructional marks, 'Present location uncertain' etc. many types		2.00
Packet stamps		2.00
Parcel stamps (on piece)		2.00
P.O.W. mail from UK camps with P.C. markings		5.00
As above from Isle of Man		25.00
P.O.W. mail from UK camps with camp cachets		10.00
As above from Isle of Man		30.00
R.E. Postal Section/R.L.O., single circle		6.00
Registered mail		5.00
Travelling Post Office markings		20.00

372   373

372 Field Post Office, double circle with thick arcs and numbers
    1–194 . . . . 0.50
373 Base Army Post Office, double circle with thick arcs and numbers
    1–20 . . . . 0.75
    Army or Field Post Office machine cancellations 0.60
    Army Post Office, Army Post or Field Post Office packet stamps 0.75
    Home Depot R.E.P.S., double circle thick arcs 0.60
    Army/Post Office, single circles 0.60
    Not with Unit/Return to Sender etc., instructional marks . . . 1.50
    Security markings, paid marks etc., preserving anonymity . . . 0.75

Post War Operations
Single circle, F.P.O. types with distinguishing numbers 0.50
Double circle Field Post Office with thin arcs 0.20

Camp Postmarks

374   Duplex   Single circle   Double circle
                       (Several types)   (Several types)
                           375   376

Skeleton   Double Arc
(Irish, double rim)   **378**
377

Camps may be listed under the name of the Camp or under location; both should be checked. Postmarks officially issued but not actually seen used are shown (?). Only main types are given. Full details of sub-types and periods of use are given by R. A. Kingston.

Earliest known date	Wording of Postmark (omitting 'Registered')	Duplex 374	Single Circle 375	Double Circle 376	Skeleton 377	Other Types
1916	Acreknowe Camp, Hawick				10.00	
1909	Aglish Camp, Fermoy				8.00	
1947	Aldergrove, Crumlin, Co. Antrim (R.A.F. Stn)			3.00		
1855	Numeral 046 (Aldershot, not duplex)	15.00				
1855	Aldershot Camp 046	15.00				
1885	Aldershot Camp 96	12.00				
1855	Aldershot Camp					Double Arc: 90.00
Victorian	Aldershot Camp B.O.					Circular Parcel: 7.50
1865	Aldershot		6.00			
1900	Aldershot Camp (with cross)			3.00		
1905	Aldershot B.O. Aldershot			4.00		
1906	Aldershot Camp B.O.			4.00		
1905	Aldershot Camp B.O. Aldershot			4.00		
1906	Aldershot Camp B.O. Aldershot		4.00			
1871	Aldershot Camp B.O. M.O. & S.B.		25.00			
1893	Field Post Office, Aldershot			6.00		
1918	Aldershot Royal Aircraft Estab. B.O.					Rectangular Parcel: 5.00
1916	Andover (Windmill Hill Camp)					Rectangular Parcel: 4.00
190?	Arborfield Camp		5.00			
1941	Arborfield Camp, Reading/Berks		3.00			
1970	Arborfield Camp/Reading Berks		0.60			
1957	Arborfield Camp, Reading Berks					Rectangular Parcel: 1.00
1917	Army Letter Office, London			4.00		
1918	Army Letter Office 1, London			4.00		
1915	Army Parcel Office, London			?		
1916	Army Post Office, London				7.00	
1918	Army R.L.O. London		?			
1954	Arncott Depot Oxford 3		3.00			
1957	Arncott Depot Bicester Oxon		3.00			
1908	Ashley Walk Camp B.O.				8.00	
1914	Ashwick Camp Dulverton				8.00	
1914	Ashwick Camp B.O. Dulverton		6.00			

	dup.	s/c	d/c	sk	
1909 Ashwick Camp Tiverton				8.00	
1909 Ashwick Camp B.O. Tiverton	6.00				
1919 Artillery Camp Grantham	?				
1944 Aston Down. Stroud. Glos	3.00				
1947 Aston Down. Stroud. Glos					Rectangular Parcel: 3.00
1939 Auchengate Camp Troon	4.00				
1916 Australian Military P.O. London (no 'Reg')					Oval Registered: 8.00
1924 Aultguish Camp. Garve. Ross-shire			5.00		
1893 Baddon Camp				8.00	
1939 Bagshot Moor Camp Hants				8.00	
1932 Ballykinler Camp. Co. Down			5.00		
1933 Ballykinler Camp, Dounpatrick, Co. Down			5.00		
1905 Ballykinler/Camp		5.00			
1934 Ballykinler Camp, Dounpatrick, Co. Down	3.00				
1957 Ballykinler Camp	1.00				
1957 Ballykinler Camp, Dounpatrick, Co. Down					Rectangular Parcel: 1.00
1916 Ballinvonear Camp, Buttevant			6.00		
1915 Ballinvonear Camp				8.00	
1943 Balivanich Lochboisdale			4.00		
1916 Balmer Camp/Lewes				8.00	
1918 Bangour War Hospital, West Lothian		5.00			
1916 Bangour War Hospital, West Lothian			4.00		
1893 Barry Camp/Dundee		5.00			
1947 Barton Stacey Camp, Winchester, Hants		3.00			
1954 Barton Stacey Camp, Winchester		2.00			
1957 Barton Stacey Camp, Winchester, Hants					Rectangular Parcel: 2.00
? Barnstaple Camp				9.00	
1970 Bassingbourne Barracks, Royston, Herts			0.60		
1916 Canadian P.O. Bath					Machine: 4.00
1937 Bawdsey Ferry, Woodbridge, Suffolk			4.00		
1915 Bears Rail Camp, Windsor					Rubber Packet: 6.00
1915 Bears Rail Camp, Windsor				8.00	
? Beaulieu Camp, Hants				8.00	
1906 Beaulieu Camp, Lymington				7.00	
1910 Camp Beaulieu				8.00	
1916 Belhus Park Camp, Aveley			3.00		
1914 Belhus Park Camp				6.00	
1915 Belhus Park Camp, Aveley				6.00	
1947 Army Pay Office, Belfast 7	3.00				
? Bellister Camp B.O., N. on Tyne				8.00	

	dup.	s/c	d/c	sk	
1914 Belton Camp, Grantham		4.00			
1915 Belton Camp, Grantham		4.00			
1914 Belton Camp, Grantham				7.00	
1914 Belton Camp, Grantham					Rubber Packet: 6.00
1919 Grantham. Belton Park Camp B.O.					Rectangular Parcel: 6.00
1916 Belton Park Camp B.O./ Grantham					Circular Parcel: 6.00
1916 Bere Island M.T.O.				10.00	
1915 Bettisfield Park Camp/ Whitechurch					Circular Parcel: 7.00
1918 Whitechurch (Bettisfield Park Camp)					Rectangular Parcel: 7.00
1915 Bettisfield Park Camp/ Whitechurch					Circular Parcel: 7.00
1915 Bettisfield Park Camp/ Whitechurch			5.00		
1917 Bettisfield Park Camp B.O. Whitechurch			5.00		
1916 Bisley Camp, Woking			3.00		
1961 Bisley Camp, Woking, Surrey			1.00		
1961 Bisley Camp, Woking, Surrey					Rectangular Parcel: 1.50
1897 Bisley Camp, Woking		4.00			
1904 Bisley Camp		3.00			
1892 Bisley Camp, Woking J62	4.00				
1902 Bisley Camp					Oval Registration: 4.00
1915 Blackdown Camp, Aldershot		3.00			
1915 Blackdown Camp, Aldershot			3.00		
1916 Blackdown Camp, Farnborough					Rectangular Parcel: 4.00
1906 Blackdown Camp, Bridestowe, S.O.Devon		3.00			
? Blackdown Camp B.O. Hants			8.00		
1915 Blackdown Camp B.O.			8.00		
1918 Blackdown Camp, Aldershot			8.00		
/ Blackdown Camp B.O. Aldershot			9.00		
1915 Military Hospital, Blackpool					Oval Registration: 5.00
1917 Military Hospital, Blackpool		6.00			
1919 Blackpool (Military Hospital)					Rectangular Parcel: 7.00
1918 Blandford Camp, Blandford			4.00		
1939 Blandford Camp, Blandford, Dorset			3.00		
1957 Blandford Camp, Blandford Forum			1.00		
1915 Naval Camp B.O./ Blandford			4.00		
? Naval Camp, Blandford			4.00		
1872 Blandford – Field Force		10.00			
? Blandford Naval Camp		5.00			
1957 Blandford Camp, Blandford Forum, Dorset		1.00			
1941 Blandford Camp, Blandford, Dorset		2.00			

	dup.	s/c	d/c	sk	
1914 Naval Camp B.O. Blandford				7.00	
1915 Blandford Naval Camp					Rectangular Parcel:?
1918 Blandford (Blandford Camp)					Rectangular Parcel: 5.00
1956 Blandford Camp, Blandford Forum, Dorset					Rectangular Parcel: 1.00
1905 The Camp, Bodmin			6.00		
1904 Field Post Office, Bordon Camp, Hants			5.00		
1904 Bordon Camp, East Liss S.O. Hants			5.00		
1907 Bordon Camp S.O. Hants			4.00		
1907 Bordon Camp, Hants			4.00		
1909 Bordon Camp				6.00	
1904 Bordon Camp, Hants		4.00			
1914 Field Post Office, Bordon, Hants				6.00	
1915 Bourley Camp, Aldershot			4.00		
1911 Bourley Camp, Aldershot				7.00	
1913 Bourley Camp				7.00	
1912 Army Post Office Bourley Camp				7.00	
1916 Bovington Camp, Poole			3.00		
1937 Bovington Camp, Wareham, Dorset			3.00		
1927 Bovington Camp, Wareham, Dst			3.00		
1916 Bovington Camp					Circular Parcel: 4.00
1907 Bovington Camp, Wareham		4.00			
1913 Bovington Camp		4.00			
1915 Bovington Camp, Poole		4.00			
1937 Bovington Camp, Wareham, Dst		3.00			
1930 Bovington Camp, Wareham, Dst		3.00			
1915 Bovington Camp, Poole				5.00	
1915 Bovington Camp, Poole					Circular Parcel: 4.00
? Bovington Camp					Rubber Packet: 4.00
1903 Bovington Camp, Wareham					Rubber Packet: 4.00
1956 Bovington Camp, Wareham Dorset					Rectangular Parcel: 2.00
1910 Bow Street Camp				8.00	
1915 Bowood Camp			5.00		
? Boyton Camp B.O.			4.00		
1915 Boyton Camp, Wilts			4.00		
1915 Boyton Camp, Warminster					Rectangular Parcel: 4.00
1916 Boyton Camp, Wilts		4.00			
1915 Boyton Camp, Wilts					Rubber Packet: 4.00
1915 Bramshott Camp B.O. (with cross)			3.00		
1914 Bramshott Camp B.O.		3.00			
1918 Bramshott Camp		3.00			
1916 Bramshott Camp, Petersfield			5.00		
1915 Canadian Base P.O. Bramshott Camp			6.00		

Year	Location	dup.	s/c	d/c	sk	
1916	Canadian P.O. Bramshott Camp, Hants			6.00		
1915	Bramshott Camp B.O.				5.00	
1919	Bramshott Camp					Krag Machine: 3.00
?	Petersfield/Bramshott Camp B.O.					Rubber Packet: 4.00
1916	Petersfield. (Bramshott Camp B.O.)					Rubber Packet: 4.00
1964	R.N.A.S. Brawdy, Haverfordwest, Pembs	2.00				
1952	Brean Camp, Burnham on Sea				5.00	
1904	Bridestowe Camp, North Devon	4.00				
1904	Camp. Bridestowe Devon	4.00				
1902	Camp Bridestowe R.S.O. Devon	4.00				
1904	Camp Bridgetown, Devon				8.00	
1916	Canadian Base P.O. Brighton		5.00			
?	Canadian P.O. Brighton		5.00			
1917	Brocton Camp, Stafford	?				
1915	Brocton Camp, Stafford		5.00			
1916	Brocton Camp B.O. Stafford		5.00			
1916	Stafford (Brockton Camp B.O.)					Rectangular Packet: 5.00
1901	Buddon Camp	3.00				
1911	Buddon/Camp	3.00				
1914	Buddon Camp		3.00			
1914	Buddon Camp, Dundee		3.00			
1906	Buddon Camp				5.00	
1913	Buddan/Gamp (error)				10.00	
1915	Bulford Camp, Salisbury	3.00				
1914	Bulford Camp B.O. Salisbury	3.00				
1939	Bulford Barracks, Salisbury, Wilts	3.00				
1898	Field Post Office, Bulford Camp 1		3.00			
1898	Field Post Office, Bulford Camp 2		3.00			
1904	Bulford Camp B.O., Salisbury		3.00			
1918	Bulford Camp, Salisbury		3.00			
1934	Bulford Camp, Salisbury, Wilts		3.00			
?	Bulford Barracks, Tidworth, Hants		3.00			
1912	Bulford Camp, Salisbury			5.00		
1904	Bulford Camp B.O.			5.00		
1947	Bulford Barracks, Salisbury, Wilts					Krag Machine: 1.00
1961	Bulford Barracks/Salisbury/ Wilts					Rubber Packet: 0.75
1947	Bulford Barracks, Salisbury, Wilts					Rectangular Parcel: 1.00
1917	Salisbury. Bulford Camp					Rectangular Parcel: 3.00
1914	Bullswater Camp, Woking			5.00		
1939	Burley Camp, Ringwood			3.00		
1938	Barrowhead Camp B.O., Newton Stewart			3.00		

Year		dup.	s/c	d/c	sk	
1904	Bushey Down Camp				4.00	
1908	Bustard Camp B.O. Devizes		4.00			
1911	Bustard Camp B.O. Salisbury		4.00			
1909	Bustard Camp, Devizes		4.00			
1924	Bustard Camp. Salisbury		4.00			
1912	Bustard Camp, Salisbury				5.00	
1903	Bustard Field P.O. Devizes				5.00	
1903	The Bustard Field P.O. Devizes				5.00	
1939	Butlins Camp, Skegness, Lincs		6.00			
?	Canadian P.O.					
	C.D.D. Buxton			5.00		
1906	Royal Military College B.O., Camberley		4.00			
1906	Royal Military College, Camberley		4.00			
1947	Castle Camps. Cambridge (R.A.F. Stn)			3.00		
1917	First E. G. Hospl. Cambridge				6.00	
1905	The Camp, Camelford			5.00		
1873	Cannock Chase F.P.O. G19	25.00				
1913	Caterham Barracks		3.00			
1947	Caterham Barracks, Caterham, Surrey		3.00			
1947	Caterham Surrey, Caterham Barracks					Rectangular Parcel: 2.00
1915	Catterick Camp, Yorks			3.00		
1931	Catterick Camp, Richmond, Yorks			3.00		
1937	Catterick Camp. Yorkshire			3.00		
1918	Catterick Camp. Yorks		3.00			
1942	Catterick Camp. Yks		3.00			
1957	Catterick Camp. Yorkshire D.		3.00			
1916	Catterick Camp. Yorks					Oval Registration: 4.00
1916	Catterick Camp					Universal Machine: 1.00
1916	Catterick Camp					Krag Machine: 2.00
1957	Catterick Camp, Yorkshire					Rectangular Parcel: 1.00
1916	Darlington (Catterick Camp)					Rectangular Parcel: 3.00
1919	Chatham Marines		?			
1915	Chatham Royal Engineers		?			
1918	Royal Marine Engineers, Chatham		?			
1916	Naval Barracks B.O., Chatham/Kent		3.00			
1974	Naval Barracks, Chatham, Kent		1.00			
1920	Dockyard B.O. Chatham		3.00			
1930	Chatham Naval Barracks B.O.					Rectangular Parcel: 3.00
1959	Naval Barracks, Chatham, Kent					Rectangular Parcel: 1.00
1906	Chelsea Barracks, S.W.		4.00			
1914	Pimlico Road, Chelsea Barracks, S.W.		4.00			
1915	Chisledon Camp, Wilts			4.00		
1915	Chisledon Camp, Wilts		4.00			
1916	Chisledon Camp, Wilts				5.00	

		dup.	s/c	d/c	sk	
1917	Chisledon Camp, Swindon					Rectangular Parcel: 4.00
1915	Chisledon Camp/Wilts					Circular Parcels: 4.00
1853	Chobham Camp					Double Arc: 150.00
1915	Churn Camp, Oxford			4.00		
1915	Churn Camp, Oxford		4.00		5.00	
1968	Churchill. Helensburgh		4.00			
1915	Chyngton Camp, Seaford			4.00		
1915	Chyngton Camp B.O. Seaford			4.00		
1914	Chyngton Camp, Seaford, Sussex		4.00			
1919	Chyngton Camp/Seaford					Circular Parcel: 4.00
1917	Chyngton Camp/Seaford/ Sussex					Circular Parcel: 4.00
1915	Chyngton Camp, Seaford			5.00		
1914	Clandeboye Camp			6.00		
1911	Claughton Territorial Camp			7.00		
1950	Clay Lane, Oxford			2.00		
1954	Clay Lane, Oxford		2.00			
1915	Clipstone Camp, Notts			6.00		
1915	Clipstone Camp B.O. Notts					Rubber Packet: 3.00
1915	Clipstone Camp, Notts			3.00		
1917	Clipstone Camp			3.00		
1915	Mansfield (Clipstone Camp)					Rectangular Parcel: 4.00
1915	Clipstone Camp/Notts					Circular Parcel: 4.00
1974	Clyde Sub. Base, Helensburgh					Rectangular Parcel: 1.00
1967	Clyde Submarine Base Helensburgh		1.00			
1920	Garrison B.O. Colchester			3.00		
1914	Clockheil Camp, Campbeltown				4.00	
1915	Codford St. Mary Camp					Circular Parcel: 7.00
?	Colsterdale Camp, York			?		
1915	Colsterdale Camp, Yorks				5.00	
1915	Colsterdale Camp, Yorks			5.00		
1946	H.M.S. Collingwood/ Fareham, Hants		2.00			
1950	Collingwood, Fareham, Hants		2.00			
1974	Collingwood, Fareham, Hants					Rectangular Parcel: 1.00
1941	Compton Bassett Camp, Calne, Wilts			2.00		
1947	Compton Bassett Camp, Calne, Wilts		2.00			
?	Compton Bassett Camp					Rectangular Parcel: 2.00
1916	Cooden Camp, Bexhill on Sea				4.00	
1919	Bexhill on Sea (Cooden Camp B.O.)					Rectangular Parcel: 4.00
1914	Coolmoney Camp				5.00	
1915	Coolmoney/Camp				5.00	
1913	Coolmoney Camp, Co. Wicklow				5.00	
1916	Canadian P.O. Coombe Down, Bath			5.00		
1904	Cork Barracks. Mil.Tel.Off		5.00			
1940	Cosford Camp, Wolverhampton, Staffs		3.00			

		dup.	s/c	d/c	sk	
1959	Cosford Camp/ Wolverhampton/Staffs					Rectangular Parcel: 2.00
1906	Cothill Camp				7.00	
1944	Crimond R.N.A.S.P.O. Lonmay		5.00			
1947	Cranwell, Sleaford, Lincs		3.00			
1916	Cranwell, Sleaford, Lincs	4.00				
1934	Crookham Camp, Aldershot	3.00				
1922	Crookham Camp B.O., Aldershot	3.00				
?	Crookham Camp B.O., Aldershot, Hants	3.00				
1947	Crookham, Aldershot, Hants					Rectangular Parcel: 2.00
1939	Crookham Camp, Aldershot, Hants	3.00				
1924	Crookham Camp B.O., Aldershot		3.00			
1931	Crookham Camp, Aldershot, Hants		3.00			
1941	Crossapol Isle of Tiree	4.00				
1917	Crowborough Camp B.O.					Rectangular Parcel: 3.00
1918	Tunbridge Wells (Crowborough Camp)					Rectangular Parcel: 3.00
1914	Camp Hill Camp. Crowboro					Circular Parcel: 4.00
1916	Crowborough Camp, B.O.			5.00		
1916	Crowborough/Camp					Circular Parcel: 4.00
1915	Canadian P.O. Crowborough Camp, Sussex		5.00			
1918	Crowborough Camp, Tunbridge Wells		4.00			
1915	Crowbrough Camp, Tunbridge Wells	4.00				
1914	Camp Hill/Crowboro Camp		5.00			
1914	Camp Hill Camp/Crowboro		5.00			
1914	Crowboro/Camp		5.00			
1916	Crowborough Camp B.O.		5.00			
1915	Crowborough Camp, Tunbridge Wells		5.00			
1917	Canadian P.O. Crowborough Camp, Sussex					Oval Registered: 5.00
1917	Crowborough Camp B.O.					Rubber Packet: 4.00
1963	Culdrose R.N. Air Stn., Helston, Cwll		1.00			
1963	RNA Stn Culdrose, Helston, Cornwall					Rectangular Parcel: 1.00
1956	Culdrose RNA Stn Helston, Cwll			1.00		
1956	RN Air Stn Culdrose, Helston, Cwll			1.00		
?	Curragh Camp					Scroll Type: 450.00 Double Arc: 85.00
1857	The Curragh Camp					
1860	Curragh Camp, 455	10.00				
1862	Curragh Camp		4.00			
1905	Curragh Camp. M.O. & S.B.		10.00			

	dup.	s/c	d/c	sk	
1904 Curragh Camp				4.00	
1911 Curragh Camp T.O.				8.00	
1905 Curragh Camp					Rubber Packet: 3.00
1897 Curragh Camp/1			4.00		
1902 Curragh Camp (with bars)			4.00		
1920 Curragh Camp (with cross)			3.00		
1912 Fleet Post Office, Dale		5.00			
1951 Dalcross East, Inverness			2.00		
1917 D.A.L.O. London			4.00		
1873 Dartmoor F.P.O. G17	12.50				
1873 Dartmoor R.S.T. G18	12.50				
1935 Deepcut Camp, Aldershot			2.00		
1942 Deepcut Camp, Aldershot		2.00			
1905 Deepcut Camp, Farnborough		2.00			
1911 Deepcut Camp, Farnborough				5.00	
1947 Deepcut Camp, Aldershot, Hants					Rectangular Parcel: 3.00
1917 Deepcut Camp, Farnborough (under Aldershot)					Rectangular Parcel: 3.00
1915 Detling Camp, Maidstone			5.00		
1914 Deganwy Camp				8.00	
1915 Depot Royal Marines, Deal		?			
1916 D.L.S. Canadian P.O., C.C.A.C. Folkestone		?			
1941 Military Camp, Devizes			3.00		
1906 The Barracks, Devizes		5.00			
1941 Devizes, Wilts. Military Camp					Rectangular Parcel: 3.00
1909 Dockyard B.O. Devonport		5.00			
1909 The Dockyard B.O. Devonport		?			
1868 Devonport H.M.S. 250	15.00				
? Base Fleet Mail Office, Devenport					Rubber Packet: 4.00
1914 Naval Barracks, Devonport					Circular Parcel: 4.00
1916 Dibgate Camp			4.00		
1916 Canadian Base P.O., Dibgate Camp			5.00		
1915 Canadian P.O., Dibgate Camp			5.00		
1915 Dibgate Camp, Shorncliffe			4.00		
1915 Dibgate Camp				5.00	
1915 Dibgate Camp B.O.				6.00	
1943 Digby Aerodrome		3.00			
1912 Doonfoot Camp, Ayr				8.00	
1938 Duke of Yorks School, Dover, Kent			3.00		
1914 Naval Mail Office, Dover			4.00		
1961 Duke of York's School, Dover, Kent	1.00				
1961 Duke of York's School, Dover	1.00				
1915 Naval Mail Office, Dover	4.00				
1915 Naval Mail Office, Dover					Rubber Packet: 4.00
1915 Draycott Camp, Swindon			5.00		
1915 Draycott Camp, Bradford, (Nr. Swindon)			?		

	dup.	s/c	d/c	sk	
1915 Drainie, Lossiemouth, Morayshire			5.00		
1943 Dundonald Camp, Troon, Ayrshire		3.00			
1918 Dundonald Camp, Troon, Ayrshire					Rectangular Parcel: 4.00
1916 Durrington Camp B.O., Salisbury		4.00			
1915 Durrington Camp B.O., Salisbury			4.00		
1914 Durrington Camp, Salisbury			6.00		
1942 Duxford Camp		3.00			
1900 East Down Camp, Devizes			4.00		
1908 East Anstey Camp				8.00	
1912 East Marton/Camp					Rubber Packet: 4.00
1918 Eastern General Hospital, Cambridge		5.00			
1946 R.N.C. Eaton, Chester		3.00			
1899 Higher Barracks, Exeter Devon		?			
1940 Fenton Barns, Drem, East Lothian					Rectangular Parcel: 3.00
1914 Finner Camp, Ballyshannon		5.00			
1915 Flower Down Camp, Winchester		5.00			
1915 Flower Down Camp, Winchester			4.00		
1916 Canadian Post Office C.C.A.C., Folkestone			?		
1916 Canadian P.O., C.C.A.C. Folkestone					Oval Registered: ?
? Ford Camp, Salisbury			?		
1945 Ford R.N.A.S., Arundel, Sussex		3.00			
1947 Fort Blockhouse, Gosport/Hants		2.00			
1916 Fort Matilda Camp, Greenock		4.00			
1916 Fovant Camp, Salisbury			4.00		
1918 Fovant Camp, Salisbury		4.00			
1917 Fovant Camp, Salisbury				5.00	
1915 Salisbury, Fovant Camp					Rectangular Parcel: 4.00
1915 Frensham Common Camp, B.O. Farnham			4.00		
1915 Frensham Common Camp B.O. Farnham		4.00			
1915 Frensham Common Camp					Oval Registered: 5.00
1909 Frogmore Camp, East Liss, Hants		5.00			
1900 Gailes Camp, Irvine/602		6.00			
1916 Gailes Camp/Irvine		5.00			
1915 Gailes Camp Irvine				5.00	
1912 Gargrave/Camp					Oval Registered: 5.00
1912 Glamis Camp			8.00		
1914 Glanrheidol Camp			9.00		

		dup.	s/c	d/c	sk	
1901	Glen Imaal Artillery Camp		5.00			
1905	Glen Imaal S.O.					
	Co. Wicklow		4.00			
?	Glen Imaal B.O.,					
	Co. Wicklow		4.00			
1901	Glen Imaal Artillery Camp				7.00	
1905	Glen Imaal Camp				7.00	
1927	Gipsy Bottom Camp,					
	Aylesbury				8.00	
1921	Gormanston Camp, Co. Meath		4.00			
1922	Gormanston Camp, Co. Meath				6.00	
1948	Grazeley Camp, Reading, Berks		3.00			
1918	Greenhill Camp, Sheffield		4.00			
1919	Greenhill Camp, Sheffield				5.00	
1918	Grantham (Harrowby Camp BO)					Rectangular Parcel: 4.00
1965	F.M.O. Greenock		1.00			
1915	Gosforth Park Camp,					
	Newcastle on Tyne		4.00			
1974	Sulton, Gosport, Hants		1.00			
1930	Guards Camp, Goodwood, Sx.				6.00	
1914	Hagley Park Camp				8.00	
1914	Halton Camp, Tring			4.00		
1917	Halton Camp/Bucks			4.00		
1941	Halton Camp,					
	Aylesbury, Bucks			3.00		
1914	Halton Camp, Tring		4.00			
1920	Halton Camp, Bucks		4.00			
1915	Halton Camp B.O. Tring		4.00			
1915	Halton Camp, North Tring		4.00			
1920	Halton Camp, North Bucks		4.00			
1936	Halton Camp, Aylesbury, Bucks		3.00			
1917	Halton Camp, Bucks				6.00	
1921	Halton Camp					Oval Registration: 5.00
1917	Halton Camp B.O. Bucks					Rectangular Parcel: 4.00
1915	Tring. Halton Camp B.O.					Rectangular Parcel: 4.00
1947	Halton Camp, Aylesbury, Bucks					Rectangular Parcel: 4.00
1937	Hampton Court Camp,					
	Kingston on Thames		3.00			
1919	Hampton Court Camp				6.00	
1937	Hampton Court Camp,					
	Kingston on Thames, Sy.					Rubber Packet: 4.00
1916	Harrowby Camp, Grantham		4.00			
1954	Harrowden, Bedford			2.00		
1954	Harrowden, Bedford		2.00			
1915	Hare Park, Gerragh Camp		4.00			
1913	Fleet Post Office, Harwich		4.00			
1940	Haslar Hospital/Gosport		2.00			
1974	Haslar Hospital, Gosport, Hants		1.00			
1913	Haslar Hospital B.O. Gosport		4.00			
1915	Haynes Park Camp, Bedford		4.00			
1917	Canadian P.O. Hastings			5.00		
1915	Hazeley Camp, Winchester			5.00		
1915	Hazeley Camp, Winchester		5.00			
1917	Winchester (Hazeley Camp)					Rectangular Parcel: 5.00

	dup.	s/c	d/c	sk	
1942 Hednesford Camp, Hednesford, Staffs	2.00				
1957 Hednesford Camp, Hednesford, Staffs					Rectangular Parcel: 3.00
1908 Helmsley Camp B.O.				8.00	
1941 Hemswell Aerodrome, Lincoln		3.00			
1928 Henlow Camp, Beds		4.00			
1944 Henlow Camp, Henlow, Beds		3.00			
1944 Henlow Camp, Henlow, Beds	3.00				
1957 Henlow Camp, Henlow, Beds					Rectangular Parcel: 2.00
1915 Heytesbury Camp, Wilts		3.00			
1916 Heytesbury Camp, Wilts	3.00				
1915 Heytesbury Camp, Wilts					Rubber Packet: 3.00
1915 Heytesbury Camp					Rectangular Parcel: 3.00
1915 Warminster, Heytesbury Camp					Rectangular Parcel: 3.00
1915 Heytesbury Camp					Circular Parcel: 3.00
1910 Hindlow Camp, Buxton			8.00		
1915 Holkham Camp, Wells, Norfolk			8.00		
1935 Hollom Dn Barn Camp, Hants			8.00		
1903 Holmsley Camp, Ringwood			8.00		
1960 Honington Camp, Bury St. Edmunds, Sfk		1.00			
1962 Honington Camp, Bury St. Edmunds, Suffolk		1.00			
1959 Honington Camp, Bury St. Edmunds, Suffolk	1.00				
1974 Honington Camp, Bury St. Edmunds, Suffolk					Rectangular Parcel: 0.50
Hornchurch, NZ Base Depot					Octagonal Type: 10.00
1935 Horsebridge Camp, Hants			8.00		
1902 Houndean Camp, Lewes			8.00		
1935 Houghton Down Camp, Hants			8.00		
1947 Houndstone, Yeovil, Somerset			6.00		
1965 Houndstone, Yeovil, Somerset					Rectangular Parcel: 2.00
1914 Hunmanby Camp, Yorkshire			8.00		
1916 Hurdcott Camp, Salisbury			5.00		
1915 Hurdcott Camp, Salisbury	5.00				
1915 Hurdcott Camp					Circular Parcel: 5.00
? Hursley Camp, Winchester			7.00		
1915 Hursley Park Camp, Winchester			4.00		
1915 Hursley Camp, Winchester	4.00				
1915 Hursley Park Camp, Winchester	4.00				
1910 Hurst Castle Signal Station		?			
1908 Ibsley Camp, B.O.			8.00		
1959 Immingham Dock Grimsby, Lincs					Rectangular Parcel: 2.00
1915 Inverness A.M.D.O.(Naval)			?		
1917 Invergordon Dockyard B.O.					Rectangular Parcel: ?
1954 Royal Hospital School, Ipswich, Sfk	2.00				
1955 Jurby R.A.F.P.O./Ramsey/ Isle of Man					Rubber Packet: 30.00

	dup.	s/c	d/c	sk	
1956 RAF/Jurby/I.O.M./Post Office					Rubber Packet: 30.00
1958 Jurby R.A.F.P.O./Ramsey, Isle of Man		25.00			
1960 R.A.F. Jurby/Ramsey/ Isle of Man					Rubber Packet: 30.00
1937 Kensington Gdns Camp W2		3.00			
1937 Kensington Gardens Camp, W2					Oval Registration: 3.00
1919 A.P.O. Kensington Gdns Camp				7.00	
1921 Kensington Gardens Camp				7.00	
1914 Naval Barracks B.O. Keyham, Devonport		4.00			
1922 Naval Barracks B.O., Keyham, Devonport				6.00	
1954 Kidlington, Oxford			2.00		
1954 Kidlington, Oxford		2.00			
1907 Kilbridge Camp, Dublin		5.00			
1905 Kilbridge Camp				8.00	
1899 Kilworth Camp S.O. Co. Cork		5.00			
1913 Kilworth Camp, Co. Cork		5.00			
1905 Kilworth Camp B.O. Co. Cork		5.00			
1899 Kilworth Camp S.O. Co. Cork				7.00	
1915 Kinmel Park Camp B.O. Rhyl		4.00			
1916 Kinmel Camp B.O./Rhyl			4.00		
1915 Kinmel Park/Camp B.O.		4.00			
1919 Kinmel Park/C.P.C. Registered				8.00	
1915 Kinmel Park Camp B.O./ Rhyl					Circular Parcel: 4.00
1917 Kinmel Park Camp, Rhyl				6.00	
1921 King Edward VII Sanatorium Midhurst		7.00			
1916 Kinross/Camp		6.00			
1947 Kirkham Camp, Preston, Lancs		2.00			
1947 Kirkham Camp, Preston, Lancs					Rectangular Parcel: 2.00
1915 The Camp, Knockaloe, Peel			45.00		
1908 Knockaloe Camp, Peel				75.00	
1953 Lakenheath Camp, Brandon, Suffolk			2.00		
1957 Lakenhall Camp, Brandon, Suffolk		2.00			
1911 Lamphey Camp, Pembroke					Rubber: 5.00
1915 Landguard Camp, Felixstowe			4.00		
1913 Lark Hill Camp B.O., Salisbury			4.00		
1915 Lark Hill Camp, Salisbury			4.00		
1929 Lark Hill Camp, Salisbury, Wilts			4.00		
1910 Lark Hill Camp B.O., Salisbury		4.00			
1907 Lark Hill Camp, Salisbury				5.00	
1908 Lark Hill Camp				5.00	
1915 Lark Hill Camp					Circular Parcel: 3.00
1915 Salisbury (Lark Hill Camp)					Rectangular Parcel: 4.00
1947 Larton R.A.F. Camp, Wirral, Ches			3.00		

Year	Place	dup.	s/c	d/c	sk	Notes
1947	Larton R.A.F. Camp, Wirral, Cheshire		3.00			
1915	Latham Park Camp, Ormskirk			4.00		
1916	Latham Park Camp, Ormskirk		4.00			
1948	Naval Barracks, Lee-on-the-Solent		3.00			
1958	Lee-on-the-Solent Naval Barracks					Rectangular Parcel: 2.00
?	Littlemore Camp, Plymouth		5.00			
1929	Littlemore Camp, Weymouth				8.00	
1911	Lisnegar Camp				7.00	
1913	Lisnegar Camp					Rubber Packet: 4.00
1904	Brigade Depot Barracks, Litchfield		5.00			
1971	Llanmiloe, Carmarthen		5.00			
1914	Loch Doon Camp, Ayrshire			5.00		
1947	Locking Camp, Weston Super Mare, Som		3.00			
1954	Locking Camp, Weston Super Mare, Som 2		2.00			
1957	Locking Camp, Weston Super Mare, Somerset					Rectangular Parcel: 1.00
1906	Lodmore Camp, Weymouth				8.00	
1904	Longmoor Camp, East Liss S.O. Hants			4.00		
1906	Longmoor Camp, East Liss B.O. Hants			4.00		
1918	Longmoor Camp, East Liss, Hants			4.00		
1948	Longmoor Camp, Liss, Hants			3.00		
1904	Longmoor Camp	4.00				
1948	Longmoor Camp, Liss, Hants	4.00				
1916	Longmoor Camp, Petersfield	4.00				
1915	Longmoor Camp, East Liss S.O. Hants			4.00		
1912	Longmoor Camp, East Liss				4.00	
1918	Longmoor Camp, East Liss, (under Petersfield)					Rectangular Parcel: 4.00
1957	Longmoor Camp, Liss, Hants					Rectangular Parcel: 2.00
1940	Lopcombe Camp, Salisbury			5.00		
1919	A.L.O. 2, London					Oval Registration: 7.00
1915	Canadian Contingent S.W.		?			
1910	Lovesgrove Camp				8.00	
1912	Lovesgrove Camp, Aberystwyth				8.00	
1911	Lulworth Camp, Wareham				8.00	
1915	Lydd Camp			4.00		
1915	Lydd Camp/Kent	4.00				
1909	Lydd, Kent				7.00	
1942	Machrihanich North, Campbeltown			3.00		
1952	Machrihanich N. Cambeltown, Argyll	2.00				
1905	Magilligan Camp, Londonderry		4.00			

		dup.	s/c	d/c	sk
1911	Malahide Camp, Co. Dublin		4.00		
1908	Manby-Louch. Lincs				
	Aldershot			5.00	
1915	Maresfield Park Camp,				
	Uckfield			5.00	
1910	Marlborough Lines, Aldershot			2.00	
1908	Marlborough-Lines, Aldershot			2.00	
1947	Marlborough Lines, Aldershot		2.00		
1951	Marlborough-Lines,				
	Aldershot, Hants		1.00		
1915	Marlborough Lines, Hants				4.00
1914	Marlborough Lines, Aldershot				4.00
1917	Aldershot (Marlborough Lines)				Rectangular Parcel: 2.00
1957	Aldershot, Hants,				
	Marlborough Lines				Rectangular Parcel: 1.00
1914	Marske Camp by Sea, Yk				8.00
1909	Martinhoe Camp, Barnstaple				8.00
1968	Medmenham R.A.F.P.O./				
	Marlow, Bucks		4.00		
1968	R.A.F. Post Office/				
	Medmenham, Marlow, Bucks				Rubber Packet: 10.00
1947	Melksham Camp,				
	Melksham, Wilts		2.00		
1957	Melksham Camp,				
	Melksham, Wilts				Rectangular Parcel: 1.00
1916	Milton Depot,				
	Steventon, Berks			4.00	
?	Milton Depot				Rubber Packet: 4.00
1911	The Camp, Minehead S.O.,				
	Som		4.00		
1914	Morfa Camp, Conway		4.00		
1918	Conway (Morfa Camp B.O.)				Rectangular Parcel: 4.00
1915	Morn Hill Camp, Winchester			4.00	
1915	Morn Hill Camp, Winchester		4.00		
1918	Morn Hill Camp, Winchester			6.00	
1918	Winchester: (Morn Hill Camp)				Rectangular Parcel: 3.00
1912	Moor Park Camp			8.00	
1915	West Signal Station, Mumbles		5.00		
1913	Mytchett Camp			7.00	
1914	Mytchett Camp, Farnborough			7.00	
1919	Mytchett Camp, Aldershot			7.00	
1928	Mytchett Camp, Aldershot		4.00		
1926	Mytchett Camp B.O.,				
	Aldershot			7.00	
1900	Netley Hospital, Southampton		5.00		
1927	Nettlebed Camp, Hently Ths			6.00	
?	North Denes Camp			8.00	
1904	North Sway Camp (with cross)			7.00	
1904	North Sway Camp B.O.			7.00	
1905	North Sway Camp S.O.			7.00	
1906	B.O. North Sway Camp			7.00	
1958	Norton Barracks, Worcester		2.00		
1934	Okehampton Camp B.O.,				
	Okehampton			3.00	

		dup.	s/c	d/c	sk
1938	Okehampton Camp, Okehampton			3.00	
1907	Okehampton Camp B.O., Okehampton (22m)		5.00		
1910	Okehampton Camp B.O., Okehampton (24m)		5.00		
1958	Orsett Camp, Grays, Essex			2.00	
1958	Orsett Camp, Grays, Essex				Rectangular Parcel: 2.00
1917	Osterley Park Camp, Isleworth			?	
1916	Park Hall Camp, Oswestry			4.00	
1917	Park Hall Camp, B.O., Oswestry			4.00	
1915	Otterpool Camp/Shorncliffe			5.00	
1916	Park Hall West Camp, Oswestry			4.00	
?	Park Hall Camp West, Oswestry			4.00	
1919	Park Hall Camp, Oswestry		4.00		
1915	Park Hall Camp B.O., Oswestry		4.00		
1948	Park Hall Camp, Oswestry, Shropshire		3.00		
1916	Park Hall West Camp, Oswestry		4.00		
1918	Park Hall Camp, Oswestry				4.00
1916	Park Hall Camp/Oswestry				Circular Parcel: 4.00
1916	Park Hall/West Camp B.O./Oswestry				Circular Parcel: 4.00
1959	Park Hall Camp 1, Oswestry, Shropshire				Rectangular Parcel: 4.00
1915	Otterpool Camp B.O.				8.00
1916	Canadian P.O., Otterpool Camp				Oval Registration: 5.00
1938	Oxney Camp, Bordon, Hants				8.00
1941	Padgate Camp, Warrington, Lancs		3.00		
1947	Padgate Camp, RAFPO, Warrington, Lancs		3.00		
1954	Padgate Camp, Warrington, Lancs				Rectangular Parcel: 2.00
1937	Panfield Camp, Braintree				8.00
1928	Parham Park Camp, Sussex				8.00
1900	Parkhouse Camp B.O., Salisbury			4.00	
1900	Parkhouse Camp B.O., Salisbury/1			4.00	
1900	Parkhouse Camp B.O., Salisbury/2			4.00	
1916	Parkhill Camp, Salisbury			4.00	
1940	Parkeston Quay/Harwich, Essex			3.00	
1915	Park Royal Camp N.W.		?		
1916	Australian Field P.O., Park House Camp		4.00		

	dup.	s/c	d/c	sk
1916 Peas Pottage Camp, Crawley			5.00	
1908 Peel Camp/Douglas				£175
1915 Penkridge Bank Camp, Stafford			4.00	
1915 Penkridge Bank Camp B.O., Stafford			4.00	
1918 Perham Down Camp, Andover			4.00	
1899 Field Post Office, Perham Down/1			4.00	
1899 Field Post Office, Perham Down/2			4.00	
1900 Field Post Office, Perham Down/3			3.00	
1906 Field Post Office, Perham Down			3.00	
1904 Field Post Office Perham Down Camp			3.00	
1900 Field Post Office, Perham Down Camp/2				3.00
1907 Field Post Office, Perham Down Camp		3.00		
1908 Perham Down Camp, Andover		3.00		
1915 Perham Down Camp B.O.				5.00
1916 Perham Down Camp, Andover				5.00
1916 Andover (Perham Down Camp)				Rectangular Parcel: 3.00
1915 Perham Down Camp/Andover				Circular Parcel: 3.00
1940 Penley Hall Camp, Wrexham, Denb.			3.00	
1872 Pewsey Field Force		12.00		
1914 Pirbright Camp B.O. Woking			4.00	
1936 Pirbright Camp B.O., Woking, Surrey			4.00	
1905 Pirbright Camp B.O. Woking		4.00		
1937 Pirbright Camp B.O., Woking, Surrey		4.00		
1915 Pitt Camp, Winchester			?	
1915 Pitt Camp, Winchester		5.00		
1915 Plessey Camp, Cramlington				8.00
1957 Plymouth, Devon Naval Barracks				Rectangular Parcel: 2.00
1954 Plymouth, Devon The Dockyard				Rectangular Parcel: 2.00
1919 Plymouth Marines		?		
1939 The Dockyard, Plymouth/Devon		2.00		
1941 Naval Barracks, Plymouth/Devon		2.00		
1908 Pond Farm Camp, Devizes		4.00		
1914 Pond Farm Camp B.O., Devizes				7.00
1914 Pond Farm Camp, Salisbury				7.00
1918 Experimental Ground, Porton, Salisbury			4.00	

	dup.	s/c	d/c	sk	
1918 Experimental Station, Porton, Salisbury			4.00		
1935 Experimental Stn, Porton, Salisbury			4.00		
1923 Portobello Barracks B.O.				8.00	
1949 Portland Dock B.O., Portland/Dorset		2.00			
1908 Portland Harbour S.O. Dorset		?			
1947 Portsmouth Dockyard/ Portsmouth, Hants		2.00			
1915 Portsmouth R.M.A.		?			
1936 Naval Barracks/Portsmouth		3.00			
1947 Naval Barracks, Portsmouth, Hants		2.00			
1900 Fort Grange, Portsmouth		?			
1957 Portsmouth, Hants Naval Barracks					Rectangular Parcel: 1.00
1915 Prees Heath Camp B.O., Whitchurch			4.00		
1916 Prees Heath Camp B.O., Whitchurch		4.00			
1917 Prees Heath Camp				7.00	
1916 Whitchurch, (Prees Heath Camp)					Rectangular Parcel: 3.00
1917 Barracks. Preston		4.00			
1947 Barracks. Preston, Lancs		4.00			
1916 Barracks. Preston					Circular Parcel: 4.00
1907 Puddaven Camp				8.00	
1914 Purfleet Camp				7.00	
1915 Purfleet Camp. Grays		5.00			
1957 The Raleigh, Torpoint, Cornwall			2.00		
1954 Raleigh. Torpoint, Cornwall		2.00			
1954 Raleigh. Torpoint, Cornwall					Rectangular Parcel: 2.00
1945 Ranikhet Camp, Reading, Berks		2.00			
1914 Ravensworth Camp, Gateshead				8.00	
1885 The Barracks, Reading		12.00			
1938 The Barracks, Reading, Berks		4.00			
1937 Regents Park Camp, N.W.1				8.00	
1919 Reed Hall Camp B.O., Colchester			4.00		
1915 Reed Hall Military Camp, Colchester			?		
1915 Reed Hall Military Camp, Colchester		4.00			
1919 Reed Hall Camp B.O., Colchester		4.00			
1915 Reed Hall Camp					Circular Parcel: 4.00
1915 Reed Hall/Camp					Circular Parcel: 4.00
1915 The Remount Depot, Romsey		4.00			
1915 Remount Depot/Romsey					Circular Parcel: 4.00
1912 Military Camp, Rhayader					Rubber Packet: 5.00
1914 Rheidol Camp				8.00	
1915 Richmond Camp B.O.			4.00		

	dup.	s/c	d/c	sk	
1915 Richmond Camp B.O. Yorks			4.00		
1915 Richmond Camp B.O. Yorks		4.00			
1915 Richmond Camp. Yorks B.O.					Rectangular Parcel: 4.00
1915 Ripon Camp/1			3.00		
1915 Ripon Camp/2			3.00		
1918 Ripon Camp/1		3.00			
1915 Ripon Camp M.O.S.B.		10.00			
1917 Ripon Camp					Rectangular Parcel: 4.00
1915 Ripon. Ripon Camp					Rectangular Parcel: 4.00
1917 Richborough Camp, Sandwich, Kent		5.00			
1908 Rochford Camp B.O.				8.00	
1915 Roehampton Camp S.W.		5.00			
1915 Rolleston Camp, Salisbury			4.00		
1915 Rollestone Camp, Salisbury			4.00		
1915 Salisbury. Rollestone Camp					Rectangular Parcel: 4.00
1911 Rolleston Camp B.O. Salisbury		4.00			
1909 Rolleston Camp B.O. Devizes		4.00			
? Australian Field P.O., Rollestone		?			
1915 Romsey Camp. Romsey			4.00		
1915 Romsey Camp/Romsey					Circular Parcel: 4.00
1915 Roomer Camp/Masham				8.00	
1917 Royal Aircraft Factory, (B.O.) Aldershot		?			
1918 Royal Aircraft Estab. (B.O.) Aldershot		?			
1916 Rugeley Camp, Stafford			4.00		
1915 Rugeley Camp B.O. Stafford			4.00		
1917 Rugeley Camp, Stafford		4.00			
1917 Rugeley Camp B.O. Stafford		4.00			
1918 Rugeley/Camp				6.00	
1916 Stafford (Rugeley Camp B.O.)					Rectangular Parcel: 4.00
1916 Rushmoor Camp, Aldershot			4.00		
1915 Rushmoor Camp, Aldershot				6.00	
1898 Field Post Office Salisbury/1			4.00		
1898 Field Post Office Salisbury/2			4.00		
1898 Field Post Office Salisbury/3			4.00		
1915 Canadian Base P.O. Salisbury			5.00		
? Salisbury (Durrington Camp)					Rectangular Parcel: ?
1915 Park House Camp, Salisbury					Circular Parcel: 4.00
1958 St. Athan Main Site, Barry, Glam		2.00			
1944 St. Athan Station, Barry, Glam		2.00			
1914 St. Anthony Camp, Falmouth			4.00		
1913 St. Anthony Camp, Falmouth				7.00	
1914 St. Anthony Camp, Falmouth					Rubber Packet: 4.00
1937 St. Giles Camp. Wimborne, Dst				7.00	
1937 St. Giles Camp, Wimborne				7.00	
1914 St. John's Camp, Crowboro					Circular Parcel: 5.00
1907 St. Leonard's Camp, Ringwood				8.00	
1915 Canadian Field P.O., St. Martins Plain			4.00		

	dup.	s/c	d/c	sk	
1916 Canadian F.P.O., St. Martins Plain					Oval Registration: 5.00
1915 Sand Hill Camp, Wilts		5.00			
1915 Warminster. Sand Hill Camp, Wilts					Rectangular Parcel: 4.00
1915 Sandling Camp, Folkestone		4.00			
1915 Sandling Camp, Shorncliffe		4.00			
1915 Canadian Field P.O., Sandling Camp		4.00			
1915 Sandling Camp, Shorncliffe			5.00		
1916 Sandling Camp					Oval Registration: 5.00
1916 Canadian F.P.O., Sandling Camp					Oval Registration: 6.00
1920 Scarborough Race Course Camp, Scarborough		5.00			
1940 Scapa Pier, Kirkwall, Orkney		6.00			
1915 Canadian Base P.O., Seaford Camp		4.00			
1917 Canadian P.O. Seaford		4.00			
1916 Canadian P.O. Seaford Camp, Sussex		4.00			
1913 Seaford Camp, Lewes			5.00		
1914 The Camp, Seaford. Sx			5.00		
1914 The Camp, Seaford, Sussex			5.00		
1914 North Camp, Seaford, Sussex	4.00				
1919 Canadian P.O., Seaford Camp, Sussex					Oval Registration: 5.00
1914 North Camp/Seaford, Sussex					
1918 Sedbury Camp, Chepstow		4.00			
1918 The Seldown Camp		4.00			
1918 Sedgeford Camp, Kings Lynn		?			
1959 Seton Camp, Longniddry, East Lothian	2.00				
1915 Shanes Park Camp, Belfast				8.00	
1919 Shanes Park Camp				8.00	
1918 Shareham Camp, Sussex (error)				12.00	
1914 Sherrington Camp				8.00	
1863 Shoebury Fort		?			
1915 Shoreham Camp, Sussex			4.00		
1916 Canadian P.O., C.D.D. Shoreham-on-Sea			?		
1916 Canadian P.O., C.D.D. Shoreham-on-Sea					Oval Registration: ?
1916 Canadian P.O., C.C.A.C. Shoreham-on-Sea			?		
1903 Shoreham Camp, Sussex	4.00				
1915 Shoreham Camp/Sussex		4.00			
1905 Shorncliffe Camp B.O./ Folkestone		4.00			
1906 Shorncliffe Camp B.O., Folkestone/1		4.00			
1906 Shorncliffe Camp/Folkestone		3.00			

	dup.	s/c	d/c	sk	
1914 Shorncliffe Camp Folkestone/1			3.00		
1915 Canadian Base, Shorncliffe			5.00		
1915 Canadian Base P.O., Shorncliffe Camp			5.00		
1871 Shorncliffe Camp		8.00			
1916 D.L.S. Canadian Base, P.O. Shorncliffe Camp		?			
1871 F46. (Numeral only)	?				
1881 Shorncliffe Camp F46	10.00				
1916 Canadian P.O. Shorncliffe					Oval Registration: 5.00
1917 Shorncliff Camp				6.00	
1913 Shorncliff Camp					Circular Parcel: 4.00
1915 Sling Camp, Salisbury			4.00		
1916 Sling Camp/Salisbury					Circular Parcel: 4.00
1915 Sling Camp				7.00	
1914 Sling Plantation Camp				8.00	
1944 H.M.S. Cabbala/Stafford					Oval Registration: 4.00
1906 Stanhope Lines, Aldershot			3.00		
1906 Stanhope Lines, Aldershot		3.00			
1963 Stanhope Lines, Aldershot, Hants		3.00			
1915 Stanhope Lines, Aldershot				5.00	
1915 Aldershot. Stanhope Lines					Rectangular Parcel: 4.00
1916 Stanhope Lines B.O./ Aldershot					Circular Parcel: 4.00
1915 Stone Farm Camp, Sandling, Hythe			?		
? Stobs Camp, Hawick		?			
1907 Stowe Park Camp				8.00	
1908 Stowe Park Camp, Buckingham				8.00	
1912 Stowe Park Camp, Bucks				8.00	
1958 Stradishall Camp P.O., Newmarket, Suffolk			2.00		
1943 Stradishall Camp, Newmarket, Suffolk		2.00			
1955 Stradishall Camp, Newmarket, Suffolk					Rectangular Parcel: 2.00
1938 Strensall Camp, York			3.00		
1912 Strensall Camp		3.00			
? Strensall Camp, Yorks		3.00			
1889 Strensall Camp, York 930	14.00				
1926 The Camp, Stroud, Glos					Rubber Packet: 5.00
1915 Summer Down Camp					Rectangular Parcel: 4.00
1915 Summer Down Camp, Eastbourne		4.00			
1917 Sunningdale Camp, Ascot		5.00			
1915 Sutton Mandeville Camp, Salisbury		4.00			
1915 Sutton Mandeville/Camp					Circular Parcel: 4.00
1916 Sutton Mandeville Camp/ Salisbury			4.00		
1916 Sutton Veny Camp, Wilts				4.00	
1915 Sutton Veny Camp, Wilts					Rubber Packet: 4.00

	dup.	s/c	d/c	sk	
1915 Sutton Veny Camp, Wilts					Circular Parcel: 4.00
1915 Sutton Veny Camp, Wilts			4.00		
1915 Sutton Veny Camp, Warminster			?		
? Sutton Veny Camp, Wilts		4.00			
1915 Sutton Veny Camp B.O. Wilts		4.00			
1912 Swanage/Camp				7.00	
1915 Swanage Camp B.O. Poole		4.00			
1915 Tadworth Camp, Epsom			4.00		
1915 Tadworth Camp, Epsom		4.00			
1915 Tadworth Camp/Epsom					Circular Parcel: ?
1929 Tain Camp, Rosshire				8.00	
1917 Army Camp, Thetford			4.00		
1911 Thetford Camp		4.00			
1911 Thetford/Camp				6.00	
1911 Tidworth Barracks B.O.			4.00		
1907 Tidworth Barracks. Andover			4.00		
1917 Tidworth Barracks, Hants			4.00		
1914 Tidworth Barracks		4.00			
1907 Tidworth Barracks, Andover M.O. & S.B.		4.00			
1914 Tidworth Barracks, Hants		4.00			
1912 Tidworth Barracks, Andover		4.00			
1903 Tidworth Park Camp, Andover		4.00			
1925 Tidworth Park Camp B.O., Andover		4.00			
1903 Tidworth Pennings Camp, Andover		4.00			
1916 Australian Military P.O., Tidworth		5.00			
? Tidworth Barracks			4.00		
1908 Tidworth Barracks B.O.			4.00		
1914 Tidworth Barracks, Hants			4.00		
1917 Tidworth Barracks, Andover			4.00		
1937 Tidworth Park Camp, Hants			4.00		
1932 Tidworth Park Camp, Tidworth			4.00		
1932 Tidworth Pk Camp, Tidworth			4.00		
1920 Andover Tidworth Barracks B.O.					Rectangular Parcel: 4.00
? Tidworth Barracks B.O. Andover					Rubber Packet: 4.00
1917 Andover. Tidworth Pennings Camp					Rectangular Parcel: 4.00
Edwardian Tidworth Barracks B.O. Andover					Circular Parcel: 4.00
1914 Tidworth Barracks, Hants					Circular Parcel: 4.00
1915 2nd Army Hdqtrs., Tonbridge Wells		5.00			
1899 Topsham Barracks, Exeter		?			
1912 Fleet Post Office, Torquay		5.00			
? Townfoot Camp, Denny			8.00		
1937 Trawsfynedd Camp		4.00			
1914 Halton Camp, Tring					

	dup.	s/c	d/c	sk	
1916 Twezeldown Camp, Aldershot			4.00		
1915 Twezeldown Camp, Farnham			4.00		
1915 Tweseldown Camp, Farnham			4.00		
1918 Tweseldown Camp (with cross)			4.00		
1917 Twezeldown Camp, Aldershot		4.00			
1915 Twezeldown Camp, Farnham		4.00			
1917 Twezeldown Camp, Aldershot				5.00	
1930 Tweseldown Camp, Aldershot				5.00	
1916 Twezeldown Camp					Circular Parcel: 4.00
1916 Central Flying School, Upavon		7.00			
1918 Upavon Central Flying School, Pewsey, Wilts		7.00			
1920 Central Flying School, Pewsey, Wilts		7.00			
1898 Wareham/Field Post Office		5.00			
1943 Weeton Camp, Preston, Lancs		3.00			
1948 Weeton Camp, Preston, Lancs					Rectangular Parcel: 3.00
1909 Wellington Barracks, S.W.		?			
1903 Welbeck Camp, Worksop				8.00	
1899 Field Post Office, West Down Camp/1			4.00		
1899 Field Post Office, West Down Camp/2			4.00		
1903 Field Post Office, West Down South		4.00			
1904 Field Post Office, West Down North		4.00			
1909 West Down South Camp, Devizes		4.00			
1908 West Down South Camp B.O. Devizes		4.00			
1911 West Down South Camp, Salisbury		4.00			
1910 West Down North Camp B.O. Devizes		4.00			
1911 West Down North Camp B.O. Salisbury		4.00			
1911 West Down North Camp, Salisbury		4.00			
1905 West Lulworth Camp				8.00	
1907 West Lulworth Camp, Wareham				8.00	
1907 West Parley Camp, Wimborne				8.00	
1947 Whale Island, Portsmouth, Hants		3.00			
1918 Whale Island		3.00			
1965 Whale Island, Portsmouth, Hants					Rectangular Parcel: 3.00
1958 H.M.S. 'Excellent' Whale Island				4.00	

	dup.	s/c	d/c	sk	
1958 H.M.S. 'Excellent' Whale Island					Rubber Packet: 2.00
1929 Whittington Barracks, Lichfield			3.00		
1908 Whittington Barracks, Lichfield		4.00			
1905 Whittington Barracks		4.00			
1929 Whittington Barracks, Lichfield, Staffs		3.00			
1957 Whittington Barracks, Lichfield, Staffs					Rectangular Parcel: 3.00
1917 Whittington Barracks, (Lichfield)					Rectangular Parcel: 4.00
1909 Whitchurch Down Camp				8.00	
1915 Prees Heath Camp, Whitchurch					Circular Parcel: 4.00
1915 Whitebread Hole Camp, Eastbourne		?			
1911 White Hill, Bordon Camp, Hants		4.00			
1914 Whitmoor Camp/Woking				8.00	
1912 Willsworthy Camp				8.00	
1877 Wimbledon Camp 801	10.00				
1877 Wimbledon Camp Z801	12.00				
1867 Wimbledon Camp		9.00			
1867 Wimbledon Camp S.W.		9.00			
1916 Wimbledon Common Camp, S.W.		4.00			
1905 Windmill Hill Camp B.O. Andover			4.00		
1905 Windmill Hill Camp B.O. Andover		4.00			
1910 Windmill Hill Camp, Andover		4.00			
1916 Andover (Windmill Hill Camp)					Rectangular Parcel: 4.00
1916 Windmill Hill Camp/ Andover					Circular Parcel: 4.00
1909 Wing Camp, Leighton Buzzard				8.00	
1914 Witley Camp, Godalming			4.00		
? Canadian Base P.O., Witley Camp			?		
1917 Canadian P.O. Witley Camp			4.00		
1914 Witley Camp, Godalming		4.00			
1918 Canadian P.O. Witley Camp					Oval Registration: 5.00
1916 Godalming, Witley Camp					Rectangular Parcel: 4.00
1915 Witley Camp, Godalming					Rubber Packet: 4.00
1914 Witley Camp, Godalming					Circular Parcel: 4.00
1944 Wittering Camp R.A.F.P.O. Peterborough		3.00			
1915 Woodbury Camp, Exeter			4.00		
1914 Woodbury Camp, Exeter					Rubber Packet: 4.00
1915 Woodbury Common Camp					Rubber Packet: 4.00
1915 Woodcote Camp, Epsom			4.00		

	dup.	s/c	d/k	sk	
1915 Woodcote Camp, Epsom		4.00			
1915 Woodcote Camp/Epsom					Circular Parcel: 4.00
1911 Woodhead Camp, K.K.		5.00			
1943 Woodside. Arbroath. Angus		3.00			
1948 Woolwich R.A. Barracks, S.E.18		3.00			
1915 Woolwich Royal Dockyard, S.E.		?			
1916 Royal Arsenal, Woolwich		4.00			
1957 London. Woolwich R.A. Barracks, S.E.18					Rectangular Parcel: 4.00
1915 Worgret Camp, Poole			4.00		
1914 Worgret Camp, Poole		4.00			
1912 Worgret/Camp				7.00	
1914 Worgret Camp, Wareham				7.00	
1971 Worthy Down, Winchester, Hants		1.00			
1947 Wroughton R.A.F. Hospital Swindon, Wilts		2.00			
1906 The Camp, Yarmouth		5.00			
1944 Yatesbury Camp, Calne, Wilts		3.00			
1947 Yatesbury Camp, Calne, Wilts					Rectangular Parcel: 3.00
1964 Yeovilton, Yeovil, Somerset		2.00			
1965 Yeovilton. R.N. Air Stn, Yeovil, Som		2.00			
1966 Yeovilton Muswum Open Day					Machine: 1.00
1942 Yeovilton, Yeovil, Somerset					Rectangular Parcel: 2.00
1965 R.N. Air Station, Yeovilton, Yeovil, Somerset					Rectangular Parcel: 200

PUZZLED?

From time to time all collectors find covers which have curious or unexplained features. Send a photocopy (with SAE or IRC) and I will send my comments or refer to a specialist in a particular field. Some of the most interesting – or ones which still cannot be explained – illustrated in the next *Collect British Postmarks*.

16. ISLANDS

Cancellations of the British Post Office and the Postal Administrations of the Channel Islands and Isle of Man. Local issues not included.

The Channel Islands

Jersey

379

380

381

382

Concave Jersey	300.00
Straight line Jersey	250.00
379 Scrolls	250.00
Jersey/Penny Post, boxed	350.00
Jersey double arc	18.00
Ship letter types	250.00
1d, red paid marks, 1840s	200.00
2d, black unpaid marks, 1840s	225.00
Maltese cross	20.00
Numeral 409	20.00
Duplex 409 types	18.00
380 Squared circles	2.50
Double circles with Maltese cross	0.75
381 Double circle with (St. Heliers)	2.00
Single circles	1.75
Krag machine marks	1.50
Universal machine marks	0.25
Machine with boxed lines	0.15
Telephone Slogans, 1930s	1.50
Other slogans, 1946–63	0.50
Holiday slogans, from 1963	0.25
Other slogans, from 1963	0.25
Oval Registration marks	2.50

Sub Offices:	Pre 1900	1900–1940	1940–45	1945–69	From 1969
Gorey	25.00	3.00	3.00	2.00	0.20
St Aubin	20.00	2.00	3.00	2.00	0.20
Others	30.00	4.00	4.00	2.50	0.25

GUERNSEY

383

384

385   386

383	Concave Guernsey	275.00
	Scroll types	250.00
	Guernsey double arc	18.00
	Ship letter types	300.00
	1d, red paid mark, 1840s	200.00
384	2d, black unpaid marks, 1840s	225.00
	Maltese cross	20.00
385	Numeral 324	20.00
	Duplex 324 types	18.00
	Squared circles	3.00
	Double circles with Maltese cross	0.75
	Large single circle	1.85
	Small single circle	3.00
	Krag machine marks	2.00
	Universal machine marks	0.25
	Machine with two horizontal bars	0.10
	Royal Wedding slogan, 1947	2.00
	'British Holiday Abroad' Slogans	0.10
	Other slogans, 1950–69	0.50
	Other slogans, 1969 onwards	0.30
386	Oval Registration marks	3.00

Sub Offices:	Pre 1900	1900–1940	1940–45	1945–69	From 1969
Cobo	25.00	10.00	2.50	2.50	0.20
St. Sampsons	20.00	2.00	3.00	2.00	0.20
Others	30.00	4.00	4.00	2.50	0.25

Alderney

387	388	389	390

387 Maltese cross 4000.00
Undated double arcs, ... 350.00
Numeral 965 . . . . 150.00
Alderney single circle 40.00
388 Alderney double circle with Maltese cross 12.00
Alderney/Ch. Is., double circle, thick arcs 5.00
Alderney/Ch. Is., single circle 3.00
389 Alderney/Guernsey, Channel Islands, single circle 2.00
390 Parcel double circle, Alderney/Channel Islands 30.00
Guernsey sub-office cancellations, from 1969 . . . . 0.50

Sark

391	392

Undated double arc type 1500.00
391 Sark single circle, as despatch mark alongside Guernsey, pre 1904 20.00
As above but cancelling stamps, 1904–27 . . . . 13.00
392 Sark, Guernsey/Channel Islands, double circle, thick arcs . . . 4.00
Sark-Guernsey/Channel Islands, single circle 4.00
Guernsey Sub-office cancellations, from 1969 . . . . 0.50

Herm

393	394

393 Herm Guernsey/Channel Islands, double circle, thick arcs,
1925–38 . . . . 250.00
Meter Mark, 1948 . . . . 100.00
394 Guernsey Sub-office cancellations, from 1969 . . . . 0.50
Parcel Post cancellation, from 1969 . . . . 4.00

ISLE OF MAN

395

396

397

398

395 Isle of Man, straight line hand stamps 100.00
    Isle of Man, double arc type 85.00
    Penny Post types 300.00
    Ship letters 1000.00
396 1840 Penny Post, P1 in red 200.00
    Douglas Isle of Man, double arc types 20.00
    Maltese Cross 25.00
    Numeral 407 types 20.00
397 Duplex 407 types 7.00
    Squared circles 2.00
    Double circles with Isle of Man, I of Man or cross 0.25
    Single circles with Isle of Man or I of Man 0.75
    Christmas crosses 250.00
    Krag machine marks 0.75
    Hey Dolphin Machine marks 1.75
    Universal machine marks 0.40
    British Goods slogan 5.00
    Post Early slogan 5.00
    Other pre 1957 slogans 10.00
    Holiday or Retirement slogan from 1963 . . . . 0.30
    Other slogans 1957–1973 . . . . 0.30
    Other slogans 1973 onwards 0.20

399

400

401

402

Ramsey/Isle of Man, boxed, from 1832 . . . . 135.00
400 Numeral 036 types 35.00
Duplex 036 types 12.50
Squared circle 20.00
Ramsey/Isle of Man double circles 0.25
Krag machine 2.50
Holiday or Retirement slogans 0.30
Other slogans, pre 1973 . . . . 0.40
Other slogans, after 1973 . . . . 0.25

401 Castletown/Isle of Man, boxed, from 1832 . . . . 180.00
Castletown – Isle of Man, double arc 35.00
Numeral 037 types 60.00
Duplex 037 types 20.00
Castletown S.O. double ring 6.00
Krag machines 0.30

Peeltown/Isle of Man, boxed, from 1832 . . . . 150.00
402 Duplex D51 . . . . 8.00
Squared circle 4.00
Peel/Douglas double ring 4.00
Peel/Douglas single ring 4.00
Peel/Isle of Man double ring 0.30
Krag Machines 0.60

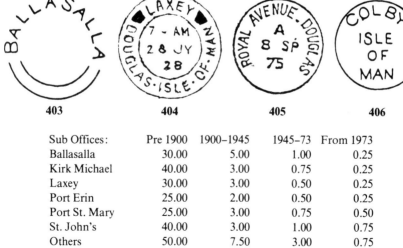

403   404   405   406

Sub Offices:	Pre 1900	1900–1945	1945–73	From 1973
Ballasalla	30.00	5.00	1.00	0.25
Kirk Michael	40.00	3.00	0.75	0.25
Laxey	30.00	3.00	0.50	0.25
Port Erin	25.00	2.00	0.50	0.25
Port St. Mary	25.00	3.00	0.75	0.50
St. John's	40.00	3.00	1.00	0.75
Others	50.00	7.50	3.00	0.75

Scilly Islands

Straight line, Scilly 100.00
Circular date stamp, Victorian 65.00
Scilly, double circle with Maltese cross 3.50
Scilly, single circle 7.50

Island Offices:	Pre 1900	1900–1939	1939–60	From 1960
St Mary's	10.00	3.00	1.00	0.20
St Martin's	15.00	4.00	1.50	0.30
St Agnes	20.00	5.00	2.00	0.30
Tresco	30.00	8.00	2.00	0.40
Bryher	50.00	15.00	2.00	0.40

Isle of Wight

	Pre 1900	1900–1939	1939–60	From 1960
Ryde, Cowes, Ventnor	2.00	0.50	0.25	0.10
Shanklin, Sandown	3.50	0.65	0.40	0.20
East Cowes, Yarmouth, Newport.	4.50	1.00	0.60	0.30
Other Offices	10.00	3.00	1.00	0.40

Other English Islands

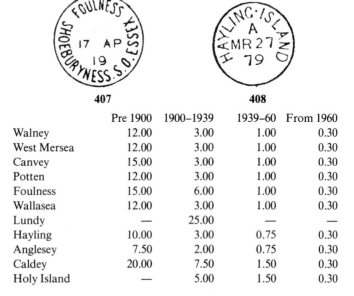

407   408

	Pre 1900	1900–1939	1939–60	From 1960
Walney	12.00	3.00	1.00	0.30
West Mersea	12.00	3.00	1.00	0.30
Canvey	15.00	3.00	1.00	0.30
Potten	12.00	3.00	1.00	0.30
Foulness	15.00	6.00	1.00	0.30
Wallasea	12.00	3.00	1.00	0.30
Lundy	—	25.00	—	—
Hayling	10.00	3.00	0.75	0.30
Anglesey	7.50	2.00	0.75	0.30
Caldey	20.00	7.50	1.50	0.30
Holy Island	—	5.00	1.50	0.30

(see also sections on Cachets and Maritime marks.)

17. CHARGE, INSTRUCTIONAL AND EXPLANATORY MARKS

London and Provincial Series

409

410

Circular marks,
More/to/Pay 8.00
409 More to Pay, with code letter at base, in red 9.00
More to Pay, with London District Initials 10.00
OS in double circle, for 'old stamp' 750.00

Pence marks, unframed, from 1870:
½d 4.00
410 1d 1.50
1d/to/Pay 3.50
2d 2.00
3d 3.00
5d 3.00

$$\frac{1}{2}\overset{D}{}\text{-}$$
458

411

412

$$\mathbf{1}\,\overset{D}{\text{-}}$$
TO PAY
723

413

Pence marks with office numbers or London District Initials, unframed, from 1870s:
411 ½D 2.00
1D 0.75
2D 1.75
3D 1.50
4D 1.75
5D 1.25
8D 1.00

Pence marks with office numbers or London District Initials, framed,
from 1870s:

	½D, oval frame	5.00
412	1D, oval frame	2.50
	1D, circular frame	5.00
	5D, circular frame	2.50
	6D, oval frame	2.50
	7D, oval frame	3.00

Pence marks with office numbers or London District Initials, unframed, with
TO PAY, black or green, from 1920s:

	½D	2.00
413	1D	0.60
	1½D	3.00
	2D	1.25
	3D	1.00
	4D	1.00
	6D	1.50
	.... D TO PAY	1.00

Boxed T shaped explanatory marks with office numbers or London District
Initials, black, purple or green (double prices for red), from 1870s:

Closed contrary to regulations 11 6	Liable to Letter Rate 407
414	415

	4D to pay	2.00
	Address Contrary to rule	5.00
	Book Post/over . . . . . oz	4.00
	Charged for/re-direction	4.00
	Closed against inspection	3.50
414	Closed contrary/to regulations	3.50
	Contains a letter in/type-writing characters	3.50
	Contains writing in the nature of a letter	3.50
	Contrary to Regulations	1.00
	Contrary to Regulations/Exceeds limits of size	3.00
	Deceased	3.50
	Exceeds limits of size	3.00
	Firm not known	3.00
	Gone Away	1.00
	Gone. No address	2.00
	Imitation typewriting/posted out of course	4.50
	Inadmissible at ½d rate	4.00

Inadmissible at printed paper rate	2.00
Inadmissible at . . . . . rate	3.00
Insufficient Address	2.00
Insufficiently Addressed	1.50
Insufficiently paid	3.00
Insufficiently prepaid	2.00
415 Liable to Letter rate	0.75
Liable to postcard rate	1.50
Misdirected	3.00
More to Pay/Above . . . . . oz (line beneath 'More to Pay')	2.00
As above but without line	1.50
No Such Street	4.00
No Such Street in	4.00
No Such Street in Liverpool	4.50
Not called for	2.00
Not certified as official	7.00
Not found	3.00
Not known	2.00
Not known as addressed	3.00
Not known at	4.00
Not to be found	2.00
Of the nature of a letter	3.00
Please advise sender of/correct Address	4.00
Posted on Ship Abroad	6.00
Posted out of course	3.00
Re-issued	5.00
Reposted more than one clear day after delivery	5.00
Undelivered for reason stated/Return to Sender	3.00
Unpaid	2.00

Early combined charge and explanatory marks, black, purple or green (double prices for red), from 1910:

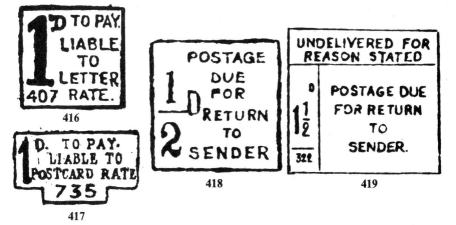

416

417

418

419

Above 2oz/1D/more to Pay, boxed T-shaped with office
number 2.50
More/to pay/above . . . . . oz/3D, boxed with office number . . 1.75
418 ½D/Postage/due/for/return/to/Sender, boxed 1.00
As above but 2D 3.00
1D/to pay/above/2oz, boxed with office number 1.75
1D/to pay/Liable to/Letter Rate, boxed T-shaped with office
number 1.00
416 1D/to pay/Liable/to/Letter/Rate, boxed with office number . 1.00
2D/to pay/Liable to/Letter Rate, boxed T-shaped with office
number 2.00
417 1D/to pay/Liable to/Postcard Rate, boxed T-shaped, with office
number 1.20
As above but blank value tablet for completion 2.00
Undelivered for/reason stated/½D/Postage/Due for/Return/
TO/Sender, boxed 2.00
As above but 1D 1.00
Undelivered for/reason stated/½D/Postage Due/For Return/
To Sender, boxed with double frame and office number . . 2.00
419 As above but single frame and 1½D 1.50
As above, single frame, 2D 0.75
As above, single frame 2½D 1.00
As above, single frame, space for amount to be inserted . . . 0.50
Unpaid 2D to pay/Posted too late for ½D rate, boxed 4.00

420   421

*Boxed marks with double frame, value panel above office number or London
District Initials, black or green, from 1930s:*
1D/More to/Pay/letter rate/above . . . . . oz 3.00
1D/More to/Pay/Printed Paper/Rate/above . . . . . oz 3.00
420 D/More to/pay/letter rate/above . . . . . oz, blank panel 1.00
D/More to/pay/Newspaper/rate/contains . . . . . newspapers,
blank panel 2.75
D/More to/pay/ . . . . . rate/above . . . . . oz, blank panel . . . 1.00
D/To pay/contrary to/regulations/liable to/ . . . . . rate, blank
panel 2.50
D/To pay/Form not/appropriately/printed/Liable to/Letter
rate. 3.50

D/To pay/inadmissible/Sample rate/liable to/letter rate/above	
..... oz, blank panel	3.50
2D/To pay/liable to/letter rate	3.00
D/To pay/liable to/letter rate, blank panel	1.00
D/To pay/liable to/postcard/rate, blank panel	1.25
2D/To pay/Posted/unpaid	3.00
D/To pay/Posted/Out of/course	2.50
D/To pay/posted/unpaid/above ..... oz, blank panel	1.00
D/To pay/posted/unpaid, blank panel	1.00

Boxed marks, fixed value above office number or London District Initials, (size of box, letters, thickness of frame varies). Black, green or purple, from 1940s:

2D/More to/Pay/Insufficiently/Prepaid, no internal panel lines	0.60
2D/More to/Pay/Letter Rate/Above ..... oz	0.60
3D/More to/pay/letter rate/Above ..... oz	0.65
As above but 2 oz	0.65
3D/More to/Pay/ ..... rate/Above 2 oz	0.65
421 2D/More to/Pay/ ..... rate/Above ..... oz	0.65
As above but 3D	0.65
7D/More to/Pay/Insufficiently/Prepaid	0.65
2D/To pay/imitation type/circular not/specially posted/liable to/letter rate	1.20
1D/To pay/liable to/letter rate	0.50
As above but 2D	0.50
3D/To Pay/Liable to/letter rate/Above ..... oz	0.65
As above but 2 oz	0.65
1D/To pay/Liable to/postcard/rate	0.60
As above but 2D	0.75
7D/To pay/posted/underpaid	0.50
2D/To pay/Posted/unpaid	0.50
As above but 4D	0.50
As above but 5D	0.60
As above but 6D	0.60
As above but 8D	0.40
3D/To pay/Posted Unpaid/Too late for 1D rate	1.00
5D/To pay/Posted Unpaid/Too late for 2D rate	1.00
8D/To pay/Posted/Unpaid/Too late for/3D rate	1.00

 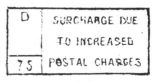

422   423

Boxed marks, blank panel above office number or London District Initials (Size of box, letters, thickness of frame varies). Black, green or purple, from 1940s:

D/More to/pay/insufficiently/prepaid, no internal panel lines   .   0.50
D/More To/Pay/Letter Rate/above . . . . . oz 0.60
D/More to/pay/Printed Paper/rate/above . . . . . oz 0.70
D/More/To pay/ . . . . . rate/above . . . . . oz 0.45
D/More to/pay/ . . . . . rate/above . . . . . oz 0.60
423 D/Surcharge Due/to Increased/Postal charges 0.60
D/To Pay/closed/contrary to/Regulations/Liable to/Letter rate   1.00
D/To pay/contrary to/regulations/liable to . . . . . rate   . . .   0.85
D/To pay/imitation type/circular, not/specially posted/liable
    to/ . . . . . rate 0.90
D/To pay/liable to/letter/rate 0.50
D/To pay/liable to/letter rate/ . . . . . oz 0.55
D/To pay/Liable to/postcard/rate 0.55
D/To pay/liable to/Printed Paper/rate/above . . . . . oz   . . .   0.70
422 D/To pay/posted/unpaid 0.35
D/To pay/posted/unpaid/above . . . . . oz 0.45
    As above but without office number 0.75
    Undelivered for reason/stated/Postage due for/return to sender,
      with D and office number at bottom right 1.00

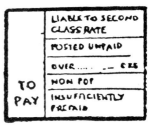

424   425

Boxed marks, decimal currency, from 1971:

3P/More to/Pay/over . . . . . oz, with office number 0.45
P/More to Pay/ . . . . . Rate/Above . . . . . oz, as above 0.45
P/More To Pay/ . . . . . Rate/Above . . . . . Grms, as above   . . .   0.40
P/Surcharged/To Increased/Postal charges 1.00
424 Surcharge due/To Increased/Postal charges 0.50
P/To pay/More to/Pay over/ . . . . . oz, ...   0.45
P/To pay/Posted/Unpaid, blank panel above office number   . .   0.35

Multipurpose charge box, green or purple, 1970s:

1p in left hand panel 0.15
2p in left hand panel 0.15
6p in left hand panel 0.15
11p in left hand panel 0.20
14p in left hand panel 0.20
425 Blank left hand panel for amount to be inserted 0.10
As above but ozs removed after metrication 0.10
As above but new type, TO/PAY central and OVER . . . Grms
(or G) 0.10

The Inland Section

426

427

428

With I.B. (Inland Branch) above figures, from 1870s:

1D 5.00
2D 4.00
426 10D 10.00

Large figures, code letters beneath or uncoded, black or green from 1900s:				*Small figures, uncoded, black or green, from 1900s:*			
½D	4.00	4D	1.75	½D	—	4D	1.75
427 1D	1.00	5D	1.50	1D	3.00	5D	1.75
1½D	2.00	6D	1.50	1½D	—	6D	1.75
2D	1.75	9D	3.00	2D	2.50	9D	—
2½D	5.00	1/-	2.00	2½D		1/-	—
3D	1.50	1/6	2.00	**428** 3D	2.00	1/6	—
3½D	4.00						

429

430

Other Marks:

Above . . . . . oz/1D/More to pay/I.S., boxed, T-Shaped	1.50
Address illegible/I.S., boxed, T-shaped	2.50
Charge not paid/I.S., boxed, T-shaped	2.50
Contrary to Regulations/I.B., boxed, T-shaped	3.00
Found Torn/and enclosed at/Inland Section, boxed, in purple .	1.00
Insufficiently Addressed/I.S., boxed, T-shaped	2.00
I.S. in triangle, Inspectors mark	1.50
3D/I.S./More to/pay/ . . . . . rate/above . . . . . oz, boxed, in green	1.50
10D/I.S.M.P./To pay/posted/underpaid, boxed in green . . .	1.00
Liable to letter Rate/I.B., boxed, T-shaped	3.00
Liable to Letter Rate/I.S., boxed, T-shaped	1.50
More to pay/above . . . . . oz/I.S., boxed, T-shaped, in green . .	1.50
8D/M.P.I.S./To pay/posted/unpaid, boxed	1.00
Not on board/Return to Sender, not boxed	7.00
Posted on Board Ship/I.S., boxed T-shaped	15.00
Posted out of course, boxed	2.50
Posted/out of/course/I.S., boxed	3.00
R.L.D.I.S./Surcharge duty/To pay, boxed	2.00
Return to Sender/Address Insufficient/I.S., boxed, T-shaped .	3.00
429 To Pay/I.S., boxed	3.00
To pay/R.L.D.I.S., boxed	2.00
1/- To pay/R.L.D.I.S., boxed	3.00
Undelivered for/Reason Stated/2D/Postage due/for return/to/	
Sender, in green	1.50
Unpaid 2D to pay/Posted too late for ½d rate/I.S., boxed . . .	3.00

Taxe Marks on Surcharged mail sent to or from abroad, from 1880:

Hexagonal framed T with 5, L for London beneath	1.50
As above but 10	1.50
430 As above but 15	1.50
As above but 30	1.50
As above but manuscript value	1.00
As above, manuscript value and order letters beneath	2.00
As above, 10, office number beneath	2.50
Large hollow T, in green	0.35
Unframed T	1.00

The Foreign Section

431

432

	Type 431	Type 432	As Type 432 but decimal	
½D	4.00	—	½p	0.75
1D	1.00	2.00		
1½D	3.00	—		
2D	2.00	2.00		
2½D	3.00	—		
3D	2.00	2.00		
3½D	—	4.00		
5D	4.00	—	5½p	0.75
6D	2.00	0.75		
7D	—	0.85		
9½D	—	3.00		
1/-	—	1.00		

Other Marks:

Contrary to Regulations/F.B., boxed, T-shaped	2.50
Express Fee Paid, boxed	1.50
Insufficient/Address, boxed	0.80
Insuffiently Addressed, boxed, FS in panel at right	1.50
Liable to Letter Rate/F.S., boxed, T-shaped	2.00
More to/Pay/ . . . . . Rate/above . . . . . /oz with FS and blank panel to left	2.00
Not transmissible unpaid/Postage required, boxed	1.25
Postage Paid/(F.S.), boxed	1.00
Posted out/of course, boxed	0.85
Returned for/better address, boxed, with FST inside right panel	1.50
Return to Sender/Open Panel F.S./Contrary to regulations, see page . . . . . P.O. Guide, boxed, purple	4.00
Stamps not valid, with F.S., boxed	0.50
T/15c in hexagon, with F.S. beneath	2.00
As above but manuscript value	2.00
Undelivered for reason stated/Returned to Sender, with FSR inside panel to right	1.50

Returned Letter Office, London

1D To Pay/Ldn. R.L.B. unframed	3.00
As above but 3d	2.00
As above but 4d	1.75
As above but 5d	1.75

Miscellaneous Marks

CHARGE NOT COLLECTED / FRESH LABEL REQUIRED

433

Liable to LetterRate

434

POSTAGE CANNOT BE PREPAID
BY MEANS OF INCOMPLETE
FRANKING IMPRESSION

435

Address Defective/Please advise sender, boxed, in purple . . .	0.75
433 Charge Not collected/X/Fresh label required, boxed	0.30
CH, in circle	1.50
. . . . . D To Pay, boxed	2.50
Delayed through being/posted in a letter box/for 'Country' letters/please advise sender, crinkly frame	5.00
Delayed through being/posted in a letter box/for 'London' letters/please advise sender, crinkly frame	5.00
Gone away, boxed or unboxed	0.50
Gone away/Address Not known, boxed	0.75
Gone away/1/2, boxed	0.65
Imperfect Impression/6d To Pay, boxed	1.50
Insufficiently Paid, boxed	1.00
Insufficiently paid/ . . . . . d to pay, boxed, with or without office number, in green	0.40
Insufficiently paid/ . . . . . to pay, boxed with office number, in green	0.40
Insufficient Postage 1st Class/Transferred to 2nd class, boxed, green	0.65
Invalid Revenue/Stamp, boxed, in green	2.00
Invalid Stamps Used/Postage Due . . . . . , boxed	1.00
Irregularly included by poster/in a bundle of late posted/meter-franked printed papers, framed in green	0.70
Late Fee/Paid, boxed	5.00
434 Liable to Letter Rate, boxed.	1.50
Liable to Postage surcharge/imperfect Meter franking, unframed in green	0.85

Liable to Surcharge/Imperfect/Meter franking, boxed with office
number 0.85
£SD stamps/Now Invalid, boxed in green 2.00
Mail opened and disposed/of at Liverpool (etc), boxed 4.00
Misdirected To, unframed 2.00
No post town, boxed or unboxed 0.50
No Service/Return to sender, boxed, divided horizontally, purple 1.00
No such street/Greenford Middx, many similar types, boxed, or
unboxed 0.40
No such street/(or place) in . . . . . unframed 0.40
Not known, boxed or unboxed 0.50
Not known at address stated/Forwarding particulars not
available, boxed 5.00
Not known/Southport,/Lancs, many similar types, boxed or
unboxed 0.40
Open Panel/Return to sender/Inadmissible for/Transmission
Abroad, boxed, purple 0.80
Over Grammes/ . . . . . d More to Pay, with office number . . . 2.00
Please inform sender/of your correct address, boxed 0.60
Postage cannot be/prepaid by means/of incomplete/franking
impressions, boxed in green 0.65
435 Postage cannot be prepaid/by means of incomplete/franking
impressions, unframed in green 0.85
Postage cannot be prepaid/with an incomplete/franking
impression, boxed in green 0.65

14P	POSTED
TO	UNPAID
PAY	SECOND CLASS

436

20P TO PAY

437

UNDELIVERED FOR REASON STATED

RETURN TO SENDER

438

P.T.O., boxed or unboxed 0.50
Return to sender/Undelivered for reasons stated, boxed, without
horizontal division, purple. 0.50
Ship Sailed, boxed 4.00
Stamp Invalid, unframed 2.00
Stamps/Missing/in/Transit, boxed, in red 0.50
Surcharged/Stamps invalid, boxed, in purple 0.30
Too late – ship sailed, unframed in black 3.00
To Pay/13p, boxed, green 0.50

To Pay/14p, boxed, green	0.50
4D To/Pay	0.60
12p To Pay unframed, green or red	0.30
As above but 18p to pay	0.30
437 As above but 20p to Pay	0.30
As above but 22p to Pay	0.30
13p/To Pay/Posted/Unpaid, boxed	0.40
436 14p/To/Pay/Posted/Unpaid/Second Class, boxed	0.60
To Pay/liable to/Postcard Rate, rectangular with blank panel for amount and office number.	0.80
To pay/on return/to sender/Postage/deficiency, in three sections with blank panel for amount and office number.	0.40
To Pay/Postage cannot be/prepaid by means/of an incomplete/ franking impression/liable to . . . . . rate, boxed with blank value tablet to left and office number or London District letters, green, black or purple	0.45
Trapped in machinery/Liverpool MLO (etc), single circle	1.00
Unclaimed, boxed or unboxed	0.50
438 Undelivered for reason stated/return to sender, boxed in two horizontal sections in purple, black or green, (red 0.50)	0.10
As above but 'reasons'	1.00
Undelivered for reason stated/to be returned to sender/at the address shown on cover, boxed in two horizontal sections	1.00
Underpaid overseas surcharge box, in green	0.30
Unpaid, boxed or unboxed	0.50
Writer of a letter addressed/to	0.50
Your correct postal address is/Any other form of address may lead/to delay. Please advise sender.	0.45
Boxed multi-purpose explanatory box, blank value tablet at left, without office number, green	0.75
Boxed number (e.g. 41, London E9; 42, Chelmsford)	0.75
Circular Returned letter marks:	
Returned Lr Office/London, etc	1.50
Edinburgh/R.L.O. etc.	1.50
R.L.B./Bristol etc.	2.50
Modern purple RLB types	0.45
Multipurpose mark explaining non-delivery, framed or unframed, some with office name	0.35
Multipurpose Overseas Surcharge box, in green	0.30
Small oval London E.C. marks, e.g. E.C. 18, in purple	0.50
Small triangle, apex downwards, with London District initials.	2.00
Small triangle, apex upwards, London District initials, telegraph code letters or office numbers	0.75
Surcharge box on mail from abroad, underpaid, incorporating + 11p Surcharge Fee	0.50
As above + 15p	0.50

18. NEWSPAPER, PARCEL, REGISTRATION, EXPRESS AND TRIANGULAR POSTMARKS

Newspaper Branch (prices are for large pieces or Newspaper Wrappers)

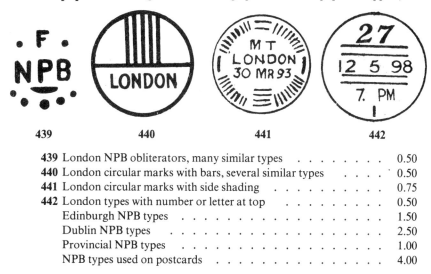

| 439 | 440 | 441 | 442 |

439 London NPB obliterators, many similar types 0.50
440 London circular marks with bars, several similar types 0.50
441 London circular marks with side shading 0.75
442 London types with number or letter at top 0.50
    Edinburgh NPB types 1.50
    Dublin NPB types 2.50
    Provincial NPB types 1.00
    NPB types used on postcards 4.00

Parcel Postmarks (prices are for large pieces)

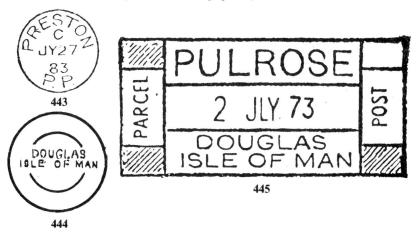

443

445

444

443 Single circles with 'Parcels office', 'Parcels Depot', 'P.P.' or
    'P.P.O.' 1.50
    As above but on Parcel Post Label 3.00
    Squared circle parcel marks 3.50
    Scroll parcel marks 4.50

444 Circular marks with office name and horizontal bars	0.50
As above but with vertical bars	0.50
As above but office name across double circles	0.40
445 Label type rectangular parcel marks, several types	0.20
Roller parcel cancellations	0.20
Oval marks in red for paid parcels	0.15

Registration

446

447

446 Crown with 'Registered' below	10.00
447 Oval Registered marks	0.50
Distinctive town types	4.00

Express

448

Straight line types	20.00
448 Oval types	3.00

Triangular Handstamps

449

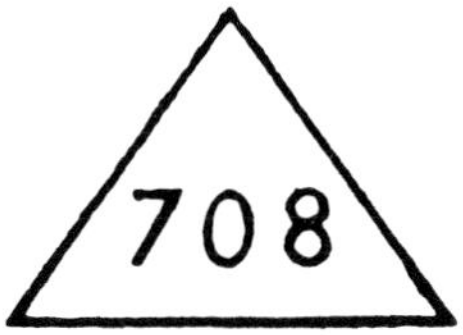

450

449 With telegraph code letters	0.50
With London District initials	0.80
With London Head Office initials, S.H., K.E., M.T.P, F.B., F.S	
or I.S	0.50
450 With provincial office numbers	0.60

(see also 'Machine Cancellations' and 'Charge and Instructional Marks')

19. CHRISTMAS POSTMARKS

Posted in Advance for Delivery on Christmas Day, 1902–09

451
Type 1

452
Type 2

453
Type 3 (Parcels?)

454
Type 4

455
Type 5: Columbia Machine

Town	Telegraph Initials (Type 2)	Date	1	2	3	4	5
Aberdeen	AB	1903	?				
Altrincham	ADJ	1903	£250				
		1904	£250				
		1905	£200				
		1906				£120	
		1907				£120	
		1908				£120	
		1909				£120	

Town	Telegraph Initials (Type 2)	Date	1	2	3	4	5
Ashton Under Lyme		1906				£250	
		1907				£250	
		1908				£250	
		1909				?	
Birkenhead		1906				£130	
		1907				£90	
		1908				£90	
		1909				£90	
Bolton	BL	1903		£150			
		1904		£150			
Bradford	BD	1904		£250			
Bury	BC	1903 red		£150			
Carlisle	CE	1904		£300			
Cheltenham	CM	1903		?			
Clevedon	CJJ	1903		?			
Cork	CK	1903		?			
Coventry	CV	1903		?			
Douglas, IOM		1906				£300	
		1907				£250	
		1908				£250	
		1909				£250	
Dover	DR	1903		£300			
Dukenfield		1906				£250	
		1907				£250	
		1908				£250	
		1909				£250	
Eccles	ECC	1905		?			
		1906				£180	
		1907				£180	
		1908				£130	
		1909				£130	
Glasgow	GW	1904		£150			
Glossop		1906				?	
		1907				£250	
		1908				£250	
		1909				£250	
Greenock	GK	1903		?			
Heywood	HIL	1903		?			
Hull	HU	1903 red		£200			
Hyde		1906				£300	
		1907				£300	
		1908				£300	
		1909				£300	

Town	Telegraph Initials (Type 2)	Date	1	2	3	4	5
Knutsford	KU	1903		£300			
		1906				£250	
		1907				?	
		1908				£250	
		1909				?	
Leicester	LE	1903 red		£180			
		1904		£150			
		1908				£80	
Leigh, Lancs		1906				?	
		1907				£200	
		1908				?	
		1909				£250	
Liverpool		1906				£85	
		1907				£85	
		1908				£75	
		1909				£75	
Macclesfield	MC	1903 red		£250			
Manchester	MR	1903		£90			
		1904		£85			
		1905		£70	£120 purple £70 black		
		1906			£100	£80	£75
		1907				£60	£75
		1908				£60	£75
		1909				£50	£75
Newton Le Willows		1906				£250	
		1907				£300	
		1908				?	
		1909				?	
Norwich	NC	1903		?			
		1907				£150	
		1908				£130	
Oldham		1906				£150	
		1907				?	
		1908				£125	
		1909				£150	
Ormskirk		1906				£300	
		1907				?	
		1908				£250	
		1909				?	
Plymouth	PY	1903		?			
Portsmouth	PT	1903		?			
Prescot		1906				?	
		1907				£300	
		1908				?	
		1909				£250	

Town	Telegraph Initials (Type 2)	Date	1	2	3	4	5
Preston	PR	1904		£250			
Reading		1908				£300 £400 red	
Rochdale	RO	1902 red	£175				
		1902 black	£175				
		1903	£100				
		1904	£100				
		1905	?				
Runcorn		1906				?	
		1907				£300	
		1908				?	
		1909				?	
St. Helens		1906				£180	
		1907				£180	
		1908				?	
		1909				?	
Sale	SCR	1903		£200			
		1904		£200			
		1905		£140			
		1906		£140			
		1907		£140			
		1908		£120			
		1909		£120			
Shrewsbury	SY	1903		?			
Southport	SP	1903		£200			
		1904		?			
Stalybridge		1906				?	
		1907				£300	
		1908				?	
		1909				?	
Stockport	SP	1903		£180			
		1904		?			
Wakefield	WF	1903 red		£180			
Walsall	WL	1903		£150			
Warrington	WA	1903		£180			
		1904		£180			
		1905		£150			
		1906				£140	
		1907				£140	
		1908				£140	
		1909				£140	
Waterford	WT	1903		?			

Town	Telegraph Initials (Type 2)	Date	1	2	3	4	5
Widnes	WIP	1904	£300				
		1905	£300				
		1906		£250			
		1907		?			
		1908		?			
		1909		?			
Wigan	WI	1903	£170				
		1904	£140				
		1905	£140				
		1906		£110			
		1907		£110			
		1908		£110			
		1909		£110			

Items marked (?) are thought to exist but have not been seen.

Other Christmas Postmarks

December 25th cancellations . . . . Double Normal
Christmas period, untimed hand stamps or machines . . . . . Normal
Tempy. Office, London machine marks, 1930s 3.00
Reinderland postmarks, in red 1.00

(See also Christmas Slogans and Special Event Postmarks)

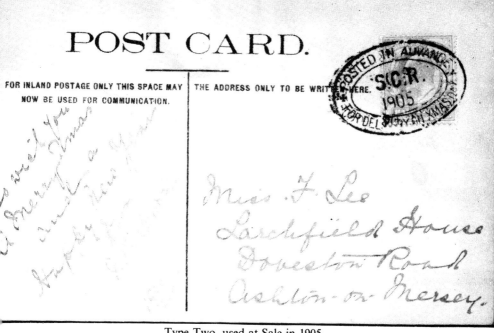

Type Two, used at Sale in 1905

20. ROYALTY

| 456 | 457 | 458 |

456 Scroll type with central VR 200.00
Scroll type with V.R at base 75.00
Scroll type with E.R at base 400.00
Circular type with ER VII, surmounted by crown 50.00
457 As above but GVR 25.00
Boxed type with ERI/VIII 30.00
Circular type with GRI/VI, surmounted by crown 15.00
As above but GVIR 10.00
458 As above but EIIR 1.00

| 459 | 460 | 461 |

Abergeldie Castle/Aberdeen, Skeleton 1955 . . . . 40.00

459 Royal Pavilion. Aldershot, single circle with crown, 1915 . . . 100.00

Balmoral, single circle 25.00
Balmoral Castle, single circle with crown at base 40.00
Official Paid/Balmoral Castle, single circle 1.00
Official Paid/Ballater, double circle with thick arcs 15.00
Balmoral Castle Aberdeenshire, parcel label type 3.50

Buckingham Palace, single circle 20.00
Buckingham Palace/S.W.1 single circle 10.00
Buckingham Palace S.W.1/Paid, single circle with GR cypher . 10.00
London S.W.1 official Paid/9, double circle with thick arcs . . 10.00
460 Registered/Buckingham Palace, oval 3.50
As above but Registered/Buckingham Palace S.W.1 . . . . 3.50

461 Dublin Castle, single circle with cross at base, 1911 . . . . . . 150.00

462 **463** **464**

Hampton Court, single circle 50.00

Holyrood Palace, single circle with cross at base 25.00
Edinburgh/Official Paid, double circle with thin arcs 1.50

Osborne, single circle with name across circle 35.00
Osborne/I. of Wight, single circle, from 1897 . . . . 20.00
Osborne, I.W., parcel double circle type 20.00

Sandringham, single circle 30.00
Official Paid/Sandringham. R.S.O. Norfolk, single circle . . . 10.00
462 Official Paid/Sandringham. Nfk, single circle 10.00
Official Paid/Sandringham House Nfk, single circle 10.00
Official Paid/King's Lynn, single circle 10.00
Sandringham House/Norfolk, double circle with thin arcs . . . 2.00

463 Westminster Abbey, 1911 double circle with cross 150.00

Windsor Castle, single circle 30.00
Windsor Castle Windsor/Berks, single circle 1.00
Official Paid/Windsor, Berks, double circle with thick arcs . . . 5.00
464 Windsor Great Park, Windsor/Berks, single circle 5.00
Cumberland Lodge/Windsor, single circle 7.00
Frogmore, single circle 25.00
Frogmore/Windsor, single circle 20.00

Note: The early single circles, eg 'Windsor Castle', 'Hampton Court' etc. were issued for telegraphic purposes. Prices quoted are for loose stamps with clear cancellations.

465

466

467

465 HMY Osborne/Cowes, 1901 skeleton for Cowes Regatta . . . 150.00
His Majesty's Yacht, single circle with crown at base. 30.00

466 King's special wire, as above, used on 'Victoria and Albert' . . 150.00

The King's Flight, double circle with Royal Cypher 25.00
The Queen's Flight, as above 7.00

467 Official Paid, single circle with crown at base 15.00

468

OFFICE OF
HRH THE DUKE
OF GLOUCESTER
Kensington Palace
London W3

469

468 Privy Purse/Buckingham Palace, oval with crown 3.00
PH/EIIR/Buckingham Palace, oval with crown 3.00
Lord Steward/M.H./Buckingham Palace, oval with crown . . 7.50
Master of the Horse/The Royal Mews, S.W., oval with crown . 7.50

Lord Chamberlain/St. James's Palace, oval with crown 4.00
Central Chancery of the Orders/St. James's Palace/London
S.W.1/of Knighthood, oval with crown 7.50

Office of/Kensington Palace/H.R.H. The Princess Margaret,
double oval 1.50
469 Office of/HRH The Duke/of Gloucester/Kensington Palace/
London W.3, oval 1.00

Office of the/Court Postmaster, double circle with GVR cypher
used at Osborne. 50.00
Master of the Horse/The Royal Mews Windsor, oval with crown 7.00
Master of the Household's Department/Windsor Castle, double
oval with crown 7.00
Royal Gardens/Windsor, oval with crown 7.00

21. METER MARKS AND PPIs

Meter Marks (struck in red)

470 A   471 B   472 C   473 D

(Town dies and slogans omitted from illustrations)

470 Type A, from 1922   . . . .   0.50
471 Type B, from 1927   . . . .   0.10
    As above but value central, crown and cypher low 0.10
    As above but Edward VIII types 0.40
    As above but George VI types 0.10
    As above but Elizabeth II types 0.08
472 Type C, from 1959 (several settings and sizes) 0.05
473 Type D, from 1968 (several sizes) 0.05

(Machines were often kept in use well into the following reign. Different types are used by the Postal Administrations of Jersey, Guernsey and Isle of Man)

Postage Paid Indicators

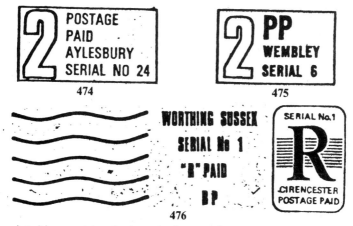

474   475

476

Preprinted in a variety of colours by large mail users, many other types. Value from 2p each at present but PPIs often have a very short life and are the Postal History of the future.

22. CACHETS

Private postal markings applied by sponsors of tourist locations to enhance the novelty value of the mail. Prices are for items with stamps and postmarks. Cachets on unused cards are worth about a third to a half of the prices stated.

Beachy Head

BEACHY HEAD.

477

478

479

477 Beachy Head, straight line, unframed, purple	4.00
Watch Tower on Beachy Head, England. Harry Randall, circular	4.00
Watch Tower/Beachy Head/1910, purple	4.00
478 The Watch Tower/Beachy Head, in buckle, purple or black . .	2.00
Watch Tower/Beachy Head, double framed diamond, black or purple	0.75
479 Watch Tower/Beachy Head, oval, purple or black	0.50
As above but with lighthouse in centre, purple	0.50
Printed cachets	0.30

Blackpool Tower

480

480 Posted From Top of/Blackpool/Tower/518 Feet High, oval, black	0.75
Posted/from/the/top/of/Blackpool/Tower 518 illustrated, purple	0.50

Island Cachets

| PO STE D AT |
| 25 AUG 1909 |
| ETTRICK BAY |

481   482   483

Post Office/R.E. Office/Alderney, oval, violet 75.00
Boxed cachet for visit of Queen and Duke to Alderney 5.00
Alderney THE Channel Island, blue 2.00
Modern tourist cachets of Alderney 0.50

481 Posted at/date/Ettrick Bay, boxed (Isle of Bute) 10.00

Cow Lane/St. Martin's/Old Guernsey, black 17.00
Boxed cachet for visit of Queen and Duke to Guernsey 3.00
Modern tourist cachets of Guernsey 0.50

Herm, single line, black 75.00

St Helier's Bazaar, double circle, violet 35.00
Wolf Caves, Jersey, double circle, violet or red 12.50
Boxed cachet for visit of Queen and Duke to Jersey 3.00
Modern tourist cachets of Jersey 0.50

Jethou Island/date, two line, black 50.00
482 Jethou Island/date/Chan. Isles, circular, violet 45.00

Posted at/the/Cunningham/Holiday Camp/Douglas/I.O.M.,
     boxed, purple 60.00
Peel Castle/Isle of Man, horizontal diamond, purple 40.00

Snaefell Summit:
Upright diamond in black or purple 7.00
     As above but green or red 25.00
Horizontal diamond in purple (several types) 6.00
     As above in blue 1.50
     As above in black 0.50

Tholt-y-will/Sulby Glen, upright diamond, black 40.00
     As above in green 60.00

Boxed cachet for visit of Queen and Duke to Sark 4.00
Isle of Sark/1565 Charter 1965/Quater Centenary, boxed . . . 4.00

St Kilda/date, unframed 12.00
   As above but boxed with indented corners, purple 10.00
483 St. Kilda/The furthest station west, circular with puffin, purple .   8.00
   St. Michael's Mount, boxed, with crinkly border 2.00

John O'Groats

484   485   486

484 John O'Groats/N.B./House, in triangle, black or purple   . . .   10.00
   John O'Groats House, large circle, purple 2.00
485 John O'Groats House, small circle, purple 2.00
486 John O'Groats/House, hexagon, purple 1.50

Land's End

487   488   489

From the/Old Man at the/Land's End, rectangle with indented
   corners, from 1901, purple or green 1.00
487 Land's End, double triangle with hatched border, from 1903,
   black, purple or blue 0.30
First and Last Refreshment House/By E. James/Lands End,
   double oval, from 1905, black 1.50
   As above but without 'By E. James', from 1907, black or purple   1.00
First & Last House/Lands End, unframed two line, from 1913,
   purple or red 0.50
   As above but Land's End, from 1928, purple or red 0.50
First and Last House/Lands End, unframed two line, from 1930,
   grey or red 0.50
488 Lands End, small double oval, from 1911, blue, purple or green   1.00
   As above but larger, from 1921, purple 1.00
   As above but large single oval, from 1921, purple 2.00
   Lands End, single triangle, from 1926, purple 0.50

First & Last House,/Lands End, boxed, from 1931, red	0.75
The First & Last House/In England/Land's End, boxed, from 1932, red	0.50
First and Last House/In England,/Land's End, boxed, from 1932, red	0.50
The First and Last/House in England/Land's End, boxed from 1935, red	0.50
First and Last Hotel/In England. Land's End, boxed, from 1934, red	0.75
First and Last House/In England/Land's End, boxed with illustration, from 1935, red	0.90
489 Lands End on pennant beneath shield showing light house, from 1935, purple	1.20
Lands End between pairs of two wavy bars, printed in black, from 1952	0.20
As above but between a pair of four wavy bars, from 1942 . .	0.30
Sennen/Post Office/Lands End, single circle, black	2.50
Land's End Hotel Ltd/Land's End, circular with shield, black .	2.50

Llanfair P.G.

490

491

Village name, unboxed straight line, several sizes	2.00
490 Village name round rim with 'Posted At' in centre	0.50
As above but 'Posted From' in centre	0.75
As above but with dragon in centre	0.75
As above but with map in centre	0.75
As above but with WYN BACH in centre	—
As above but nothing in centre	0.50
Oval with blank centre	1.00
Circular type with National Trust emblem	0.50
491 Oval type with Anglesey Column	0.50

Snowdon

| 492 | 493 | 494 |

492 Summit/of/Snowdon, single circle, 25 mm, blue or purple . . . 2.00
493   As above but double circle, 36 mm, purple or black 2.00
494   As above, single circle, 21 mm, purple or black 2.00
     As above, double circle, 24 mm, purple 1.75
     As above, single circle, 32 mm, purple or black 0.85
     As above, single circle, 35 mm 0.50

HMS Victory, Portsmouth

495

Illustration of ship, no wording 1.00
495   As above but smaller and Posted/on board/H.M.S. Victory,
    blue or black 0.50
    Posted In/H.M.S. Victory, blue, unframed 1.00
    Large boxed ship illustration with name of commanding officer,
    red 0.50

Other cachets

THIS CARD WAS POSTED AT THE SUMMIT OF THE GREAT ORME, LLANDUDNO

496

497

Posted at the/Grand Pump Room/Bath, boxed 5.00
Posted at the/Pump Room/Bath, England, boxed 0.50

Ben Nevis Summit/J. Miller/Hotel, double oval, date beneath . 3.00

Central Spa/Town Hall, rectangle with indented corners, used at
Cheltenham 2.50

Dartmoor Cachets for Fur Tor, Duck's Pool or Cranmere Pool . 1.00

Maritime Museum/Posted/Bucklers Hard, illustrated 0.50

Haddon Hall/date/Bakewell, single circle 1.00

Posted at/Hampton Court, boxed, with Henry VIII 0.50

Hotel Cachets 0.50

496 This card was Posted/at the Summit of the/Great Orme,
Llandudno, boxed, blue, black or red 0.60

497 Cruise of "The Northern Belle", 1933–9 . . . . 50.00

Penny Park/House/Coventry, double circle 1.00

498   **499**   **500**

498 Ragley/Hall, small double circle, purple 1.00

499 Shell Grotto, double circle, black 3.00

Stationers' Cachets 0.30

Posted on Southend Pier 20.00

Posted in the Tower of London, with picture of Tower 0.50

500 Posted in/Wookey/Hole, boxed, with Witch on broomstick . . 0.50

Wrekin Hill/Wellington Salop, decorated two line cachet . . . 0.50

23. BRITISH POST OFFICES ABROAD

Postmarks to be found on GB stamps (or GB overprints) used abroad. Prices quoted are for loose stamps pre-1900 (often 1d red perf.); covers are usually worth considerably more. Some overseas numerals were later used inland so prices relate solely to issues during the period stated. Prices of twentieth century items are for a cover or a card.

Africa

Ascension (1855–1922)

Ascension, single circle on Victorian loose stamp 15.00

As above but Edward VII or George V card or cover 30.00

Fernando Póo (1874–77)

247, upright oval numeral 350.00

Morocco Agencies (1907–57)

501	502	503

	Single circle	Double circle	Oval Registration
Alcazar	6.00		
Casablanca	3.00	2.00	7.50 **503**
Fez	4.00		10.00
Fez (Mellah)	10.00		25.00
Larache	8.00		15.00
Marrakesh	6.00		12.00
Marrakesh (Mellah)	10.00		25.00
Mazagan	8.00		
Mequinez **501**	8.00		
Mogador	7.00		
Rabat	7.00		15.00
Saffi	6.00		
Tetuan	7.00		12.00

Tangier:

Undated double arc, 'Tangiers' . . . . ?

Small single circle without British P.O. 15.00

Ship Letter/Tangier . . . . ?

Missent to Tangier . . . . ?

British Post Office/Tangier, single circle 1.00

502	As above but double circle	1.00
	Registered oval cancellation	3.00
	Universal machine	1.00
	As above but with 1953 Coronation slogan	5.00
	Packet type	5.00
	Parcel type	7.50

Nigeria (1888–99)

Cancellations on GB stamps used in Niger Coast or on Oil Rivers overprints. Known types include single circles, squared circle, double ring parcel, oval registered, double oval and boxed varieties.

504	505	506

Abutshi	Buguma	Opobo River
Akassa	Burutu	Qua Iboe River
Bakana	Forcados River	Sapele
Benin River	Lukaja	Sombreiro River
Bonny River	Old Calabar	Warrj
Brass River	Old Calabar River	

	○	✉
From	4.00	50.00

Zululand (1888–93)

507	508	509

Abombo (or Ubombo)	Lower Umfolozi	Qudeni
Entonjaneni	Melmoth	Rorkes Drift/Natal
Eshowe	Nkandhla	Rorkes Drift/Zululand
Hlobisa	Nandweni	Ulundi
Lower Tugela/Natal	Nongoma	
Lower Tugela/Zululand	Nqutu	

	○	✉
From	2.50	20.00

Americas

510 511 512 513

	Horizontal oval	Upright oval	Duplex	Single circles
Argentine: Buenos Ayres (1860–73), B32	8.00	10.00	7.00	
Bolivia: Cobija (1865–78), C39	150.00	150.00		
Brazil (1866–74): Bahia, C81		15.00		
Brazil (1866–74): Pernambuco, C82		25.00		
Brazil: Rio de Janeiro, C83		12.00		
British Honduras: (1856–66), A06	200.00			
Chile (1865–81): Caldera, C37	16.00			
Chile (1865–81): Coquimbo, C40	16.00			
Chile (1865–81): Valpariso, C30		12.00	10.00	
Colombia (1865–81): Cartagena, C56	15.00			
Colombia (1865–81): Cartagena, C65 error	25.00			
Colombia (1865–81): Colon, E88		15.00		
Colombia (1865–81): Panama, C35	7.50		6.50	
Colombia (1865–81): Santa Martha, C62	20.00			
Colombia (1865–81): Savanilla, F69			511 20.00	
Cuba (1865–77): Havana, C58	17.50		15.00	
Cuba (1865–77): St. Jago de Cuba, C88			40.00	
Danish W. Indies (1865–79): St. Thomas, C51	10.00	15.00	10.00	
Danish W. Indies (1865–79): Spanish Mail Pkts, D26		350.00		
Dominica (1869–81): Porto Plata, C86		15.00		15.0
Dominica (1869–81): San Domingo, C87		20.00		20.0
Ecuador (1865–80): Guayaquil, C41	510 20.00			
Haiti (1865–81): Jacmel, C59	15.00			
Haiti (1865–81): Port-au-Prince, E53		20.00	20.00	
Mexico (1865–76): Tampico, C63	25.00			
Nicaragua (1865–82): Greytown, C57	20.00	20.00	512 20.00	
Peru (1865–79): Arica, C36	12.00	15.00	12.00	
Peru (1865–79): Callao, C38	8.00	10.00	8.00	
Peru (1865–79): Iquique, D87		20.00		
Peru (1865–79): Islay, C42	14.00			
Peru (1865–79): Paita, C43	20.00			
Peru (1865–79): Pisagua, D65		?		
Peru (1865–79): Pisco, D74		250.00		
Puerto Rico (1865–77): Aguadilla, F84		20.00		25.0
Puerto Rico (1865–77): Arroyo, F83		20.00		513 25.0
Puerto Rico (1865–77): Mayaguez, F85		15.00		20.0
Puerto Rico (1865–77): Naguabo, 582		150.00		
Puerto Rico (1865–77): Ponce, F88		15.00		20.0
Puerto Rico (1865–77): San Juan, C61	8.00	10.00	8.00	
Uruguay (1864–73): Montevideo, C28	20.00	25.00		
Venezuela (1865–80): Cuidad Bolivar, D22		30.00		35.0
Venezuela (1865–80): La Guayra, C60	15.00			20.0

Europe

514   515

Cyprus (1878–81), upright ovals:

942, Larnaca	18.00	981, Paphos	150.00
969, Nicosia	45.00	982, Famagusta	250.00
974, Kyrenia	125.00	D47, Polymechia	300.00
975, Limassol	50.00	D48, HQ Camp, Nicosia	300.00

Gibraltar (1857–85)

G, horizontal oval	10.00
514 A 26, horizontal oval	10.00
A 26, duplex with horizontal oval	8.00
As above but upright oval	10.00
Gibraltar, small single circle	7.00

Malta (1855–85)

Wavy Lines obliteration	600.00
M, horizontal oval	30.00
515 A 25, horizontal oval	4.00
As above but upright oval	10.00
A25, duplex with horizontal oval	8.00
As above but upright oval	7.50

Levant

516   517

Alexandria (1839–82)

516 B01, horizontal oval	8.00
As above but upright oval	6.50
B01, duplex	5.00

Beyrout (1873-1914)

G06, upright oval 8.00
British Post Office/Beyront, single circle 3.50
Beyrout/British Post Office, scroll type 10.00
Registered/Beyrout, oval 10.00
517 Beyrout/British Post Office, single circle 10.00

518

519

520

521

Constantinople (1857-1914)

518 C, horizontal oval 2.00
As above but upright oval 3.50
519 British Post Office/Constantinople, unframed circular 10.00
As above with PAID 20.00
Constantinople/Ship-Letter, boxed . . . . ?
520 British Post Office/Constantinople, single circle 6.00
Registered/Constantinople, oval 10.00

— Stamboul Sub Office (1884-1914)

British Post Office/Constantinople S., single circle 15.00
521 S., upright oval (with full stop) 5.00
British Post Office/Stamboul, single circle 12.00

522

523

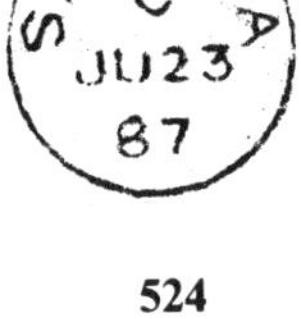

524

525

Salonica (1900-14)

S, upright oval (without full stop) . . . . ?
522 British Post Office/Salonica, single circle 20.00
523 As above but double circle 15.00

Smyrna (1872–1914)

F87, upright oval	6.00
524 Smyrna, small single circle	15.00
British Post Office/Smyrna, single circle	10.00
Registered/Smyrna, oval	10.00

Suez (1860–82)

525 B02, horizontal oval	7.00
As above but upright oval	10.00
B02, duplex	7.00

West Indies (horizontal ovals)

Antigua (1856–6): St. John's, A02	100.00
English Harbour, A18	1500.00
Bahamas (1857–8): Nassau, A05	180.00
British Guiana (1856–8): Georgetown or	
Demarara, A03	75.00
New Amsterdam or	
Berbice, A04	100.00
Dominica (1856–73), A07	175.00
Grenada (1856–60): St. George, A15	160.00
Jamaica (1858–60): Alexandria, A27	120.00
Annotto Bay, A28	50.00
Bath, A29	55.00
Black River, A30	35.00
Brown's Town, A31	130.00
Buff Bay, A32	100.00
Chapleton, A33	75.00
Claremont, A34	120.00
Clarendon, A35	75.00
Dry Harbour, A36	180.00
Duncans, A37	180.00
Ewarton, A38	—
Falmouth, A39	25.00
First River, A40	80.00
Gayle, A41	100.00
Golden Spring, A42	115.00
Gordon Town, A43	350.00
Goshon, A44	90.00
Grange Hill, A45	25.00
Green Island, A46	110.00
Highgate, A47	80.00
Hope Bay, A48	110.00
Kingston, A01 **529**	15.00
Twin A01 **530**	100.00
Duplex A01 **531**	20.00
Lilliput, A49	60.00
Little River, A50	—
Lucea, A51	35.00
Manchioneal, A52	135.00
Mandeville, A53	30.00
May Hill, A54	30.00
Mile Gully, A55	110.00
Moneague, A56	110.00
Montego Bay, A57	25.00
Montpelier, A58	500.00
Morant Bay, A59	35.00
Ocho Rios, A60	55.00
Old Harbour, A61	85.00
Plantain Garden	
River, A62	55.00
Pear Tree Grove, A63	—
Port Antonio, A64	170.00
Port Morant. A65	60.00
Port Maria, A66	40.00
Port Royal, A67	220.00
Porus, A68	50.00
Ramble, A69	110.00
Rio Bueno, A70	60.00
Rodney Hall, A71	60.00
Saint David, A72	110.00
St. Ann's Bay, A73	55.00
Salt Gut, A74	110.00
Savanna-La-Mar, A75	25.00
Spanish Town, A76	25.00
Stewart Town, A77	110.00
Vere, A78	35.00
Monserrat (1856–66), A08	300.00
Nevis (1856–60), A09	185.00
St. Christopher (1856–69): Basse	
Terre, A12	140.00
St. Lucia (1855–60): Castries, A11	150.00
St. Vincent (1855–60): Kingstown,	
A10	185.00
Tobago (1856–79): Scarborough,	
A14	150.00
Virgin Is. (1856–66): Tortola, A13	750.00

INFORMATION

Abbreviations

Many different abbreviations have been used in British postmarks and this is the first attempt to provide a list for ready reference. The list omits abbreviations of place names (eg IOW, Isle of Wight) and telegraphic codes (eg BHK, Bishop Auckland). Those shown with ? have not been confirmed and more information is needed for those without explanation.

ALO	Army Letter Office	GNR	Great Northern Railway
AMDO		GP	General Post
APO	Army Post Office	GPO	General Post Office
		GR	
B		G(R)SD	Giro (Remittances) Services Dept.
BA	British Association		
BAPO	British Army Post Office	H	
BFPO	British Forces Post Office	H&K	Holyhead and Kingstown
BL		HD	Howe Depot
BMM	British Military Mission	HO	Head Office
BO	Branch Office	HP	House of Peers
		HPO	Head Post Office
C	Collection	HS	Highland Show
CCAC			
CDD		IB	Inland Branch
CH	Clearing House?	IE	International Exhibition
CL	Late Matter Collection	IS	Inland Section
CO	Chief Office	ISMLO	Inland Section Mechanised Letter
CR	Caledonian Railway		Office
CS	Cannon Street	ISMP	Inland Section Mount Pleasant
CX	Charing Cross		
		KE	King Edward St
DALO		KL	
DLS			
DO	District Office	L	Late
DSC	District Sorting Carriage	LB&SC	London, Brighton and South Coast
DSO	District Sorting Office?	LC	
		LPS	
E	Evening	LTR	
ED	Eastern District	LX	
EDO	Eastern District Office		
EX	Exchange	M	Morning
		MB	Moveable Box
F		MLO	Mechanised Letter Office
F&CPP	Foreign and Colonial Parcel Post	MO&SB	Money Order and Savings Bank
FB	Foreign Branch	MOO	Money Order Office
FBO	Foreign Branch Office?	MP	Mount Pleasant
FD		MPIS	Mount Pleasant Inland Section
FDM	French Day Mail?	MPO	Mobile Post Office
	Foreign Day Mail?	MPPO	Mount Pleasant Parcel Office
FMO		MS	Missent
FNM	French Night Mail?	MT	
	Foreign Night Mail?	MTO	Military Telegraph Office
FO		MTP	
FPM	French Parcel Mail?		
	French Packet Mail?	NB	
FPO	Field Post Office	ND	Northern District
FRH	Floating Receiving House	NDO	Northern District Office
FS	Foreign Section	NE(TPO)	North Eastern TPO
		NMT	Night Mail Tender
		NPB	Newspaper Branch
		NW(R)	North Western Railway

OC		S	Stationery Office	
OS	Old Stamp	SC	Sorting Carriage	
		SD	Southern District	
PB		SDO	Southern District Office	
PC	Prison Censor	SDSO	Southern District Sub Office	
PDO	Postmens Delivery Office	SEDO	South Eastern District Office	
PO	Post Office	SH		
POW	Prisoner of War	SM	St Martins Le Grand	
PP	Penny Post or Parcel Post	SMP	St Martins Place	
PPO	Parcel Post Office	SO	Station Office or Sub Office or	
PS			Sorting Office	
PSC	Parcel Sorting Carriage	SOC		
PSO	Postmens Sorting Office	SPDO		
PTO	Please Turn Over	ST	Sorting Tender	
PTS(HPO)		SW(R)	South Western Railway	
		SWDO	South Western District Office	
R	Railhead			
RDO	Rural District Office?	T	Telegraph or Taxe	
	Railway District Office?	TD	Telegraph Department	
RE(office)	Registered Envelope?	TO		
RH	Receiving House	TP	Two Penny	
RL	Ride Letter	TPO	Travelling Post Office	
RLB	Returned Letter Branch			
RLDIS	Returned Letter Department Inland	W		
	Section	WCDO	Western Central District Office	
RLO	Returned Letter Office	WDO	Western District	
RMS	Royal Mail Steamer	WDO	Western District Office	
RNAS		WDSO	Western District Sub Office?	
RNC		WH		
RO	Registered Office or Railway Office	WR	Willesden Ride	
RPO	Railway Post Office			
RRH		Y		
RSC	Railway Sorting Carriage			
RSO	Railway Sorting Office or Railway			
	Sub Office			
RST	Railway Sorting Tender			
RW	Railway?			

PUZZLED?

From time to time all collectors find covers which have curious or unexplained features. Send a photocopy (with SAE or IRC) and I will send my comments or refer to a specialist in a particular field. Some of the most interesting – or ones which still cannot be explained – illustrated in the next *Collect British Postmarks.*

BOOKS

The best and most comprehensive book on British Postal markings remains the classic *The Postmarks of Great Britain and Ireland* by R. C. Alcock and F. C. Holland, published by R. C. Alcock Ltd, 1940. Copiously illustrated and embracing the whole history of the British postmark, this book was originally published to celebrate the centenary of the Uniform Penny Postage. Long out of print it fetches up to £100 when bought at auction. Some fifteen supplements were produced in subsequent years in *The Philatelic Adviser* also published by the House of Alcock. Some of these were consolidated into a small *Part Two* and *The Philatelic Adviser Annual* of Christmas 1963 contained supplements No. 1 and 9–15. An abridged version of the whole work *British Postmarks: A Short History and Guide* by R. C. Alcock and F. C. Holland, Revised Edition, 1977 is, in the opinion of the Compiler of this Handbook, the single most useful book on British Postmarks currently available. It is recommended without reservation: buy it before it goes out of print! Some of the supplements to the original volume are also still available. R. C. Alcock Ltd, 11 Regent Street, Cheltenham, Glos.

Also highly recommended are the series of books of James A. Mackay, *English and Welsh Postmarks since 1840* (published 1980), *Scottish Postmarks from 1693 to the Present Day* (published 1978), *Irish Postmarks since 1840* (published 1982), together with supplements in the *Postal History Annuals 1979, 1980, 1981 and 1982*. These publications are available from the author at 11 Newall Terrace, Dumfries DG1 1LN, Scotland.

Another classic very valuable for the pre-stamp and earliest cancellation periods is *The Encyclopaedia of British Empire Postage Stamps, Vol. 1. Great Britain and The Empire in Europe*, written and published by Robson Lowe, Second Edition 1952, reprinted in two parts by HJMR as Billig Philatelic Handbook Vols 34 and 35.

This Handbook could not have been compiled without the many specialised studies published in recent years. Often published in limited edition at personal expense, these publications are frequently the result of years of erudite study. Collectors are urged to acquire their own copies of books in fields that interest them for these specialised studies rapidly go out of print and become collectors' items in their own right. Books are listed below in the corresponding order to the sections of this Handbook.

England's Postal History to 1840, written and published by R. M. Willcocks, 1975
The Postal History of Great Britain and Ireland, A Summarised Catalogue to 1840,
  written and published by R. M. Willcocks and B. Jay, Second Edition 1980
Postal Markings of Scotland to 1808, Bruce Auckland, 1978
Handbook of Irish Postal History to 1840, David Feldman and William Kane,
  published D. Feldman Ltd, 1975
Herewith my Frank, J. W. Lovegrove (also two supplements)
The Provincial Local Posts of England 1765–1840, G. F. Oxley
British County Catalogue, R. M. Willcocks and B. Jay, 1980

The Maltese Cross Cancellation of the United Kingdom, R. C. Alcock and F. C. Holland, Second Ed. 1970, pub. R. C. Alcock Ltd.

List of 1844 Obliterations, T. Mountford

British Post Office Numbers 1844–1906, G. Brumell, pub. R. C. Alcock Ltd.

A Provisional Guide to the Valuation of the Numeral Cancellations of the British Isles, Part 1 England and Wales, M. R. Hewlett, Picton Philatelic Handbook No 1, 1979.

The Sideways Duplex Cancellations of England and Wales, R. G. Traill and F. C. Holland, pub. R. C. Alcock, 1975

Priced check list of horizontal oval single cancellations with the number in a circle, J. C. Parmenter

Postal cancellations of London 1840–1890, H. C. Westley, pub. H. F. Johnson

London Cancellations, L. Dubus

The Spoon Experiment, 1853–58, written and published by R. M. Willcocks and W. A. Sedgewick

British Post Office Numbers, 1924–69, J. A. Mackay, 1981

Squared Circle Postmarks, W. G. Stitt Dibden, reprinted Harry Hayes, 1974
Unpublished notes of the late K. Willington

The Skeleton Postmarks of Great Britain, G. F. Crabb, pub. The British Postmark Society, 1960

Unpublished notes on scroll cancellations by M. R. Hewlett

Early Stamp Machines, W. G. Stitt Dibden, pub. The Postal History Society, 1964

Current Machine Postmarks of the United Kingdom, J. Bruce Bennett, C. R. H. Parsons, G. R. Pearson, pub. The British Postmark Society, 1963

U.K. Machine Marks, J. Peach, pub. Vera Trinder Ltd, 1979

Slogan Postmarks of the United Kingdom, 1917–69, C. R. H. Parsons, C. G. Peachey, G. R. Pearson, pub. by the authors, 1974

Local Publicity Slogan Postmarks, C. R. H. Parsons, C. G. Peachey, G. R. Pearson, pub. by the authors, 1970

Slogan Postmarks of the U.K. 1970–73, C. R. H. Parsons, C. G. Peachey, G. R. Pearson, pub. by the authors, 1974

Slogan Postmarks of the Seventies, C. R. H. Parsons, C. G. Peachey, G. R. Pearson, pub. by the authors, 1980
Annual Supplements to the above and Bulletins of the British Postmark Society

Special Event Postmarks of the United Kingdom, G. R. Pearson, pub. by the author, 1973
Bulletins of the British Postmark Society

Railway Station Postmarks, D. P. Gowen, pub. Railway Philatelic Group, 1978

An Introduction and Guide to the Travelling Post Offices of Great Britain, A. M. Goodbody, Railway Philatelic Group

T.P.O. A History of Travelling Post Offices of Great Britain: Part One, England – "The Specials" and associated T.P.O.s, 1975, Part Three, Scotland and Ireland, 1977, H. S. Wilson, pub. Railway Philatelic Group

The Maritime Postal Markings of the British Isles, written and published by A. Robertson, 1958

Paquebot cancellations of the world, written and published by R. Hosking, 1977

Floating Post Offices of the Clyde, James A. Mackay, 1979

Naval Mails 1939–49, J. Goldup, pub. T.P.O. and Seapost Society, 1950

The Transatlantic Post Office, written and published by R. Hosking, 1979

British Army Field Post Offices, 1939–1945, Locations and Assignments, G. R. Crouch and N. Hill, pub. Lara, 1951

The Postal History of the British Army in World War I, A. Kenedy and G. Crabb, 1977

Camp Postmarks of the United Kingdom, R. A. Kingston, pub. Forces Postal History, 1971, Supplement 1974

History of British Army Postal Service, Vol 1 1882–1902 Vol 2 1903–27, E. B. Proud, pub. Proud-Bailey Co Ltd

Handbook and Catalogue of the Stamps and postmarks of the Islands of Great Britain, pub. Woodcote Stamps, 1961

Channel Islands Stamps and Postal History, Stanley Gibbons, 1979

Isle of Man Stamps and Postal History (YPM4), Dr J. T. Whitney, BPH Publications, 1981

Catalogue of Great Britain Surcharge and Explanatory Dies, compiled and published by C. M. Langston

Newspaper Branch Cancellation, W. G. Stitt Dibden, published by The Postal History Society, 1971

Telegraphic Codes of the British Isles, 1870–1924, J. A. Mackay, 1981

The Parcel Post of the British Isles, J. A. Mackay, 1982

A Christmas Story, C. W. Meredith and C. Kidd, pub. R. C. Alcock, 1954

Posted in advance for delivery on Christmas Day, C. Kidd, pub. Robson Lowe, 1974

Meter Stamps of Great Britain and Ireland, J. C. Mann, Second edition, 1972

The Postal History of the Manx Electric Railway, A. Povey and J. T. Whitney, pub. by the authors, 1979

Land's End Cachets, G. Beckwith and J. Lawrence, pub. by the authors, 1981, Second edition, 1982

Postmark Collecting, R. K. Forster, pub. Stanley Paul, 1960

Collecting Postmarks, R. K. Forster, pub. Stanley Gibbons Guides, 1977

Introducing Postal History, A. Branston, pub. Stanley Gibbons Guides, 1978

Post Offices of the United Kingdom, The Post Office.

Collect First Day Covers, BB Publications

The above list excludes studies of localities. Many of the Societies publish a journal containing articles relevant to their speciality. Particularly useful are the *Bulletins* of the British Postmark Society and *Postal History* published by the

Postal History Society. *The Philatelic Journal of Great Britain* is published four times a year by Robson Lowe Ltd and contains frequent history studies. *Postal History International* is the monthly journal published by Proud-Bailey Co Ltd.

Publications currently in print can be obtained from Vera Trinder Ltd, 38 Bedford St, Strand, London WC2E 9EU, Harris Publications Ltd, 42 Maiden Lane, Strand, London WC2E 7LW or G. Barrington Smith, Cross Street, Oadby, Leicester LE2 4DD. Out of print books can often be found in the auctions of Harry Hayes, 48 Trafalgar Street, Batley, West Yorkshire WF17 7HA.

CURRENCY, ETC

Some overseas readers have asked for an explanation of British usages.

Until 1971 Britain used a unique system of currency (though it was also used in many parts of the Empire and Commonwealth). This divided the pound (£) into twenty shillings (s). The shilling was divided into twelve pence (d), itself subdivided into two halfpennies ($\frac{1}{2}$d) or four farthings ($\frac{1}{4}$d). A sum in all three denominations was written £1-16-3$\frac{3}{4}$ or £1 16s 3$\frac{3}{4}$d while smaller sums were expressed as 16s 3$\frac{3}{4}$d or 16/3$\frac{3}{4}$d.

On 15 February 1971 Britain adopted a decimal currency system, the pound being divided into one hundred new pence or, simply, pence (p). Modern usage is to show four pounds and twenty-three pence as £4.23. Valuations in this book are shown either in whole pounds or large sums, eg £100, or without symbols for smaller amounts, eg fifteen pounds would be 15.00 and fifteen pence 0.15.

Weights and measures are in process of metrication. Those effecting postal history are as follows. There were 16 ounces (oz) to the pound weight (lb) prior to 29 September 1975 when postal services were metricated to grams and kilograms. The ounce was equivalent to approximately 25gms and the pound 450gms.

The mile is still in use but has not been relevant to postal history since 1840. The mile is approximately 1.6 kilometres.

CURIOUSER AND CURIOUSER!

Some collectors are interested by the odd names which can be found in postmarks of all countries. There are only a few of those used in Great Britain at the present time or in the past.

World's End	Jump	Old	Sandwich
Ugley	The Lizard	Decoy	Battlefield
Lovely Lane	Isle of Dogs	Sound	Box's Shop
Barking	Freezywater	Good Easter	Bethlehem
Yelling	Loggerheads	Hope	Nazareth
Clatter	Sudden	Deception Island	Clock Face
Knock	London Apprentice	Forty Foot	Halfpenny Green
Tooting	Adelina Patti – Hospital	Hammer	Foxholes

DESCRIPTIVE POSTMARKS

This term is used of postmarks relating to a particular building rather than a town or village. Some were used regularly for special events, others continuously and at least two, those used at the Houses of Commons and Lords, are still in use. Many of the cancellations at shows or exhibition centres were only used in Registered Mail and Certificates of Posting. Others of the list following were used only for telegraphic purposes and so can only be found on loose stamps, not covers. Many other similar marks are known.

Halifax/Cricket Ground
Newmarket/Grandstand
Derby/Grandstand
Sandown Park/Grandstand
Kempton Park/Grandstand
Manchester/Grandstand
Lincoln/Grandstand
Ascot/Grandstand
Aintree/Grandstand
Westminster Palace Hotel/S.W.
Langham Hotel, London
Shelbourne Hotel, Dublin
Covent Garden Market/W.C.
Smithfield Market
Manchester Fish Market
Manchester/Stock Exchange
Swansea Docks
Brighton/West Pier
Glasgow/Kelvin Hall
Kelvin Hall, Glasgow
Showgrounds Belfast
Mobile Post Office
Ampleforth College/York
Earls Court Exhibition/S.W.
Registered Earls Court Exhibition/
Earls Court Exhibition B.O.S. W.5
Olympia/West Kensington W.
Olympia/West Kensington W.14

Somerset House/W.C.
Athletic Ground. Richmond/Surrey
Stockbridge/Grandstand
Stock Exchange/E.C.
Stock Exchange/Glasgow
British Legion Village/Maidstone, Kent
Easington Colliery
Blackhull Colliery
Shankhouse Colliery
Aycliffe Trading Estate, Co Durham
Bata Estate, Essex
Fish Docks, Grimsby
Royal Automobile Club
Duke of York's School, Dover
Ushaw College, Durham
The Pier, Bournemouth
Parliament House
House of Commons S.W.1
House of Lords S.W.1
Commercial Sale Rooms/E.C.
Baltic Coffee House/E.C.
Alexandra-Palace/N.
Agricultural Hall/London N.
Crystal Palace
Registered/Olympia B.O.W.4
Olympia B.O./W. Kensington/London W14
Shepherds Bush/Exhibition B.O.W.

ERRORS

Many different kinds of errors may be found in postmarks, eg wrong numeral types, errors in place name spellings, inverted or reversed dates, inverted or omitted datestamps in machines, inverted slogans, missing or inverted letters in skeletons, wrongly used charge and instructional marks, paid marks struck in black or unpaid marks in red.

FIRST DAY OF ISSUE

Over 200 offices now regularly provide Special First Day cancellations when new stamps are issued. Linked special event cancellations are also sometimes available elsewhere. All FDI cancels are listed by the *Bulletins* of the British Postmark Society and some of the most popular are listed and priced by *Collect First Day Covers*.

PHILATELIC HANDSTAMPS

Since 1969 a number of offices have regularly used special handstamps, often pictorial in design, on philatelic mail. This list was drawn up by members of the British Postmark Society.

National Postal Museum	Birmingham
Guernsey Postal Museum	Blackpool
Northernmost Post Office, Haroldswick	Bournemouth
Branch Office, Trafalgar Square	Cambridge
Chief Office, London EC1	Cardiff
Windsor, Berks	Colchester
Oldest Post Office, Sanquhar	Glasgow
Brighton, Sussex	Leeds
Heathrow Airport	Liverpool
Cardiff	Manchester
Edinburgh	Newcastle-u-Tyne
Belfast	Norwich
Caernarfon	Oxford
Shakespeare, Stratford	Sheffield
Stoke on Trent	Southampton
York	

POSTAGE RATES

Inland Letter Rates

1638–1839

All rates quoted are for single letters, i.e. letters written on a single sheet of paper tucked round as an 'Entire'. Double and treble letters were charged at double and treble rates. Quadruple rates applied per ounce.

	First stage	Subsequent stages
1638	2d Under 80 miles	4d 80–140 miles.
		6d over 140 miles
		8d London to Scotland
		9d London to Ireland

1653	2d Under 80 miles	3d over 80 miles
		4d London to Scotland
		6d London to Ireland
1711	3d 80 miles	4d over 80 miles
		6d London to Edinburgh
		6d London to Dublin
1765	1d One Post Stage	2d between one and two post stages
		3d between two Post stages and 80 miles
		4d over 80 miles
		6d London to Edinburgh
784	2d One Post stage	3d between one and two Post stages
		4d between two Post stages and 80 miles
		6d 80–150 miles
		7d London to Edinburgh
1796	3d 15 miles	4d 15–30 miles
		5d 30–60 miles
		6d 60–100 miles
		7d 100–150 miles
		8d over 150 miles
1801	3d 15 miles	4d 15–30 miles
		5d 30–50 miles
		6d 50–80 miles
		7d 80–120 miles
		8d 120–170 miles
		9d 170–230 miles
		10d 230–300 miles
1805	4d 15 miles	5d 15–30 miles
		6d 30–50 miles
		7d 50–80 miles
		8d 80–120 miles
		9d 120–170 miles
		10d 170–230 miles
		11d 230–300 miles
		1d each additional 100 miles or part
1812	4d 15 miles	5d 15–20 miles
		6d 20–30 miles
		7d 30–50 miles
		8d 50–80 miles
		9d 80–120 miles
		10d 120–170 miles
		11d 170–230 miles
		1/- 230–300 miles
		1d each additional 100 miles or part
1838	2d 8 miles	4d 8–15 miles
		Other rates as from 1812

Scotland

1710	2d Under 50 miles	3d 50–80 miles
		4d over 80 miles
		6d Edinburgh to London
1765	1d One Post stage	2d between one Post stage and 50 miles
		3d 50–80 miles
		4d over 80 miles
		6d Edinburgh to London
1784	2d One Post stage	3d between one Post stage and 50 miles
		4d 50–80 miles
		5d 80–150 miles
		6d above 150 miles
		7d Edinburgh to London
1796	3d One Pos. stage	4d between one Post stage and 50 miles
		5d 50–80 miles
		6d 80–150 miles
		7d above 150 miles
		8d Edingurgh to London
1801		Scottish rates made same as English.

Ireland (between 1784 and 1827 rates were for Irish miles)

1660	2d 40 miles	4d over 40 miles
		(1/- per ounce over 40 miles, raised to 1/4 in 1711)
1765	1d One Post stage	2d between one Post Stage and 40 miles
		4d over 40 miles
1784	2d Under 15 miles	3d 15–30 miles
		4d over 30 miles
1796	2d Under 15 miles	3d 15–30 miles
		4d 30–50 miles
		5d 50–80 miles
		6d over 80 miles
1805	3d Under 15 miles	4d 15–30 miles
		5d 30–50 miles
		6d 50–80 miles
		7d over 80 miles
1810	4d Under 15 miles	5d 15–30 miles
		6d 30–50 miles
		7d 50–80 miles
		8d over 80 miles

1813	2d Under 10 miles	3d 10–20 miles
		4d 20–30 miles
		5d 30–40 miles
		6d 40–50 miles
		7d 50–60 miles
		8d 60–80 miles
		9d 80–100 miles
		10d over 100 miles
1814	2d Under 7 miles	3d 7–15 miles
		4d 15–25 miles
		5d 25–35 miles
		6d 35–45 miles
		7d 45–55 miles
		8d 55–65 miles
		9d 65–95 miles
		10d 95–120 miles
		11d 120–150 miles
		1/- 150–200 miles
		1/1 200–250 miles
		1/2 250–300 miles
		1d each aditional 100 miles
1827		Irish rates made same as English rates of 1812. Reckoning now measured in English miles.

By the 1830s postal charges had become insupportable. To send a single sheet from London to Edinburgh cost 1/1½ while sending a letter the same weight as the 1980 minimum charge cost 8/8½d. About two weeks pay was required to send a letter of the same weight inside Great Britain! Opposition came from the newly enfranchised middle classes and the agitation led by Robert Wallace MP and Rowland Hill. A House of Commons Select Committee, appointed November 1837, reported in August 1838 and recommended the adoption of Hill and Wallace's proposals. A uniform rate was to be charged, regardless of distance. After a brief experimental rate of 4d, a penny rate was introduced from 10th January 1840. Handstamps were used from this date, adhesive stamps and printed stationery being issued on 6 May 1840. In 1890 an anniversary publication commented, 'one of the greatest social reforms ever introduced was, to speak plainly, given as a bribe by a tottering Government to secure political support'.

POST OFFICE REGULATIONS.

On and after the 10th January,
a Letter not exceeding **half an ounce in weight,** may be sent from any part of the United Kingdom, to any other part, for **One Penny,** if paid when posted, or for **Twopence** if paid when delivered.

THE SCALE OF RATES,

If paid when posted, is as follows, for all Letters, whether sent by the General or by any Local Post,

Not exceeding ½ Ounce ....**One Penny.**

Exceeding ½ Ounce, but not exceeding 1 Ounce.. **Twopence.**

Ditto   1 Ounce................2 Ounces **Fourpence.**

Ditto   2 Ounces ....3 Ounces **Sixpence.**

and so on ; an additional Two-pence for every additional Ounce. With but few exceptions, the WEIGHT is limited to Sixteen Ounces.

If not paid when posted, double the above Rates are charged on Inland Letters.

COLONIAL LETTERS.

If sent by Packet Twelve Times, if by Private Ship Eight Times, the above Rates.

FOREIGN LETTERS.

The Packet Rates which vary, will be seen at the Post Office. The Ship Rates are the same as the Ship Rates for Colonial Letters.

As regards Foreign and Colonial Letters, there is no limitation as to weight. All sent outwards, with a few exceptions, which may be learnt at the Post Office, must be paid when posted as heretofore.

Letters intended to go by Private Ship must be marked " *Ship Letter.*"

Some arrangements of minor importance, which are omitted in this Notice, may be seen in that placarded at the Post Office.

No Articles should be transmitted by Post, which are liable to *injury*, by being stamped, or by being crushed in the Bags.

It is particularly requested that all Letters may be *fully* and *legibly addressed*, and *posted as early* as convenient.

January 7th, 1840.

By Authority :—J. Hartnell, London.

The Post Office notice announcing the introduction of Uniform Penny Postage on January 10th 1840.

1839–1968

Date of start of new rate:	First stage:		Subsequent stages:
1839, Dec. 5th	4d	½oz	(4d was the maximum charge. The 2d rate still applied up to 8 miles. Pre-paid London local letters, were charged at 1d, unpaid at 2d or 3d.)
1840, Jan. 10th	1d	½oz	1d for next½oz. 2d for each subsequent ounce (or part) to maximum of 16oz. Unpaid letters were charged double.
			1847, 16oz. limit abolished.
			1865, 1d for next ½oz and each succeeding half oz.
			1872, initial weight step raised to 1oz. ½d for second oz. ½d for each succeeding 2oz (or part) to 12oz, thereafter 1d per ounce.
			1882, 12oz limit abolished.
			1897, initial weight step raised to 4oz. ½d for each succeeding 2oz (or part).
			1915, initial weight step reduced to 1oz. Between 1oz and 2oz 2d, ½d for each succeeding 2oz (or part).
1918, June 3rd.	1½d	4oz.	½d for each succeeding 2oz.
1920, June 1st.	2d	3oz.	½d for each succeeding ounce.
1922, May 29th	1½d	1oz	2d for 3oz; ½d each succeeding ounce.
			1923, initial weight step raised to 2oz; ½d each succeeding 2oz.
1940, May 1st.	2½d	2oz	½d each additional 2oz.
			1952, ½d for next 2oz, 1d for each 2oz thereafter.
1957, Oct 1st.	3d	1oz	1½d for each succeeding 2oz.
1965, May 17th	4d	2oz	2d for each succeeding 2oz up to 1lb then 3d per 2oz.

1968–present day

Date of new charge.	Max. weight for minimum charge	First class minimum charge	Second Class minimum charge
1968, Sept. 16	4 oz	5d	4d
1971, Feb. 15 (decimalisation)	4 oz	3p	$2\frac{1}{2}$p
1973, Sept. 10	2 oz	$3\frac{1}{2}$p	3p
1974, June 24	2 oz	$4\frac{1}{2}$p	$3\frac{1}{2}$p
1975, March 17	2 oz	7p	$5\frac{1}{2}$p
1975, Sept. 29 (metrication)	60 g	$8\frac{1}{2}$p	$6\frac{1}{2}$p
1977, June 13	60 g	9p	7p
1979, August 20	60 g	10p	8p
1980, February 4	60 g	12p	10p
1981, January 26	60 g	14p	$11\frac{1}{2}$p
1982, February 1	60 g	$15\frac{1}{2}$p	$12\frac{1}{2}$p

Postcards:

1870	$\frac{1}{2}$d	1940	2d
1918	1d	1957	$2\frac{1}{2}$d
1921	$1\frac{1}{2}$d	1965	3d
1922	1d		

A separate postcard rate disappeared with the advent of Two Tier post in 1968.

SOCIETIES

The following Societies actively cater for aspects of British Postal History and will be glad to hear from those interested in membership. An SAE or IRC should accompany all enquiries.

THE POSTAL HISTORY SOCIETY
J. G. S. Scott, 5 Bywater Street,
London SW3 4XD

GB GROUP OF THE PHS
A. J. Kirk, 123 Benhill Road,
London SE5 7LZ

BRITISH POSTMARK SOCIETY
A. J. Haward, 9 Gainsborough Avenue, Marple
Bridge, Stockport, Cheshire SK6 5BW

WELSH PHILATELIC GROUP
O. M. Richards, 'Cartrefle', 4 St. Simon's Road,
Cherry Willingham, Lincoln LN3 4LN

KENT POSTAL HISTORY GROUP
J. Wilkes, 42 St. George's Road, Hastings,
East Sussex TN34 3ND

**EAST ANGLIA POSTAL HISTORY
STUDY CIRCLE**
J. Wilton, 76 Rushmere Road, Ipswich,
Suffolk IP4 4JZ

LONDON POSTAL HISTORY GROUP
Rev. A. J. Potter, St. Hugh's Old Hall Green,
Ware, Herts. SG11 1DR

YORKSHIRE POSTAL HISTORY GROUP
W. A. Sedgewick, 25 Hunters Lane,
Sheffield S13 8LA

IRISH PHILATELIC CIRCLE
H.K. Jamieson, 3 Cleves Way, Hampton,
Middx. TW12 2PL

SCOTTISH POSTMARK GROUP
D.C. Jeffries, 11 Criagcrook
Avenue, Edinburgh EH4 3QE

RAILWAY PHILATELIC GROUP
P. Johnson, 20 Rockley Rd,
Leicester LE4 0GJ

PHS OF LANCS. AND CHESHIRE
E. Hebdon, 410 Rossendale Road, Burnley,
Lancs. BB11 5HN

FORCES POSTAL HISTORY SOCIETY
M. Dobbs, 80 Addison Gardens,
West Kensington, London W14 0DK

WESSEX POSTAL HISTORY GROUP
I.M. Warn, 1 Knowsley Road,
Fishponds, Bristol BS16 2AD

CHANNEL ISLANDS SPECIALISTS' SOCIETY
B. Cropp, 17, Westlands Ave,
Huntercombe, Slough SL4 6AG

ISLE OF MAN POSTAL HISTORY SOCIETY
G. Holland, Yn Druin, Glen Tramman,
Lezayre, Nr Ramsey, Isle of Man

MARITIME P.H. CLUB
6 Devon Terrace, Totnes,
Devon TQ9 5AZ

Any other Societies who would like to be included in future editions are asked to send details to Dr Whitney. The above societies are asked to notify any changes of officers or addresses.

1874 entire, underpaid with ½d cancelled by Tring duplex with fine London S.W. circular surcharge MORE TO/PAY and 1d charge mark.

1846 envelope to Great North Railway Office at Darlington with fine early FARNHAM skeleton datestamp and 292 (Farnham) cancelling 1d pink embossed.

To mark the site of the General Letter Office, destroyed by the Great Fire in 1666, the Corporation of London has now put up a plaque. Here, the City of London's postmaster Colin Burbage visits the spot where Bishop's postmark was first used in 1661.

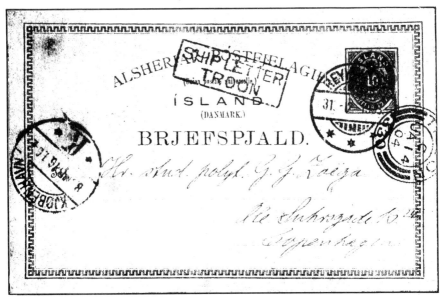

1904, card from Iceland to Copenhagen with very scarce Troon Ship Letter mark. Sold 1976 by Robson Lowe for £340.

Information needed . . .

'I have left the stamp as Fig. 840 until now, although there are two schools of thought as to whether it should be included in Scottish or English listings.

One school of thought is that it indicates 'Lancaster and Carlisle Railway', the other that it indicates 'London-Caledonian Railway'. All that is known is that it is recorded from March 1858 to May 1866 on letters from London to Scotland.

The theory that it is a variation of the Caledonian handstamps seems logical, in that all the letters are to addresses in Scotland and none to places served by the Lancaster and Carlisle Railway. Against this, however, is the arrangement of the letters. If it is a variation of the 'C.R.' stamps, then L/CR would be more logical than LC/R.'

H. S. Wilson

(T.P.O. History, Part Three, Scotland and Ireland)

The British Coronation Crown.

The Wrench Series Nº 1170

1902, Coronation cachet on picture side of viewcard. Back bears ½d EVII cancelled London W.C. squared circle for 6 June 1902. Information needed about the status of this cachet.

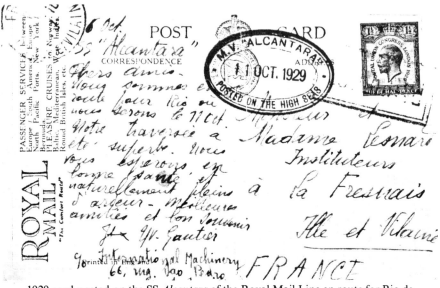

1929 card posted on the SS *Alcantara* of the Royal Mail Line en route for Rio de Janeiro. The card received a ship's cachet, a Rio Paquebot mark and a receiving cancel in France.

A lucky find! It pays to buy *Collect British Postmarks*! 1912 card posted on the SS *Snowden* one of the small coastal vessels plying the North Wales Coast. The dealer who sold this (at 10p) thought the card was posted on the mountain. The cachet is catalogued at £175.

Mr Roy Maltson sent this photo of a 1904 postcard bearing two different duplex marks, two single circles, and three double circles, one of them three times. Many thanks to Roy and all the others who sent entries. A free copy of *Collect British Postmarks* goes to him. Can anyone beat this record of seven different British postmarks legitimately used on the same cover?

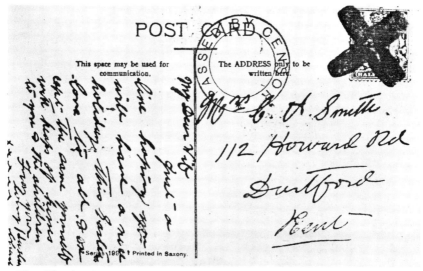

First War dumb cancel, probably Naval usage with censor mark alongside.

Rubber cancellations often deteriorated rapidly, probably due to the acid in the ink acting on the rubber. Milton Depot/Berks became almost illegible between Apr 11 and May 24 1918.

1872 THE STOCK EXCHANGE FORGERY
1/– GREEN

It is generally accepted that this is the most unusual and interesting Postal Forgery. Discovery by Charles Nissen did not take place until 1898 and then only of Plate 5. Another London dealer located 35 examples of Plate 6 in 1910.

Fred J. Melville wrote a pamphlet entitled "The Mystery of The Shilling Green" and more recently Dr. Carl Walske contributed a comprehensive study throwing a new light on the production of these forgeries.

Cdr. Malcolm Burnett reporting on a recent find contributed an erudite resumé in the September 1979 issue of the P.J.G.B.

Two datestamps were used on the stamps noted by Malcolm Burnett as follows. Easy identifications are:

TYPE A: Year date much higher than in B. Month abbreviation level with stroke of T. No stop after C.

TYPE B: Year date nearer to E.C. Month abbreviation at slightly diagonal angle. Stop after C.

TYPE X: Spaced date. STOCK-EXCHANGE with hyphen. E.C. (no stop). This cancel is only found on pieces of telegraph forms, not on the stamps.

Non-postal use of the £5 Q.V. orange with fine oval Account Branch/P.O. Glasgow.

Some postmarks with curious names –

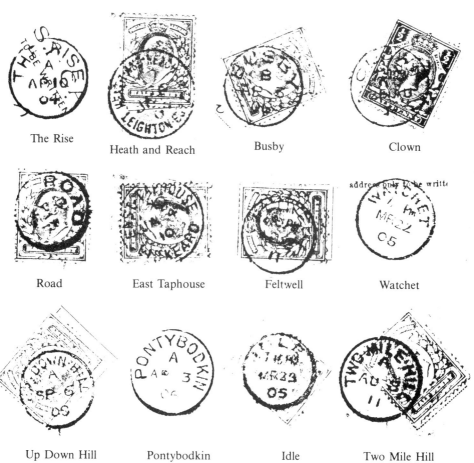

The Rise

Heath and Reach

Busby

Clown

Road

East Taphouse

Feltwell

Watchet

Up Down Hill

Pontybodkin

Idle

Two Mile Hill

Fishponds   Sticklepath

Some puzzling postmarks . . . any comments welcome.

FOUND-IN-F.N.D. (or O?)/WITHOUT CONTENTS on 1893 cover from
Bradford to Yorks. A similar mark is also known on a cover from Bloemfontein
to the Hague. What is F.N.D.?

1903 postcard from Duncoon to Glasgow.   O.S.&W.R.P.O./Up Night.
What is the circular mark?   1901 Possibly foreign T.P.O.

1918 card from Denmark to Hull with unusual 'Part of a Mail/Captured by the/ Germans and delayed.' Any comments on the history of this mark?

1915 Express letter from an unidentified camp. North Leam Camp is shown as N.B. which means 'North Britain' an abbreviation often used of Scotland.

The explanation of these strange items is probably that a hamlet near Ironville lost its datestamp so had to press a cork into emergency use. Ironville placed its datestamp alongside, at one period using a skeleton.

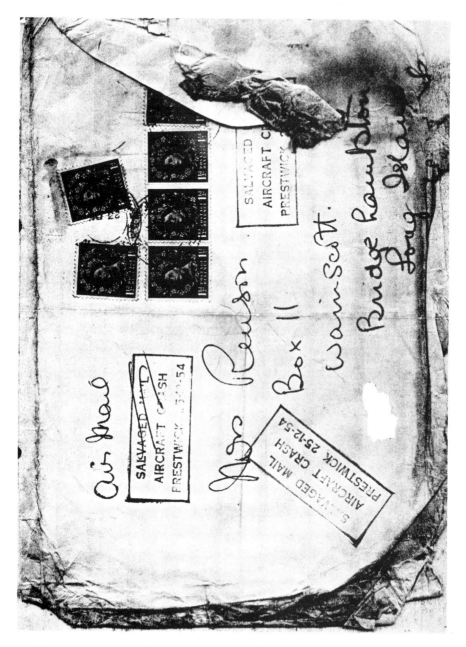

1954, Salvaged Cover. Such rare items are, of course, exceptions to the usual rules about condition. (See *A History of Wreck Covers*, A. Hopkins, Robson Lowe.)

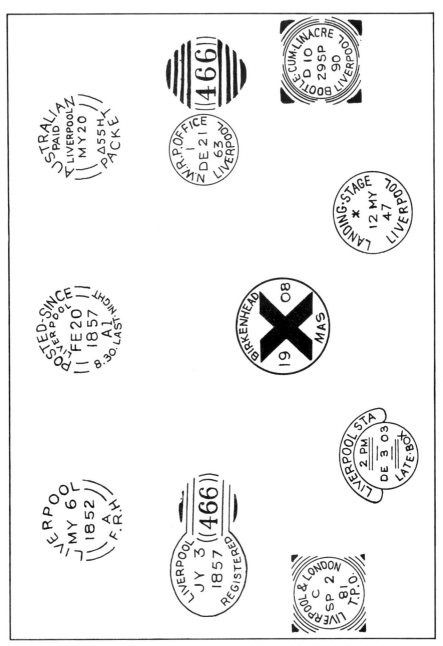

Reverse of special postcard produced by Merseyside Philatelic Society to commemorate its 75th anniversary on 26 Feb 1981. The drawings of old Liverpool postmarks were made by Mr J. Howard.

1844 entire to the famous Baptist leader Rev Joseph Angus bearing pair of 1841 1d red imperfs each cancelled by the rare Alderney Maltese Cross. Endorsed 'By private Steamer, via Southton (ie Southampton) with speed'.

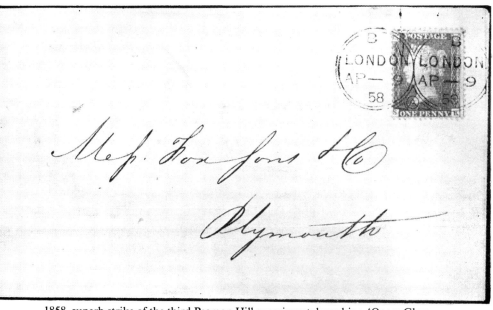

1858, superb strike of the third Pearson Hill experimental machine, 'Opera Glass Type'.

1840, cover from Dublin to Boyle. Illustrated envelope bearing 1d black cancelled with red Maltese Cross. Sold by Robson Lowe in 1979 for £1,300.

1857, illustrated cover extolling the cause of 'Ocean Penny Postage' bearing 1d red stars cancelled by London Inland Section numeral 20.

1857, Glasgow to Mexico via United States. Fine Glasgow duplex cancellations and 'Vera Cruz' and '4' applied in Americas.

1843 cover from London to Edinburgh forwarded on to Glasgow. Twopenny blue imperf cancelled by London Maltese Cross with 2.

PICTON PUBLISHING
Citadel Works, Bath Road, Chippenham, Wilts SN15 2AB

SHIPS ON STAMPS *by E. W. Argyle* £2.00* each
One: The Royal Navy. **Two**: Passenger Liners. **Three**: Early Sailing Ships and Canoes. **Fou.** Sailing Ships. **Five**: Local Craft. **Six**: Cross-Channel, River & Lake Passenger Ships. **Seven**: Cargo Ships, Oil Tankers. **Eight**: Sail & Paddle Auxiliary Vessels. **Nine**: Ships of the World's Navies. **Ten**: Miscellaneous Vessels, Index. **Eleven**: The Royal Navy (New Issues). **Twelve**: Passenger Liners of the World over 4,000 tons.

MUSIC ON STAMPS *by Sylvester Peat* £2.00*,each
One: A–B, Bach, Beethoven, Berlioz and Bartok. **Two**: C–F, Chopin, Debussy, Dvorak and Elgar. **Three**: G–L, Grieg, Handel, Haydn and Liszt. **Four**: M–R, Mahler, Mendlessohn, Mozart and Ravel. **Five**: S–Z, Schubert, Sibelius, Strauss and Tchaikovsky. **Six**: Musical Monarchs and National Anthems. **Seven**: Native and Folk Instruments.
    Now available, a new series
MORE MUSICIANS ON STAMPS Parts 1 & 2 £2.00* each

ISLE OF MAN STAMPS AND POSTAL HISTORY (YPM 4) *by Dr J. T. Whitney* £20.00† each
This is the first handbook to cover all aspects of the philately of this fascinating island. Part One 'The Postal History' contains about 1,000 illustrations, many of them never before published. Part Two 'The Stamps' has illustrations of all the major issues and examples of those used in Local Delivery Services, Strike Posts, etc. This is a *priced* catalogue enabling you to acurately value your collection, but it is also a work of scholarship which has become the standard reference book on the subject frequently quoted by authorities such as Stanley Gibbons. Sized 210 x 148 mm and casebound with 300 pages, no ot Isle of Man philatelist can afford to be without this work.

THE GREAT RAIDS *by Air Commodore J. H. Searby, DSO DFC.*
A series of books on the raids by RAF Bomber Command during World War II. Each book in the series contains information and documents not before published, a complete list of the squadrons and crews who took part and is written superbly by an expert on the subject. He was there.
Part One: PEENEMUNDE. Soft Cover £4.50† Library Edition £7.50†
Part Two: ESSEN. THE BATTLE OF THE RUHR. Soft Cover £5.50† Library Edition £7.50†

TERRIERS IN THE TRENCHES The History of the Post Office Rifles *by Charles Messenger* £12.95†
THE RIFLE VOLUNTEERS 1859–1908 *by Ray Westlake* £9.95†
ISLANDERS DEPORTED *by Roger Harris*
The story of the Channel Islanders deported to Germany during WWII. £4.20†
ADMIRAL SEYMOUR'S EXPEDITION & TAKU FORTS 1900 *by Colin Narbeth* £7.50†
THE DISTINGUISHED SERVICE MEDAL 1939–1946 *by W. H. Fevyer* £20†
BRITISH GALLANTRY AWARDS 2nd Edition *by P. E. Abbott & J. Tamplin* £18●
1933 CENTENARY ISSUE OF THE FALKLAND ISLANDS *by R. N. Spafford* £5†
1983 PICTON'S PRICED POSTCARD CATALOGUE
by Ron Mead, Joan Venman & Dr J. T. Whitney £4.95†
PRE-VICTORIAN STAMPS AND FRANKS *by Hewlett & Picton-Phillips* £4† *(new edition)*
THE WHALE'S TALE *by Frederick P. Schmitt* £3.50†
PRINTERS AND PRINTING IN PHILATELY *by John Alden* £3.50†
OFFICIAL RAILWAY POSTCARDS OF THE BRITISH ISLES: Part 1 L&NWR £4* **Part 2** GWR and Others £6*
RAILWAYS ON STAMPS *by A. M. Goodbody and C. A. Hart* £2.00* each
PICTON'S PHILATELIC HANDBOOK No. 1 £4.00†
A CORSHAM BOYHOOD: The Diary of Herbert Spackman 1877–1891
by Faith Sharp with Heather Tanner and illustrations by Robin Tanner £5.95†
THE CURSE OF MACBETH & OTHER THEATRICAL SUPERSTITIONS *by Richard Huggett* £7.95†
FRENCH ISLANDS A Priced Catalogue to the Postal History of the Islands of the North & West Coasts of France
by O. W. Newport & J. T. Whitney £9.95†
THE STAMPS OF ALDERNEY Illustrated Priced Guide & Handbook *by P. Kelley & P. E. Newell* £3.50*
ROADWAYS The History of Swindon's Street Names *by Peter Sheldon & Richard Tomkins* £2.95*
SWINDON IN CAMERA A Photographic Journey 1850–1979 *by Peter Sheldon* £4.50*

These titles available direct from PICTON PUBLISHING or your local bookseller.
Please send SAE (6" x 8½") for free catalogue of all titles.

Postage and Packing
*=55p †=£1.00 ●=£1.50

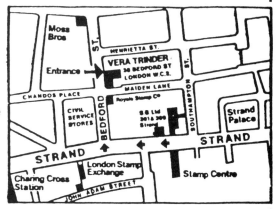